Profitably Managing Your Rental Properties

R. Dodge Woodson

JOHN WILEY & SONS, INC.
New York • Chichester • Brisbane • Toronto • Singapore

Copyright © 1992 by John Wiley & Sons, Inc.

Library of Congress Cataloging-in-Publication Data:

Woodson, R. Dodge (Roger Dodge), 1955–
    Profitably managing your rental properties / by R. Dodge
Woodson.
        p.   cm.
    Includes index.
    ISBN 0-471-57564-X (cloth : alk. paper).—ISBN 0-471-57565-8
(paper : alk. paper)
    1. Rental housing—Management.   2. Real estate management.
3. Real estate investment.   I. Title.
HD1394.W66   1992
333.5'068—dc20   92-6198

Printed in the United States of America

10 9 8 7 6 5 4 3 2 1

To my daughter, Afton Amber Woodson,
who has been a great inspiration to me.
Afton, you have changed my life.
I thank you and I love you.

Acknowledgments

I would like to thank my parents, Maralou and Woody, for their contributions to my success. Their support over the years has made many ventures possible. Thanks, Mom and Dad.

A special thanks is due to my good friend, Ken Luce. Ken has helped me to enjoy enough time away from normal business matters to get this book published sooner than it might otherwise have been. Ken, thank you for all your help. Working with you is the next best thing to writing.

I would like to thank my editor, Mike Hamilton, for allowing me to write this book for such a respected publisher. Mike has been a pleasure to work with.

My thanks extend to everyone involved in the production of this book. Many of these people are never known by name, but without their diligent efforts, the book would never be produced. Thank you all.

My acknowledgments would be incomplete without thanking my wife, Kimberley. She has always been an active partner in my dealings. Her support and encouragement have enabled me to reach goals that would have gone unattempted without her. Kimberley, thanks for the past twelve years. I look forward to the rest of our lives together.

R.D.W.

Contents

Introduction

Profitably Managing Your Rental Properties is for the active investor. The examples it provides are based on proven techniques. Unlike some books, this one has been written from firsthand knowledge. The advice you will find here is the result of many years of my own property management experience.

I have been involved with real estate for twenty years. Having watched my grandfather turn many deals, I was able to make a profit with my first venture, a piece of raw land. As time passed and my experience grew, I went on to land developing, building, remodeling, brokerage, buying, renting, and selling.

At one time, I controlled more than fifty properties that ranged from single-family homes to multifamily apartment buildings. Some of these I extensively remodeled. In addition to managing my own properties, I have served as a professional property manager and consultant for many clients.

My experience has been hard-earned and expensive. What I have learned will, I hope, help you run your buildings profitably while avoiding many pitfalls and problems in owning and managing rental property.

I have written this book to help you become a better property manager. However, the information should not be taken as legal or tax advice. I have made every effort to achieve accuracy in the text and sample forms, but I cannot guarantee it. Good books have long shelf lives, and some of their information may become outdated. The forms here are only samples, intended to help you understand the text; they are not meant as legal documents. Before using the information in this book, confirm its suitability to your circumstances with local professionals.

Chapter 1

Evaluating Your Ability to Manage Rental Property

Should you manage your own rental property? This is a serious question, and it is not always an easy one to answer. Not everyone is cut out to be a landlord. There is a big difference between owning rental property and managing it. When your rental portfolio starts to grow, management duties can erode your time and patience. Many investors never stop to consider their ability to manage their properties. Instead, they look only at the cost of hiring a management firm and decide to try their own management to decrease operating expenses. While such landlords are not spending money for a management firm, they may be losing more money than they are saving.

What is your time worth? Can you afford to spend an hour waiting for a prospective tenant who never shows up for your scheduled meeting? Will your people skills allow you to control your tenants—without losing them? The income property management business is not an easy one. It takes special skills and a certain temperament to be successful at it.

This chapter is going to help you evaluate your position as a property manager. You may find that you are ideal for the job and can save thousands of dollars managing your own property. Or you might discover that you would be much better off hiring a professional management team to do what they do best, so that you can do what you do best. After you have read this chapter, take the quiz at the end of it. It may not provide conclusive evidence for what is right for you, but I believe it will reveal much about your personal desires and abilities in managing rental property.

What Are the Basic Qualities of a Property Manager?

Property managers must assume many roles and balance numerous tasks simultaneously. They must be firm yet flexible. A good manager will enjoy working with the public and not be afraid to take control of a situation. Equally important, the manager will have a strong background in the laws and principles of property management, for without this knowledge, he may wind up in court for violating a tenant's rights. A professional manager must also be willing to work nights and weekends, since that is when her customers are available to do business. These few examples are only the beginning of what it takes to be a successful property manager.

How Is Your Business Sense?

Many real estate investors have no idea how difficult it can be to run their own rental property. If you are unprepared, being a landlord may change the way you look at your real estate investments. After a year of bad experiences, you may never want to see another tenant. Even so, while property management does have its undesirable traits, it does not have to be completely discouraging. With the proper knowledge and the execution of a solid business plan, your rental management endeavors can be quite successful.

Why do investors choose to manage their own properties? For some, the money saved from not paying a management fee is the primary reason. Others don't trust outsiders to operate their rental business at maximum efficiency; they want a hands-on position in the management of their rental portfolio. The possible reasons for wanting to manage rental property are as diverse as the people who invest in it.

Regardless of your reasons for entering the property management field, always treat your rental property as a business. Many investors have full-time jobs and invest in income property in their spare time. However, while it can be considered a part-time business, property management should not be considered a hobby. If you don't treat your income units as a business, you will never see all the rewards it is possible to derive from them.

In evaluating your ability to manage your income properties, you must consider your business experience. If you lack the necessary experience, you can learn much from books like this one. The key is to establish your business qualifications. Some investors are incredibly adept at finding and buying lucrative properties, but these same cunning investors can make horrible property managers. There is no shame in not having the skills and attitude to be a manager. The shame is when you are out of your element and drive your otherwise profitable rental business into the ground.

Marketing

Most investors never consider themselves as working in sales and advertising; however, successful investors are creative and accomplished in both of these fields. If your rental units are vacant, you are not receiving income from them. This defeats the purpose of owning income property. In most places, rental competition can be fierce. If you cannot put together a good marketing plan, you may fall behind the competition.

This is not to say that you must have a degree in marketing or advertising. Rather, what you must have is an awareness of the public's desires and needs. If you know what people want, you can work to meet their desires and enjoy a profitable rental operation. This requires market research and the ability to be flexible. A dry, boring advertisement is not going to attract many desirable tenants. Learn how to put some zip in your ads. With the proper advertising, you can target your demographics to obtain the tenants you want.

Anyone with reasonable intelligence can learn the skills needed for marketing. It is simply a matter of investing your time and effort to perfect your marketing plan. If you are willing to devote time and a little money to advertising and sales techniques, you can reduce your vacancy rate and ride high as a landlord.

Dealing with the Public

How do you feel about dealing with the public? Some people do not enjoy frequent contact with strangers, and if you are one of these, the property management business will be a tough one for you. As a property manager, you will be required to deal with people you have never met and may not like. The public can be cruel, especially if you are their complaint department.

When you assume the responsibility of running your own properties, you must also take on the duty of public relations. For example, it may be inconvenient when a tenant calls to see your advertised vacancy, but you must make time to take the call. Generating calls to fill vacancies is expensive, and you cannot afford to waste the interest of prospective tenants simply because the timing is bad.

If you hate playing politics, being your own property manager will not be fun. You must use tact and diplomacy to keep your buildings running smoothly. There will be times when you must hold your temper with irate tenants. A screaming property manager is rarely in control. As the captain of your rental ship, you must maintain control and avoid the many obstacles that could sink your vessel.

Maintenance

As a property manager, you must coordinate and supervise the maintenance of your properties. Do you know a closet auger from a pipe wrench? A closet auger is used to clear stoppages in toilets. Pipe wrenches are used to assemble and disassemble plumbing pipes and fittings. You don't have to know how to use these tools, but you must know enough about each trade involved in the maintenance of your building to talk intelligently with the service providers.

If your plumber tells you that your old boiler needs a new domestic coil, it is helpful to know what he is talking about. Domestic coils provide hot water for domestic purposes in the home, and if you didn't know any better, you could logically think your tenants were using dirty boiler water to bathe and cook in. However, while the domestic coil is in the boiler, the water passing through it is potable (suitable for drinking). My point to all of this is that you need a reasonable understanding of the maintenance procedures for your building.

Other Factors

Accounting. Being your own manager means doing your own bookkeeping or hiring it out to an independent bookkeeper. If you have been spoiled by a professional management firm keeping your records for you, you may be unhappy with the requirements you face as your own manager.

Computers. How do you feel about computers? They are not mandatory equipment for a successful property manager, but for most people they make the job much easier. If you are running a large number of rental units, computers will be almost essential.

Legal Matters. Legal matters abound in the property management field. If you don't have the personality for dealing with legal confrontations, you may be in the wrong business. Hiring a good attorney can ease this burden for you.

Time. Your time is a very valuable asset. You must learn to make the best use of it to run your business smoothly. Time management is critical in making the highest profits in the shortest time possible.

It is easy to get caught up talking with tenants, tradesmen, and the like. If you allow yourself to spend too much time on casual conversation, you lose time that could be producing profits. Poor time management skills will severely hamper your effectiveness as a property manager.

Paperwork. Most successful businesses run smoothly only when the proper paperwork is kept up to date. The rental business is no different. There will be lease applications, leases, inspection lists, and a pile of other papers involved with every apartment you rent. Are you willing to keep it all in order? If you despise paperwork, becoming a rental manager is not a good idea. If you ignore the extensive paperwork, you run the risk of losing your properties. If you stay on top of it, you should do fine.

The Benefits of Self-Management

The benefits of self-management are numerous. Once you learn to run your own rental business, you can make more money. This money will not always come easily, but the opportunity is there. At a minimum, you should retain about 10 percent of your gross rents, which would otherwise be paid to a management firm, by acting as your own manager. In all likelihood, your savings will be even greater.

The job of property manager will take a portion of your time. Some investors see their time as being too valuable to manage their own properties, but others enjoy the diversion. There are definite advantages to being your own manager. With a little effort and research, self-management can be profitable.

The Rest of It

There is much more to running your rental business. You will find the information you need to operate profitably in the chapters that follow. If you now have doubts about your management ability, after reading this book you will know definitely if you are cut out for the job. I believe that with the guidance available to you from this book, you will be able to successfully manage your own buildings. And if you are already successful as your own manager, this book can make you more successful.

Landlord Evaluation Quiz

	Yes	No
1. Do you enjoy working with people?	_____	_____
2. Are you well organized in your daily routines?	_____	_____
3. Are you computer literate?	_____	_____
4. Do you have maintenance and repair abilities?	_____	_____
5. Are you available to take phone calls after business hours?	_____	_____
6. Are you willing to work nights?	_____	_____
7. Are you willing to work weekends?	_____	_____
8. Do you lose your temper easily?	_____	_____
9. Are you familiar with the laws of property management?	_____	_____
10. Do you enjoy doing research work for your ventures?	_____	_____
11. Do you want to be a rental manager?	_____	_____
12. Are you willing to invest your time in long-term goals?	_____	_____
13. Do you possess strong time-management skills?	_____	_____
14. Can you keep your emotions out of your business?	_____	_____
15. Would you like to save 10 percent of your gross rental income?	_____	_____
16. Do you believe rental management is easy?	_____	_____
17. Are you a good negotiator?	_____	_____
18. Do you have sales skills?	_____	_____
19. Will it be cost effective to manage your rental property?	_____	_____
20. Can you be firm without being overbearing?	_____	_____
21. Do you believe your rental endeavors are a business?	_____	_____
22. Are you meticulous with your paperwork?	_____	_____
23. Would you like to learn more about property management?	_____	_____
24. Are you excited about being your own manager?	_____	_____

Summary of the Landlord Evaluation Quiz

Ideally, you should have answered yes to 22 questions and no to questions 8 and 16. This quiz is not scientific or perfect, but it may make you think. Assess your answers. Look at what you believe now, and take the quiz again when you finish this book. Your answers may change abruptly.

If you scored poorly, don't despair; this book may change your feelings and abilities. And, if you passed the quiz with flying colors, don't run out and start managing your properties just yet; after reading this book, you may find some chinks in your armor.

Chapter 2 begins the nuts and bolts of property management. Whether you know nothing about the rental business or are presently managing your own properties, the next 17 chapters have much to offer. Even seasoned managers will find a few new tricks. Let's get on with what you need to know to make more money with your rental properties.

The Business Side of Property Management

One of the biggest mistakes most investors make with their rental property is treating it as a hobby. This is especially true of investors with only a few units. It is crucial to your financial success to treat all of your rental property as a business. This holds true whether your portfolio consists of a single duplex or dozens of apartments. If you fail to take care of business, your properties may drive you to bankruptcy. There will be piles of paperwork, long hours, and hard work involved in reaching a goal of high profits. Your success or failure in property management will be directly related to how you run your buildings. If you are going to manage your own portfolio, you should save a lot of money, but you must invest the time to do the job properly.

As an investor, you bought income property to make money. With the correct business practices, you can make money, and lots of it. With the attitude of a weekend landlord, you will not achieve high profits, and you may lose your real estate and your credit. Often the deciding factor will be how seriously you take your landlording responsibilities. This chapter will outline and describe several of the business principles and practices you must master to control your financial future.

The Law

There are numerous laws affecting the management of rental properties. They vary from state to state and are often based on the number of rental units you own. As a landlord managing your own property, you must develop a working knowledge of these laws. You don't need a law degree, but you must learn enough to stay out of trouble.

There are several ways you can tutor yourself in real estate and rental management laws. You can read books, or you can consult with an attorney to create a checklist of rights and wrongs. You can also attend seminars on legal matters pertaining to your rental business, or you might take part-time courses in a local college to sharpen your property management skills.

The more you educate yourself in the legal aspects of property management, the fewer problems you will have down the road. Here are a few examples of the types of problems you might encounter.

If you have ever looked at generic rental agreements, those available in stores, you might have noticed that they are not all-inclusive, but leave much to be desired in protecting you and your property from bad tenants. Many landlords use these form agreements as a template to create their own lease or rental agreement. However, unless you have an attorney review and approve your homemade document, you may be in violation of the law. It is not uncommon for states to prohibit the average person from drafting a contract agreement. Even licensed brokers are very restricted in what they may draft into an agreement without the review and approval of an attorney.

Discrimination is a major consideration in the legal ramifications of property management. You may be guilty of many types of discrimination if you don't know the law. In fact, you may never consider some practices to be discriminatory until you are charged with discrimination. But by that time it will be too late, and you will be headed for court.

Eviction is an ever-present consideration in any rental business. For the unsuspecting landlord, it can be one of the worst nightmares ever experienced in rental property management. If you do not follow the proper steps in an eviction process, the tenant may have grounds to sue you. There are people who have become professionals at using the court systems to live in your apartment, rent-free, for months. Consider that it can take four to six months to get a nonpaying tenant out of your building, and you will see how expensive eviction can become. Add to this expense a violation of the tenant's rights, and you may lose much more.

Deposits made by tenants are another area where there is always a risk of trouble. Do you need a separate escrow account for each tenant's rental deposit? Can you put all of the rental deposits into one escrow account? Do you need an escrow account, or can you commingle the deposits with your personal funds? Before you start taking people's money, you had better know what to do with it.

It is never wise to commingle deposits with your personal funds. Generally, a single escrow account to hold all of your deposits should be acceptable, but check with an attorney to be sure of the law in your area. Other questions may arise about deposits. When are you required to return the deposit to a departing tenant? Is there a time limit in which you must return the deposit or notify the tenant of your intent and reason for retaining the deposit? What events allow you to legally retain the deposit?

These are simple questions, but many investors don't know how to answer them. The law is filled with facts every landlord should know and work with. If you violate the law long enough, there will come a time when your violations catch up with you. Ignorance of the law is no defense. It is your responsibility as a businessperson to know and obey the laws governing your business.

Insurance

As with any other business, property management requires various forms of insurance to operate safely. When you act as your own manager, the responsibility for insurance coverage is up to you. Depending on the size and type of your operation, there are several kinds of insurance you may need: Liability insurance is always needed; workers' compensation insurance may be required if you have employees; and fire insurance certainly should be considered mandatory. The list of possible types of insurance is long. All of these will be covered in Chapter 17.

In some cases, your tenants may be required to carry insurance, but it is your responsibility to request proof of coverage. For example, if you require all tenants with water beds to provide insurance to protect your property in the event of an accident, you should have copies of their policies on file. Simply stating such a requirement in your lease is not enough if disaster strikes. You may have a legal case against the tenant in such circumstances, but the odds of the tenant having enough money to repair the damage are not good.

An Organized Environment

All businesses run better and more profitably when they are well organized. Whether you have a battered, two-drawer filing cabinet or a high-tech computer, the key is organization. If you don't already possess good organizational skills, set a goal to improve your habits. There is extensive paperwork and recordkeeping involved with property management.

Being well organized will not only make your day-to-day activities more fruitful, it will make surviving a tax audit much easier. Good organization and time management work together to make you a more profitable investor and landlord. When you harness the power of effective time management, you can make more money without working any harder. You are simply working smarter with an organized environment and concise time management.

Market Research

Market research may be one of the most commonly overlooked factors that can increase a landlord's income. One thing it can do is tell you how much to charge for your rental units. When you buy a building, do you assess the market demand for its apartments? If you are not doing extensive market research, you may be missing big profits.

Market research can determine the type of rental business you will develop and how it will run. If you buy a building comprising only one-bedroom apartments, you can expect a high turnover of tenants. If that is what you want to allow for more rapid rent increases, fine. However, if you want stable tenants, and less time spent preparing, showing, and renting vacant apartments, then the building with all one-bedroom apartments is not such a good deal. This is only one example of how effective market research can steer your business.

Market research can also tell you how much the public is willing to pay for your rental units. If the surrounding, comparable properties are demanding high rents, your building should be able to produce high rents also. If you are contemplating an increase in your rental amounts, market research can tell you how high you can go without losing your tenants. Given the power you can gain from thorough market research, you cannot afford to ignore it.

Pricing

Setting a price for your rental units is a matter to be taken seriously. If you set the price too high, you will have an empty building. If you set it too low, your profits will suffer. Finding the right price is easy when you rely on accurate findings from market research.

In setting your rents, don't just pick numbers out of the air. Too many investors determine their desired rental amounts by looking at profit projections on a spreadsheet. Of course, you must make money, but the amount you make will often be dictated by current market conditions. You may want to see a net gain of $1,000 each month, but you may have to settle for $700. You can set your rental rate at any amount, but if you don't have tenants, you won't show a profit.

You must be realistic in your income goals. Market conditions will play a key role in your decision on how much rent is too much. If the market is flooded with vacant apartments, you should accept a lower rent to maintain a full tenancy. When housing demand exceeds supply, you can cash in with higher rents. To survive through the real estate cycles, you must monitor, project, and adapt to ever-changing market conditions.

Marketing

Without effective marketing, you cannot maximize your rental income. You may get by with dry classified advertising, for example, but a well-written ad will pull a higher number of quality tenants. Your marketing will set the trend for the type of tenants you attract. With targeted marketing you can aim your advertising dollars at a selected audience.

Creative marketing can allow you to prosper while other investors flounder. If you unleash your imagination, you can create a situation where you have more prospective tenants than empty apartments. This can hold true even in poor economic times. Market research will be a factor in your marketing. With adequate research and a winning plan, you can alleviate the worries of vacancies.

Phone Tactics

How you handle your telephone can have a dramatic effect on the success of your marketing. Advertising expenses and vacant apartments put a strain on your cash flow, so when your phone rings with a prospective tenant on the other end, you must make the most of the call. Don't let your phone behavior alienate the prospect and result in wasted time and advertising money. If you don't capitalize on each acceptable tenant, you are throwing your advertising dollars away.

When a prospective tenant calls, she will have questions for you to answer. To prequalify her you should have some questions of your own to ask. Prequalifying prospective tenants in the initial phone call saves hours of wasted time, which can then be invested in making new deals or in recreation. In either case, it makes sense to eliminate undesirable tenants as quickly as possible.

By creating a checklist, you will have all of your questions at hand when a tenant calls. You will also ensure that you don't forget to ask key questions. While the checklist adds to your paperwork, its benefits make up for the time spent on it. Phone tactics may not seem important, but they are. If you learn how to screen tenants on the phone, you will have more time to devote to other aspects of your rental business. Phone manners and methods are important steps in running a profitable rental business.

Sales Skills While Showing Property

When the time comes to show your rental units to new tenants, you must assume the role of salesperson. As real estate brokers say, "There is a difference between showing real estate and selling it," and this rule holds true in renting apartments. If you don't emphasize the features and benefits of your property, the tenant may move on to the building down the street. The first landlord to use effective sales tactics will secure the tenant.

There are many books available that can help you acquire an effective sales attitude. You do not have to use high-pressure tactics or demean your character to be good at selling. The most important part of any sale is gaining the customer's confidence. If you present a trustworthy image, your customer is very likely to do business with you.

The telephone checklist mentioned earlier will come into play with your sales maneuvers. People like to be called by their names. If you recorded the prospect's name on the phone checklist, you will be able to address her by name when showing the property. The background information you gathered on the telephone will serve to break the ice. This information gives you a known area around which to open a conversation.

How you dress and what you drive will have a mental effect on your prospective tenants. If they are wearing jeans and driving a subcompact car, your luxury car and silk suit may intimidate or degrade them. People don't like to feel they are of a lower class than the person they are dealing with. It is important to match your appearance and presentation to the level of the prospective tenant. If you allow the tenant to feel as though he is on equal ground with you, your sales efforts will be much more effective.

If you can develop sales skills, you will be well on your way to becoming an envied landlord. Other investors will struggle to fill their vacancies while you make it look easy. As you have gathered by now, you must wear many hats to be a successful property manager. All of your roles require different business principles and practices, but they are what separates the winners from the losers.

Choosing Tenants

Rental Applications

Rental applications can save you months of grief. The information they contain is invaluable when screening tenants. With a properly worded application, you will be authorized to check the applicants credit rating and references.

If she passes muster on these two points, it doesn't guarantee she is a good tenant, but it does improve your odds.

Some investors don't believe in rental applications. They meet with people and decide if they will make good tenants based on a gut reaction. Regardless of how thoroughly you investigate a tenant, you still run a risk of getting a bad one. With the expense of removing a problem tenant, anything you can do to reduce your risks is worthwhile. Rental applications can save you months of lost income and legal fees. As a part of your business practice, you should incorporate the use of a rental application into the rental of every apartment you own.

Screening

Getting a bad tenant is worse than not getting a tenant at all. Therefore, as part of your business duties, you must carefully screen all prospective tenants before making a commitment to them. This requires putting on yet another hat. All of a sudden, you must play detective. Unfortunately, bad tenants are not ashamed to lie to you. If you take the information they put on your rental application at face value, the purpose of the application is defeated.

There are people in this world who have learned how to live free off unsuspecting landlords. These professional deadbeats are hard to distinguish on looks alone, but if they were not good at fooling people, they wouldn't be able to get by for so long on so little. You must make a hard rule in your business play book to carefully screen all prospective tenants before entering into an agreement with them.

Once you put a bad tenant into your rental unit, getting him out can be all but impossible. With the tenant's rights and the judicial system, you could be forced to house the scoundrel for months without his having to pay any rent. This may not seem right, but it is the way it is. You have to learn to protect yourself from these con artists.

If you want to be a good property manager, you cannot be bashful. You must dig deep into people's backgrounds and personal lives to ensure that they will make good tenants. If you get squeamish at the thought of asking someone how much money she makes, you had better hire a professional management firm. By the time you complete your tenant screening, you should have a dossier that would make any intelligence agency proud. If you slack off on this aspect of your rental business, you are in for some hard times.

Legal Aspects of Moving In

Rental Agreements and Leases

Whether you use a rental agreement or a lease, you should have all terms of your agreement with a tenant in writing and signed by all parties. Oral agreements are legal, but they are largely unenforceable. If you are forced into going to court, only your written documents will be of value. Most of a judge's decision will be based on hard evidence. Your written agreement will serve as hard evidence and substantiate your position. The additional paperwork may take a little extra time, but always having a written agreement should be a rule you live by.

Addendum Agreements

Most experienced landlords have come to recognize the value of a written lease, but many still put themselves at risk by not requiring written addendum agreements. Any time there is a change in the terms of the original lease, you should require a written addendum to identify those changes. Without an addendum you may be helpless in court.

Let's say, for example, that you rented a unit to a single man, and he marries a woman who owns a dog. You allow the bride and the dog to move into the rental unit without a written addendum changing the terms of the original lease, and during the couple's stay, the dog destroys your apartment. Since the man did not have a dog when he rented the apartment, your lease did not address his responsibility regarding pet damages. Further, the dog doesn't belong to him but to his wife, who is not even on the original lease. Where does this leave you? It leaves you in a situation where a long litigation with a questionable outcome controls your financial destiny.

You can avoid this type of situation with addendum agreements. In the example above, if you had required an addendum that changed the terms of the original lease when the woman and dog were allowed to move in, you would have had grounds to defend your legal actions against the couple. Your position is weakened by the lack of an addendum. As a strong businessperson, you must stay up to date on your legal paperwork.

Deposits and Escrow Accounts

Handling other people's money is serious business. When it comes to security deposits and escrow accounts, you must act in a professional manner. If you approach this responsibility haphazardly, you can wind up in deep trouble. Before you begin taking deposits, consult with an attorney to learn the law in your area. There is a good chance you will be required to maintain an escrow account for the keeping of deposits. Even if the law doesn't require you to keep a separate deposit account, it is always best to do so.

Move-In Checklists

Move-in checklists, also called check-in forms, are one way of protecting your property. If you have each new tenant complete and sign one, you have an established record of the condition your property was in when the tenant took occupancy. Having this simple little form on file can save the day when a dispute arises over a security deposit. Without it you may be hard-pressed to prove a tenant has done any damage. I know it means more paperwork, but precise paperwork is what the property management business runs on.

Day-to-Day Management

Monitoring Tenants

You cannot move tenants into your property and forget about them. Even if a tenant is paying the rent regularly, you should arrange to visit the rental unit at least twice a year. Make sure when you have your lease prepared that it contains language allowing you access to the apartment at any time, with reasonable notice to the tenant.

By monitoring your tenants, you solve two potential problems. You are able to keep an eye on how the tenant is treating your property. If negligent damage is occurring, you can catch and correct it early. In addition, you can maintain good landlord–tenant relations. Your showing an interest in the tenant's living conditions should make him more respectful of you and your property. Monitoring provides multiple benefits and doesn't cost any more than a little of your time.

Property Maintenance

Most rental property requires routine maintenance. Without it, your property and its equipment will lose value and cost more to repair. This is an area where many professional management firms charge additional fees. If they must arrange and oversee repairs, they often charge a percentage of the cost of the repair to do so. As a self-manager, you avoid paying these extra fees, but you must then invest your time in doing the job yourself. If you are handy, you may be able to complete many of the routine maintenance duties personally. When you perform the work yourself, you save even more money.

Whether you plan to do the work or just oversee it, you should know something about property and equipment repairs. If you have no knowledge in this area, you are a potential victim of unsavory contractors. Take the time to learn the basics of maintenance and repairs so you can keep your contractors honest. There are many fine books available to help you develop a working knowledge and vocabulary on this subject.

Depending on the value of your time and your ability, you may do well to learn to do your own maintenance. Many routine maintenance calls are simple and do not require special tools. If you learn to be your own handyman, your savings can build to a tidy sum.

Collecting the Rent

Collecting the rent is one duty many investors hate. They want the money, but they don't want to go get it. Sometimes a property manager must aggressively seek the rent payment. Chapter 9 describes some tricks that will help you with rent collection.

I have seen countless investors put off rent collections for months just to avoid contact with a tenant. But when a tenant isn't paying her rent, you cannot afford to wait, especially since the collection process can take long enough by itself if you are forced to take legal action. When you procrastinate on initiating the collection procedure, you only worsen the situation. Follow the terms of your rental agreement and stay within the law, but get your rent on time or get rid of the tenant.

This job seems to be hardest for landlords who become too friendly with their tenants. It is all right to be cordial, but don't become best buddies. Trying to collect rent from a distressed friend is a tough job for anyone, and evicting a close friend is even harder. Keep your relationship with your tenants on a business level.

Operating Expenses

As you move along in your property management business, you will have to take control of operating expenses. These expenses are what stand between you and your net profit; if they become excessive, your net income will decrease. As the chief bean counter, the job of balancing your budget is all yours. You can yell and scream at a professional manager for his poor handling of your property's operating expenses, but when you are your own manager, there is nobody to get upset with but yourself.

Fine-tuning the cost of operating your business is a goal you should set early. Create a working budget and track your expenses on a monthly basis. If you follow your operating expenses closely, you will notice abrupt changes early enough to do something about them. If you wait until tax time, it will be too late to make adjustments for the past year.

If you have several rental properties, tracking and comparing your expenses can be tedious, but a computer will be a big help with the job. Chapter 7 will deal with computers and the many ways they can simplify your rental business. Whatever method you use, learn to control your operating costs. By streamlining expenses, you can fatten your bottom line.

Bookkeeping

Bookkeeping is an area of your business you may wish to hire out to an independent firm. Unless you are alert and good with numbers, keeping the books for multiple rental properties can be distracting. If you are not an experienced bookkeeper, it may pay to have someone else do the job for you. Before hiring someone, however, investigate using an independent bookkeeper. While subcontractors may cost more per hour than a permanent employee, when you factor in all the permanent employee's expenses, subcontractors often turn out to be cheaper.

If you don't want to share your financial information with anyone else, you can do the books yourself. Again, a computer with the right software will make a huge difference in the time you spend keeping good records. Today's software allows you to get by with a limited knowledge of accounting principles. If you plan to keep your books manually, spend the necessary time to learn the proper procedures. Mistakes in your bookkeeping can be costly at tax time.

Improvements on the Property

As your own manager, you will occasionally have to decide on improvements to your property. If you were using a professional manager, she would bring these items to your attention for a decision, but without professional advice to rely on, you must decide when to improve your property on your own.

This type of decision will vary a great deal with different locations and properties. Making the wrong improvements will not help at all; making the right improvements at the wrong time will be equally negative. Chapter 13 will help you to make wise decisions when it comes to property improvements.

Operating Capital

It will be up to you to determine how much operating capital is needed to run each of your buildings, and making this determination will require the evaluation of many factors. If you have owned the building for a while, you can pull from historical facts. By examining the past performance of the property, you can get a good idea of your future needs. If you are embarking on a new building, historical data may not be as accurate. The previous owner may not have kept accurate records and may not have run the building the way you plan to.

Without adequate operating capital, you could wind up in financial distress. Inadequate capital accounts for the failure of countless investors each year. Don't underestimate your needs. If your heating system needs to be replaced in the middle of the winter, you won't have long to come up with the money.

Financing

You are probably well aware of what it takes to obtain financing to purchase a property, but you may not know how different the tactics are when you are seeking financing to improve or repair a building. At some time, almost all investors rely on financing to maintain or expand their rental business. Chapter 10 will deal with many of the issues surrounding financing.

Since planning is essential to staying ahead of the game, line up your financing before you need it. You are the chief financial officer of your business, and thus the duty of finding suitable financing is yours. If you put your financing in place early, you will not be caught in a panic later.

Employees

As your rental business grows, you may develop a need for employees, perhaps a secretary or a part-time maintenance person. Before you hire any employees, you must determine how much they will cost you and how much they are worth to you. This is not always as easy as it sounds.

To figure out how much employees cost, you must look at much more than their hourly wages. You will be responsible for tax payments and other employee-related expenses. In most situations, you will be required to carry workers' compensation insurance on your employees, and there is the added expense of employee benefits. Costs continue to add up if you pay your employees for holidays, vacation time, or even lunch breaks. All of these expenses must be added to your employees' earnings to establish their true cost.

As a businessperson you must assess these expenses and determine if they are warranted. It is difficult to know just how much an employee is worth to you in many circumstances. On the other hand figuring the worth of your maintenance person is not too difficult. You look at what he or she does and what it would cost to hire a contractor to do the same job. When all these factors are accounted for, you can draw a conclusion to his or her value. On the other hand, your evaluation of a secretary may not be as clear cut. Secretarial duties are much harder to compare than maintenance duties. For example, you could hire an answering service to answer your phones, and that cost should be only a fraction of a full-or part-time secretary's cost. However, how much business will you lose by having an answering service handle your phones? Many people will not leave a message if they know they are talking to an answering service. In addition, it is unlikely that the service will be prepared to answer a caller's questions. Properly trained, your secretary may be very competent at expanding your business through phone contact.

Questions about employees have plagued business owners for years. The complexity of the questions often make it seem as if they have no answers. As the owner of the business, you will have to make the decision on if and when to hire employees.

Subcontractors

In some businesses, subcontractors solve the employee dilemma. For example, you may be far better off to hire independent contractors to do your maintenance and repair work than to employ a maintenance person. You will pay more per job for their work, but you will only pay them when you need them. If you must pay the in-house maintenance person to be on standby, that cost may well exceed the cost of the subcontractors.

I mentioned earlier how retaining an independent bookkeeper can be a financially sound move. If there is a specific part of your business that you are unable to do, subcontractors may be the best solution. Even so, as good as subcontractors can be, they are not without their problems. One problem is being sure the subcontractors are properly licensed and insured for the work they perform. Another is their reliability; since subcontractors are working for many people, your work may not get done quickly. Ultimately, you will have to look at your business's needs for employees or subcontractors and solve them in the way that best fits your business plan.

Projecting the Future

Further responsibility you face as a property manager will be projecting the future. For any business to run profitably on a long-term basis, it must have a sound business plan. As the owner of the business, you are responsible for coming up with a winning one.

Projecting the future of real estate and rental activity is not as hard as you might think. History has a tendency to repeat itself, and knowing this, you can use historical data to help you predict coming market conditions. Your projections may not be dead on, but you may be surprised how effective your planning is. Real estate runs in cycles. Housing needs tend to follow patterns. By looking into the past, you can get a glimpse into the future.

A trip to city hall can reveal growth plans in the community that will attract new people to the area. This type of research can provide insight into the long-range future. Something as simple as tracking the help wanted ads in the local paper can give you an idea of the needs of the near future. By projecting the future, you can build a business plan. You may have to alter your plans to accommodate unforeseen shifts in the market, but over a ten-year period, your projections should ring close to the truth.

The Cornerstone

The cornerstone to success in your rental business will be you and your actions. If you treat your rental activity as a business, you can prosper. If you treat it as a hobby, you may never see a substantial profit. This chapter has outlined many of the basic business principles and practices used in efficient property management. The remaining chapters will expand on and add to them.

When you make the decision to manage your own property, you must go into it with a serious attitude. Competition can be fierce, and the world of property management can be unforgiving. Remember, whether you have two tenants or twenty, you are running a business. Look at your actions and ask yourself if they are on a professional level. Would you pay someone to manage your properties the way you are doing the job? If you answer this question with a yes, you are on the right track. If you answer with a no, you should reconsider your decision to self-manage your income properties.

Most likely, when you bought income property you did so to make money. If the property is not well managed, you will not make as much money as you should. There is only one reason you should not be able to manage the property effectively—lack of desire. If you have the determination, you can learn the skills required to run a profitable rental business.

Chapter 3

Subsidized Rental Income

If you decide to participate in programs offering subsidized rental income, there are a few facts you should know. This chapter is going to give you those facts in easy-to-follow comparisons of the pros and cons associated with subsidized housing.

Subsidized rental income is guaranteed money, but it does not always come easily. Most programs require your rental property to meet certain minimum standards before you can participate. Moreover, the tenants you get under these programs are not always the most desirable, even though they can be.

When many landlords think of Section 8 tenants, they think of poor people who will make horrible tenants. They often assume that tenants receiving housing assistance are lazy and irresponsible, but this is not always true. Many elderly tenants receive housing subsidies, and they can be model tenants. People with physical disabilities are another example of tenants receiving subsidized rental assistance. They can be the kind of tenants any landlord would be proud to have.

If you have predetermined ideas about subsidized rental income, you may be surprised with what you can learn from this chapter. If you want to maximize the rental income of your property, you must investigate the advantages offered from subsidized rental income. On the other hand, if you choose to skip over this chapter, having already set your mind against tenants receiving financial help, you are doing yourself, and some fine tenants, a disservice.

What Is Subsidized Rental Income?

There are many government programs in existence to help people from all walks of life cope with rising rental rates. Basically, subsidized rental income is money a landlord receives from one of these programs to complement the rent a tenant pays. This is guaranteed money, there, every month, like clockwork.

Subsidized rental programs function in many ways. Rather than give you a broad-brush description, I am going to detail the most common programs available. To obtain more information, contact your local housing authority or contact the U.S. Department of Housing and Urban Development (HUD) at the following address:

Assistant Secretary for Housing
Federal Housing Commissioner
Department of Housing and Urban Development
Washington, D.C. 20410-8000

Lower-Income Rental Assistance

The Lower-Income Rental Assistance program is best known as Section 8. It is designed to help low-income people obtain safe, sanitary housing in private accommodations by covering the gap between what a tenant can afford and the market rate for available rentals. The rent charged for approved accommodations must meet the program's criteria. Eligible tenants are required to pay either 10 percent of their gross income or 30 percent of their adjusted income, whichever is higher. The program pays the difference between this amount and the required, approved rent. A tenant must meet certain criteria to qualify for this assistance.

Your building must meet safety and sanitation requirements set forth by HUD to be part of the Lower-Income Rental Assistance program. It will have to be inspected and approved before you can accept Section 8 tenants.

Rent Supplements

The Rent Supplements program depends on payments from the government to reduce the rents of some disadvantaged low-income individuals. Although current information indicates it has been suspended and is no longer available, it was established to help tenants residing in multifamily housing insured by the Federal Housing Administration (FHA). HUD paid supplemental rent to the landlord on the tenant's behalf, covering the difference between 30 percent of the tenant's adjusted income and what it determined to be the fair market rent of the rental unit. The contribution could not exceed 70 percent of the HUD-approved rent and could be paid for up to forty years.

To qualify for this assistance, a tenant had to meet one of the following criteria:

• Low-income household, qualified for public housing
• Handicapped
• Displaced by government action
• Victim of a national disaster
• Occupant of substandard housing
• Head of household serving active military duty

Section 8 Existing Housing Vouchers

The Section 8 Existing Housing Voucher program is designed to assist low-income families in securing adequate, safe, and sanitary housing in private accommodations. It gives eligible families a broader selection of rental homes by allowing them to commit to rent units where the required rent is above the fair market level. The assistance provided is based on the spread between a standard payment for a rental in the given area and 30 percent of the tenant's monthly income.

Some favoritism is shown in this program. Tenants who are living in substandard conditions, who have been involuntarily displaced, or who are paying more than 50 percent of their monthly income in rent receive first consideration. To be eligible for Section 8 existing housing, a tenant must be considered among the ranks of the very low-income. If his income does not exceed 50 percent of the area's median income, he is qualified.

As with the Lower-Income Rental Assistance program, a building must be approved by HUD as a safe, sanitary, and decent place to live to be accepted as Section 8 housing.

Finders–Keepers

The Section 8 Existing Housing Certificate program is affectionately known as Finders–Keepers. Like most Section 8 programs, it helps disadvantaged people find and secure a safe and sanitary place to live. Its term can run between two and fourteen years.

Eligible tenants must pay either 30 percent of their adjusted income or 10 percent of their gross income, whichever is higher, as their portion of the rent, and they may apply their portion of welfare assistance, as defined, for housing. The program gives preference to tenants presently living in substandard housing, involuntarily displaced, or paying more than 50 percent of their income for rent.

To qualify for Finders–Keepers, the rents being charged for the units must fall within the guidelines approved by HUD. The building must also provide safe and sanitary housing.

Section 8 Moderate Rehabilitation

The Section 8 Moderate Rehabilitation program is aimed at helping low-income tenants take residency in safe, decent, sanitary, privately owned buildings that have been renovated. It is administered by public housing agencies (PHAs), which advertise the availability of units and select landlords to participate. The selection process is a competitive one. Landlords agree to renovate their buildings to meet prescribed safety and sanitation standards.

The PHAs set rents based on cost of ownership, cost of management, cost of maintenance, and cost of rehabilitation of a property. These costs must fit within the spectrum as defined by HUD. The term of this program can extend to fifteen years.

Eligible tenants must pay either 30 percent of their adjusted gross income or 10 percent of their gross income, whichever is higher. Preference is given to those presently living in substandard housing, involuntarily displaced, or who are paying more than 50 percent of their income for rent.

Once again, your building must be decent, sanitary, safe, and rehabilitated to take advantage of this program.

Getting Your Building Approved to House Subsidized Tenants

In order for you to participate in subsidized programs, your building must provide decent, safe, and sanitary housing. The interpretation of the words decent, safe, and sanitary can vary depending upon who is setting the standards. If you work with subsidized tenants, the interpretation will be that of the people administering the programs.

To be placed on an agency's approved list, your building must be inspected by an agency representative, typically after a qualified tenant has expressed a desire to rent your unit. Section 8 tenants shop for their housing in the same way other tenants do. When they find a unit they like, they ask the landlord to allow them to rent it. At this point, the property must be inspected and approved by the program's administrator, usually the local housing authority.

Your building must be in conformance with local codes and ordinances; for example, you will be expected to have smoke detectors and adequate hall lighting. The inspection will go smoothly if your property is in average condition and not in violation of building and fire codes.

If your building fails its inspection, you have two options. You can leave the building in its present condition and not rent to subsidized tenants, or, if you choose, you can make the necessary alterations to conform with the inspector's checklist. After you make the changes, the building will be inspected again. If it is approved, it is time to negotiate the rental amount for the unit.

Negotiating the Rent and Signing the Lease

Getting an acceptable rent should not be difficult. The programs allow enough latitude for you to get fair market value. The actual amount you receive will be negotiated with the administrator in the same way you haggle with an average tenant.

The ceiling these programs work with on rental amounts excite most landlords. This is because, at first look, it appears that they can make much more money with Section 8 tenants than they can with average tenants. However, although it is possible to enjoy a higher net income under Section 8, the figures are not quite what they seem.

In the first place, the rental amounts you see are the highest amounts acceptable to the program, which you are not guaranteed of receiving. The rent you get will be negotiated and could be much lower than the upper limit. Generally, the amount will parallel the fair market rents for your area. In the second place, the rental amounts shown as a ceiling include an allowance for utilities. This allowance can reduce the amount of money you thought you would get with the Section 8 program.

Once you come to terms on the rent to be charged, it will be time to complete a lease agreement. This will be a one-year lease when you rent to a Section 8 tenant. It will be fair, and you will have the comfort of knowing that most of your money will be coming from HUD. You can think of HUD as a cosigner for the tenant.

Some Advantages to Providing Subsidized Housing

There are many advantages to participating in subsidized housing. Let's take a look at a few of them.

To start, when you participate in subsidized housing programs, you are usually able to receive maximum rents. If you can negotiate for market-rate rents, and you should be able to, you will be making just as much money with Section 8 tenants as you would with any other tenant—maybe more.

Also, when you open your doors to income-assisted tenants, you lower your vacancy rate because you have a larger base of prospective tenants to pull from. Your units will be leased for a year, and many of the tenants will renew their leases. If you treat your tenants right, they will have little reason to relocate.

Much of your income will be guaranteed when you have a lease with HUD-sponsored tenants. Your tenants will be responsible for a small percentage of the rent, but HUD will pay most of it. The portion HUD pays will be there for you on time, every time. If the tenants fail to pay their share, you may use the same procedures you would employ with average tenants to collect your rent. If they won't pay, you can evict them.

One of the best parts of subsidized housing programs is that it allows you to continue receiving most of your rent during eviction. If a tenant moves out prematurely or is being evicted, HUD will continue to pay its portion. How can you beat this deal?

The Other Side of the Coin

There can be a dark side to the subsidized rental programs. While they offer many advantages, they also have some disadvantages. Here are a few.

One disadvantage is the potential hassle of the inspections of your building to qualify it for subsidized tenants. If you maintain good living conditions for your tenants anyway, it will not be much bother, but if your building is not kept up, the inspections will require you to invest time and money in the property.

As with any government program, there is plenty of paperwork to be done with subsidized tenants. Some of it seems unnecessary, but most of it works to your advantage. Moreover, the volume of paperwork is not much more than what you should maintain with any tenant.

The quality of the tenants in subsidized housing is probably the biggest fear of most landlords, many of whom tend to assume that all subsidized tenants will be bad. Of course, this is not always the case. It is a fact that they will be low-income—they must be to qualify for financial assistance. Some may also be less educated than other tenants you could rent to, and since they are not paying all of the rent, it is possible they will be less responsible.

Yes, you could get bad tenants. Those in Section 8 programs are screened for financial consideration, but they are not rated on responsibility and dependability. It is up to you to investigate them, just as you would any others. If you perform an adequate background investigation, you can remove all but the most remote chances of getting burned. And remember, if these tenants do turn out to be bad, you can evict them and continue collecting most of your rent while you are doing it.

What Type of People Will You Get as Tenants?

The type of people who are eligible for subsidized housing are as diverse as the properties they occupy. You could be dealing with people from all walks of life. I have seen excellent Section 8 tenants, and I have seen some I wouldn't rent my doghouse to. The key to success in dealing with them is a thorough background investigation. If you select your tenants carefully, you will have no more problems than normal, and probably less.

Elderly Tenants

I have seen numerous elderly people being helped with subsidized housing. I sold a twelve-unit building that housed seven elderly tenants using Section 8 services, some of whom had lived in the building for more than twenty years. These ladies took better care of that building than most people do their own home. In essence, the building *was* their home. Not only did they maintain impeccable apartments, they scrubbed the floors in the hall.

When the building was purchased, the new owner weeded out the Section 8 tenants in an attempt to collect higher rents and avoid some of the responsibilities of being a Section 8 landlord. In less than eighteen months, all of these excellent tenants had moved out of the building. New tenants came in and problems began to arise. By the end of the next year, the twelve-unit building stood empty and boarded up. The new owner had lost his property to bankruptcy.

This building had maintained tenants and a positive cash flow for years. During the prosperous years it had housed Section 8 tenants; under new management, it went into depression and finally into bankruptcy. The Section 8 tenants didn't cause this failure—in fact, they may have been what kept the building healthy during its earlier years. I know from firsthand experience that you can get some superior tenants through subsidized housing programs.

Disabled Tenants

Disabled persons are another type of tenant you may be working with in a subsidized program. Remember, these programs help people with low incomes. That a person is unable to produce a high income because of a disability says nothing about what kind of person she is.

If you are prejudiced about people on the basis of their income, subsidized housing will not work for you. If you treat each individual as a person, you can find some very good tenants in the subsidized housing pool.

Drug Dealers and Such

I am not going to lie to you—you may wind up with drug dealers, thieves, pimps, and a host of other undesirable tenants when you participate in subsidized housing, but of course, you could end up with this same caliber of tenant in any event. As I said earlier, if you do your homework before leasing your unit, you can avoid such people.

It is safe to assume that your reputation may be affected by Section 8 tenants. Some people will perceive them as second-rate and dub you a slumlord, but the people who matter will not harbor such feelings. Instead, they will see you as a gracious landlord, a person willing to help disadvantaged people. I don't believe your reputation, or the reputation of your building, will be damaged by housing Section 8 tenants.

That doesn't mean there are no risks of renting to Section 8 tenants, but they are not much more than the risks associated with renting to any other type. In some ways, your position is stronger under Section 8 because you have HUD as a cosigner on the lease. This means you have the ability to evict the tenants while continuing to receive the lion's share of your rental income, and if a tenant skips out, HUD continues to make its portion of the rental payments. Moreover, if a tenant damages your property, HUD will pay up to two months' rent in repairs—twice as much as you would receive from most damage deposits. In many ways, the Section 8 program is much less risky than renting to average tenants.

Some Words of Advice

Give strong consideration to working with subsidized housing programs. Used properly, they can help you maximize your rental income and help unfortunate people at the same time. Take the time to sift through this chapter and consider the many benefits you could receive from being a Section 8 landlord. Talk to your competitors and see if they have experience in working with subsidized tenants. Meet with your local housing authority and get all the details on the programs available to you.

Don't jump in with both feet. If you decide to give Section 8 tenants a chance, do so in moderation. Once you allow them into your building, you must let them stay for a year unless they violate the covenants of your lease. Start with one subsidized tenant and see how things go. If you like what you see, recruit others. If you are unhappy, you don't have to allow any other Section 8 tenants in the building.

Keep an open mind toward subsidized housing programs. Don't conjure up images of bad tenants stealing your cleaning supplies and appliances. To avoid undesirable tenants, perform complete investigations on all tenants before you agree to take them in. Play by the rules. Just because these are Section 8 tenants doesn't mean you can ignore or abuse them. If their faucet is dripping, fix it.

In my experiences with Section 8 I have seen all types of people. Many are not top-quality tenants, but as the landlord, I have the right, as you do, to reject any tenant who does not meet my standards. I have found a large number of Section 8 tenants to be responsible and desirable. In fact, it is my opinion that Section 8 tenants can be the best tenants a landlord could ever have.

Regarding profits, I have seen Section 8 tenants turn troubled buildings around. For some buildings, the steady, dependable income from subsidized housing programs is a tremendous boost, especially in areas where average tenants typically are not ideal. In selling property, too, I have seen the positive impact of a building filled with Section 8 tenants. A prospective buyer of such a building knows a majority of her rental income is guaranteed. This can be a major selling point.

I have also seen the negative affects of subsidized housing. I have seen the system and the tenants abused, and I have known landlords who did not fare well either. My dealings have revealed people who would not buy a building simply because it housed Section 8 tenants.

There is always more than one way to view an opportunity. Depending upon your point of view, subsidized housing can be great or it can be a disaster. The final decision will be up to you, but I believe you owe it to yourself to at least investigate the possible gains subsidized housing can bring.

Chapter 4

Creative Marketing and Advertising

Any property manager is faced with filling vacant apartments from time to time. With some buildings, this can seem like a full-time job. Vacant rental units translate into lost revenue. If you allow units to remain empty for long, the income performance of the property sinks into the red. You might think that a responsibility of such magnitude would command the attention and respect of any property manager, but this is not always the case.

For some managers, filling vacancies is the most dreaded aspect of their job. All the time and paperwork involved with finding and moving in a new tenant can seem overwhelming, especially for part-time rental managers. Unmotivated managers can come up with countless excuses for not getting a vacant unit occupied, but none of them pay the rent. To make money with rental property, you must keep it rented.

Professional management companies strive to fill empty apartments fast, sometimes too fast. Most derive extra income from renting a vacant apartment by charging a rent-up fee. Thus, they have a monetary motivation to find a tenant. Unfortunately, in their haste to put a warm body in an empty rental unit, some companies do not screen applicants thoroughly. If your property is being managed by such a firm, you lose money twice with every bad tenant.

First, you lose money by paying a rent-up fee for a tenant you don't want and won't keep. Second, you lose money in damages or legal fees incurred while dealing with such a tenant. If you manage your own property, you don't lose a rent-up fee, but the other losses still exist. It is critical to make solid decisions when screening and selecting tenants.

As a self-manager, your monetary motivation is to stop the negative cash flow caused by vacant apartments. This should be reason enough to attend to filling vacancies, but for many part-time self-managers it is not enough. The reasons and excuses may be endless, but the result is the same: no tenants, no money! You must overcome any hesitancy you have for renting your vacant units.

Once you are motivated to fill your vacancies, you will need help. You will need something to pull tenants to your building, and that something should be aimed at pulling in quality tenants. Creative marketing and advertising can fill both of these bills. If you learn to use these tools effectively, you will find that filling vacancies does not have to be the worst part of property management.

What Does Marketing Mean to You?

Marketing is the act of making your goods or services desirable to the customer. In your case, it is the act of setting the stage to attract quality tenants to your rental property. There are many elements to consider in creating a marketing plan for rental property. Some elements you can improve, others you can't. For example, if your building is not in a desirable location, you cannot reasonably move it; however, creative marketing can help you can overcome objections to the location.

If your building pulls tenants of a lesser quality, you can change that with property improvements and marketing. In effect, improving the property to make it more desirable is a form of marketing. Also a form of marketing is your personal presentation of the property's features and benefits. Every time you describe your property to a prospect on the telephone, you are marketing your building. Many of your day-to-day activities fall into the marketing category.

Many property managers don't consider their actions as marketing. If they did, they would be more effective. In the rental business you are selling time in vacant apartments. That means you must consider yourself a salesman if you are to reach your goals. Sales skills can be used for much more than simply filling vacancies. They can be used effectively when dealing with existing tenants, bankers, appraisers, and on a host of other occasions.

If you stand back and look at your actions, you will probably see ways to improve your performance. The simple act of choosing the proper words can have an impact on your success. When you are dealing with prospective tenants, you are competing for their business. Other landlords are working to take each tenant away from you. It is not as graphic as two landlords each grabbing one of the tenant's arms and pulling, but the competition is there—in classified advertising, signs, telemarketing, and phone manners. If you don't exert yourself to secure a good tenant when you find one, some other landlord will fill his vacancy with her.

Make the Most of Your Marketing

Marketing can get expensive. Given its rising costs you must make the most of every dollar spent. Simply spending money in marketing attempts is not enough. You must design a marketing plan before you can get the most for your marketing dollar, and after you have a solid plan, you must execute it with good timing. Once the plan is in effect, you must not waste the prospects it generates.

The Marketing Plan

Drafting a marketing plan does not have to involve fancy graphs and elaborate schemes. For the average landlord, a pad of paper and a pen are all the supplies that will be needed. A computer is helpful but not necessary. The meat of a strong marketing plan is the research that goes into it.

When you are laying out a strategy to capture quality tenants, you must look below the surface. While most landlords are placing classified advertising they thought of at the last minute, you should be planning for vacancies. You know that at some point you are going to have to find new tenants. By starting early with your planning, you can make the most of it.

Decide what type of tenants you want, and then devise a method to attract them. For example, if you want college students, consider advertising in campus papers and putting notices on college bulletin boards. While students have a bad reputation as tenants, you cannot believe everything you hear.

If you are geared up to handle students, you can make more money with your income property than you might with other tenants. If your leases have been written to protect you and you monitor the students closely, you can control the situation. Not all students destroy apartments for recreation. By screening the students, you can look for the qualities you want.

The proper handling of students will make your money tree sprout new growth. Since students tend to move each year, you can increase your rents yearly to reflect rising market rates. Thus, you are likely to make more money than you would with stable tenants, who don't move for years at a time. This is just one example of how going outside the normal thinking pattern can increase your profitability.

Demographics

The foundation of your marketing plan will be research. By digging into the demographics of your area, you can plot your marketing course. Demographics can tell you almost anything you want to know about a community's people, such as income levels and average number of children. By gathering this data, you can target your marketing to specific types of tenants.

Demographic information is available from a number of sources. The local library may be a good place to begin your research. Another possible source is the many companies providing mailing lists and similar services that advertise in phone directories. Your local housing authority should be able to provide exhaustive reading material on the housing needs in your area. Collect as much data as you can to structure your marketing plan.

Building Your Marketing Plan

When you know the type of tenant you want and have completed your research into your area's needs, you are ready to formulate your marketing plan. Start by writing down all the characteristics you want in a tenant. Then check your demographics to see if these characteristics exist in the current market. It would be ridiculous to target your marketing to retired couples if your area doesn't have a significant population of retirees.

Once you have established the type of tenant you want and know that such tenants are available in the current market, all you have to do is figure out how to attract them. As part of your research you should take a close look at your competition. For example, how many bedrooms do competitive rental units have? Do the competing landlords offer incentives to new tenants? Compare your building to the competition. How does it stack up against other owners'?

Look for aspects of your property that will set it apart from the competition. Maybe it offers free parking and the competition doesn't. Perhaps you alone allow pets. Look for anything that will prevent prospective tenants from comparing apples to apples; you want your prospect to compare apples to oranges. If you set your building apart, you can justify a higher rent.

The next step to consider is how you will let people know you have rental units available. You must evaluate your advertising budget and determine the most effective way to reach your intended audience. Your advertising may be as simple as notices on community bulletin boards. Or, if you are operating a high-volume rental business, it might be as sophisticated as direct mail. Direct mail allows for very specific targeting of the market. There will be more on advertising later in the chapter.

The last step of your marketing plan concerns how you will handle prospects when they respond to your advertising. Devise a checklist or script to use when you receive phone inquiries from your ads. This element of your plan is crucial. Phone inquiries are usually your first form of contact with prospective tenants, who in a matter of seconds can form an opinion that may affect the remainder of your dealings with them. You must be well prepared to handle incoming calls. If not, much of your advertising money will have been wasted.

After your phone work is done, you are ready to move into the field. Have a plan of attack when you go out to show your rental units. Your marketing plan should include how you will show your properties and the questions you will ask your prospects. In effect, it should cover every step along your way to obtaining new tenants.

Executing Your Marketing Plan

Once you have a plan you are happy with, you will be ready to execute it when the time is right. Timing is a decisive factor in your marketing plan's success. How will you know when the time is right? You will learn from reading, research, and, most of all, experience. As you go through the highs and lows of the rental management business, you will find experience to be a strong teacher.

Management companies and landlords with large rental holdings keep their marketing plans operating almost continually. Their style of marketing is repetition. By keeping their names in front of the public they become household names. Thus, when an individual is ready to rent housing, she turns to the name she has seen over the last several months. This type of marketing is effective for big-time operators, but it is too expensive for the average landlord.

One of the biggest mistakes you can make is waiting until you need a tenant to try finding one. If you know you will have a vacancy in thirty days, start your search immediately. If you wait until the unit is empty and refurbished, it may very well sit empty for a month or more. Since good tenants give at least a thirty-day notice of their intent to vacate, you should work to find tenants a month before you need them.

The downside of this preliminary marketing is showing apartments that are still occupied by the current tenant. It can be uncomfortable for you and the prospective tenant to poke around in someone else's home. Also, the rental unit may not show as well as it would if it were empty and clean. On the other hand, it may show better with furniture and personal belongings in it; empty rental units can give the feeling of coldness and hostility.

You will have to be the judge of what circumstances will increase your chances of securing a new tenant. If you decide to show your rental units before they are vacated, make provisions in your lease to gain access for the showings. Most tenants will not object to your showing their unit as long as you give them adequate notice.

Prospecting Pointers

A good marketing plan, mixed with effective advertising, should produce an abundance of prospects. Since you will have invested time and money to generate these prospects, it is important to get a good return. To ensure a high rate of success, you must follow some sales steps in getting the prospects committed to your rental property.

Your first opportunity to use sales skills will generally come when a prospective tenant calls with questions about your advertised property. This phone call is where most landlords lose their prospects. If you lose potential tenants in the initial conversations, you have lost time and money—the time you spent developing your marketing plan and advertising campaign, the time devoted to placing ads and answering the telephone, and the money spent on your marketing efforts. You are also losing money on the unoccupied rental unit. All in all, losing prospects is very expensive. By implementing some sales approaches in your phone conversations you can save time and make the most of your marketing money.

After the barrage of phone calls, you will have to show your rental units to the interested parties. This, too, is a vulnerable time for inexperienced property managers, since mistakes made during the showing will quickly alienate the prospects and keep your units empty.

Adopting some sales skills will dramatically increase your success as a property manager. In renting apartments, as in golf, a good follow-through is needed to seal your deal. There is good advice on how to acquire the best tenants for your building in the next chapter.

Advertising

Advertising is responsible for generating prospects. If people don't know you have units available for rent, they cannot rent them. However, while advertising can make your business thrive, it can also strangle your cash flow until it dwindles to nothing more than a puddle. Advertising is expensive when done wrong and a bargain when done right. As a self-manager, you must learn to harness the power of seductive advertising.

When I talk of seductive advertising, I do not mean ads with sexy people in them. I mean advertising that piques an interest in the consumer; the seduction comes from the combination of descriptive words and selective inducements. The way you structure your ad can make a tremendous difference in the phone calls it generates. To get a feel for how two different ads for the same rental unit can produce different results, compare the two samples ads that follow.

Sample Ad 1. For rent: three-bedroom condo with one and a half baths. Large living room with view and fireplace. Modern kitchen with all appliances furnished. Exercise room and sun room on the upper level. Great location with many amenities. No pets. Lease, references, and security deposit required. $850 per month. Call 555-1919 for details.

Sample Ad 2. For rent: Available now for your inspection, this natural wood, chalet-style condo is perfect for living, loving, relaxing, working, and all-out enjoyment. A raised stone hearth surrounds a warm fireplace in the center of the huge great room. As you cuddle by the fire, you can recline and enjoy the exposed beams and vaulted ceiling. If you like the outdoors, open the mini-blinds on the fixed glass panels and let the lush sights of nature fill your home with beauty. When it's time to cook, you will appreciate the wrap-around kitchen with its time-saver appliances. An island sink accents this contemporary kitchen, abounding with cabinets and charm. Three spacious bedrooms will accommodate all your furniture and desires. The master suite offers access to its own powder room and a full bath serves the remainder of the home. As you walk up the open stairway to the balcony, you can enter the fitness center or the sun room. After a workout in your private gym, relax in the whirlpool, under the skylights of the sun room. This homey hideaway is conveniently located to work, shopping, and schools. Responsible pets will be considered. If you act now, you can capture the elegance of this stunning home for the next year with only your deposit and signature. This executive condo can be yours for the modest monthly rent of $850. Responsible tenants with references may arrange a private showing by calling Bob at 555-1919.

Evaluating Sample Ad 1

Sample ad 1 will attract some attention and will no doubt generate phone calls. But although it mentions most of the most important features of the home, it fails to demonstrate its benefits. Even so, the reader will have enough general information to make a decision about calling for further details. This sample is relatively short and therefore relatively inexpensive to run. It is adequate but not as good as it could be.

Even though sample ad 1 lacks strong pulling power, it is better than most. When property managers look at the cost of advertising, they keep the ad as short as possible. This is a mistake. After years of sales and marketing experience, I have found that descriptive ads not only generate more calls, they produce a higher-quality prospect. Descriptive advertising costs more, but the results far exceed those of mediocre ads.

Evaluating Sample Ad 2

The first obvious difference between sample ad 1 and sample ad 2 is length. Even if the second ad is no better in its content than the first, its length will catch a reader's eye. When a perusing prospect reads the classified column, he is drawn to a large ad. Since most ads are short, long ads stand out from the crowd.

Note the second difference: the first ad jumps straight to a description of the property. There is no introduction, and a cold feeling results. The second ad opens with a friendly introduction that sets the tone for what follows. It tells the reader she is in control, that the unit is available for her inspection. This adds a personal dimension to the ad.

Following the opening is descriptive text that makes the reader feel the style and appearance of the property. In the first ad, the reader knows the unit being offered for rent is a condo, but has no idea of what type. The many suggestions of potential uses for the condo in the second ad fuels the reader's imagination. All of a sudden, she can envision herself in the condo, doing what she likes best.

The first ad tells the prospect that the condo has a fireplace, whereas the second suggests a pleasing scenario to accentuate the fireplace. The exposed beams and vaulted ceiling were never mentioned in the first ad, but these special touches could be the spark needed to make the reader call you. The first ad tells the reader the unit has a view, but it doesn't indicate what the view is. A view of a parking lot or smoke stacks is hardly comparable with the view of a forest.

Most housing seekers expect a modern kitchen and appliances to be included in their rental. The first ad's description of these features does little to motivate the reader. However, the second expands on the kitchen's assets and mentions key words like cabinets, charm, island sink, timesaver appliances, and contemporary. Doesn't a contemporary kitchen sound more appealing than a modern kitchen? Timesaver appliances may be the same as any other modern appliances, but the term conjures up a level of excellence.

The sentence about the bedrooms in the second ad allows the reader to fill in the blank. It says his furniture will fit in the room, but also opens the door to his imagination for the fulfillment of his desires. The reference to a master suite is an added touch that tells the prospect this unit is designed for his kind of living. Letting the prospect know there is a powder room adjacent to the master suite may be all it takes to make your phone ring.

In the description of the stairway and the balcony in the second ad, the reader gets a feeling of open living. Open living and natural views go together well. The first ad casually mentions an exercise room. Exercise is not a pleasant thought for many people, but fitness creates an entirely different response. By a change in the wording in the second ad, the reader is impressed with the upstairs facilities of the rental property.

The description of the whirlpool and skylights in the second ad informs the reader about the ambience of the sun room. She can see that this is a house designed for successful individuals. Both ads say the location of the condo is good, but the second ad mentions the condo's surrounding privacy.

The first ad eliminates many good tenants by refusing all pets. The second gives the landlord a choice in the matter—the hint that pets may be accepted opens the door to an entirely different market. Unlike the hard, cold words of the first ad, the second ad softly makes the point about a lease and deposit. The simple use of the word responsible in the description of tenants will weed out some of the unsavory crowd.

In the second ad's closing, the reference to a private showing puts the rental property on a higher level. It indicates that this property is perfect for professionals. Also, Bob has added an important element in the rental of his condo by including a first name in the second ad. When the reader calls, he will be calling Bob, not some unknown person. This may seem like a silly difference, but people are less apprehensive if they know the name of the person they are calling. By removing apprehension, Bob has assured more calls and reduced the risks of callers putting up their protective shields during initial contact.

Comparing the Two Ads

I made many comparisons between sample ad 1 and sample ad 2 as we evaluated the second ad. Beyond those comparisons, we should consider the advantages of using the second ad over the first. Both ads were written for a condominium, but they are representative of the type of ad you could use for any rental property. Whether you are trying to rent a detached home, an apartment, or even a room, the same advertising strategies apply.

The first comment many landlords will make about the two ads is the difference in the costs to run them. Certainly, the second ad will cost more to run than the first in terms of out-of-pocket cash, but wise landlords will look beyond the obvious. The first ad is indeed less expensive to run, but if it doesn't get the job done, it is a waste of money. Likewise, the cost of the second ad will be inconsequential if it produces a high-quality tenant. You must get around the mental block of looking only at the ad cost. It is imperative that you consider results when deciding which type of ad will be the most beneficial to you.

I am confident the first style of ad will produce enough inquiries for you to fill your vacancy, but will the callers be the best tenants for your building? By using the tactics employed in the second ad, you can aim your ad at specific types of tenants. Sample ad 2 is fairly generic, but it lends itself to a professional group with stable tendencies. Sample ad 1 is not targeted to any particular group or type. There is a strong likelihood that you would receive a better tenant from the second ad than from the first. You can carry this type of targeting much further.

By using selective phrases, you can target your advertisements to a small segment of the rental population. Key words will stress the type of tenant you are looking for without being obvious or discriminating. The way you describe your property will turn some people away and other people on. In addition to the wording of your ad, as I discuss below, how you advertise, the places you advertise, and the medium of advertising will influence the type of tenant who applies for residency.

How and Where You Advertise

How you advertise your rental business will dictate the type of customers you work with. If you know the type of tenant you want, finding a suitable one will be as easy as targeting your marketing. If you prefer individuals with college degrees, you can rent a mailing list and use direct mail to aim all of your advertising at such prospects. If you like the idea of having a plumber in the house, a mailing list can also provide you with the names and addresses of all the licensed plumbers in your area.

When you don't want to go to the expense of direct mail, you can word your newspaper advertisements to attract the attention of specific groups. If you want families with children, boast about the school systems, playgrounds, and entertainment near your rental units. If you prefer to avoid children, stress your rental's adult and professional nature. By weaving your ad with key words, you can influence the type of tenant you will be dealing with.

Word-of-mouth advertising is the best kind available. It is inexpensive and produces results in the recruitment of similar tenants. If you like the tenants you presently have, make them aware of upcoming vacancies. They may spread the word among their friends and coworkers, helping you to find good prospects.

Where you advertise can be directly related to the type of prospective tenants your ads will pull. An ad in the local paper may produce varied results, but an ad in a company newsletter will target your market. Placing a notice on a bulletin board in the community grocery store is unpredictable. Putting the same notice on a bulletin board in specialized clubs or organizations is much more likely to generate the type of leads you are looking for.

The quality of the publication or the location of your advertisements will have a bearing on the type of tenants who respond. Putting fliers under the windshield wipers of cars in the shopping center may produce calls, but the nature of the prospects will be unknown. Circulating the same fliers among a selected neighborhood can produce enviable results. The point is, how you target your market will have a direct result on the type of tenants you find.

Choosing a Type of Advertising

Just as the location of an ad dictates the type of tenants you will pull, the ad's style may also influence your results. Direct mail advertisements should produce a quality tenant if you have the right mailing list. Public notices and fliers produce responses that are impossible to predict. Signs provide better qualified leads, but they may not produce the type of tenant you are looking for.

A prospect who calls from a sign on the property knows the property's location and its physical appearance. This means two possible objections have been overcome before your phone rings. Location is always a determining factor for any prospective tenant. Signs produce potential tenants who are willing to live in the area of your property.

For landlords dealing in volume, radio advertising can be effective. When you use the air waves, you aim your ads at known demographics. Any good radio station will provide you with a profile of its listeners. You can then pick your stations and times carefully to control the type of tenant who is most apt to call in response.

Newspaper ads are probably the most common form of rental property advertising. They produce the highest volume of inquiries, since the average person who needs a place to live usually turns to the classified ads first. Newspaper advertising is also usually less expensive than other effective means of advertising, and it requires the least amount of time from the property manager who is carrying out her own ad campaign. With prints ads, once the concept is conceived, a phone call is all it takes to get the ad working.

Although very few managers include it in their marketing plan, telemarketing can be considered a form of advertising. When you place calls at random to solicit tenants, you are in effect advertising your rental units. Telemarketing requires a special type of approach to be successful. Some large companies rely on it for a percentage of their new rentals, but the average landlord will never use this potentially effective marketing tool.

Other types of advertising are available to property managers, but the ones above are the most frequently used. For most landlords, print ads in local newspapers will be the extent of their advertising scheme. Let's look at each of these types of advertising and see how they may be applied to your needs.

Direct Mail. Direct mail is the best way to reach a specialized market. Particularly if you are managing high-end, executive suites, it is an excellent choice. By renting a mailing list, you can direct your advertisement to specific professions or income levels. Your list can be based on almost any criteria you set. If you want to fill your vacancy with a doctor, rent a list consisting only of doctors. You can usually obtain either their business address or their home address.

Direct mail is hard to beat if you are looking for specialized tenants. It can get your advertising into the homes of thousands of rental prospects, including those currently living in other apartment buildings. While you may be prohibited from using fliers to solicit tenants in other buildings, advertisements mailed to those tenants will be delivered. Existing tenants are already renters. If you can give them a reason to move, you can fill your empty apartments with them.

With direct mail you can keep your advertising ideas secret. If you have a gimmick that works, you will not be advertising in a way that allows every other owner to steal it. When you want to test a marketing idea, direct mail can give you fast, accurate responses. If you can afford it, it will provide you with many desirable tenants to choose from.

The drawback to direct mail is its cost, which is prohibitive if you are only renting a few units each year. Quality name lists are not cheap and neither is postage. Even if you obtain a bulk rate permit, your postage costs can be staggering. Then there is the cost of typesetting and printing, as well as having your mailer folded. If it will be sent in an envelope, stuffing the envelopes will take additional time or money. Unless you are dealing in a high-volume rental business, direct mail will probably not be cost-effective.

Fliers. Distributing fliers around the community will attract attention, but not all of it will be the kind you are hoping for. For example, if you stick fliers under the windshield wipers of every car parked at the shopping mall, you may get a notice from the mall later demanding that you clean up the parking lot. When people see a notice on their car they are not interested in, many simply drop it on the ground. If enough people do this, it makes quite a mess. Even if the mall doesn't require you to clean up the litter, it may clean it up and send you a bill for the work.

The advantage to fliers is their low cost. They are inexpensive to have printed and require only the time it takes to circulate them. Since fliers are not one of the more classy methods of advertising, you may not find the type of tenants you hope for. Except in unique circumstances, they should not be used for renting your vacant units.

Signs. Placing a sign in the window of your vacant property can be a very effective advertising tool. You know that by the time people call you from the sign they are interested in the building and the location, and this is an advantage.

A disadvantage to signs is the vandalism you invite when you place one on your property. Undesirable elements of the community may use your vacant property for shelter, parties, or other more destructive events. A sign in the window of a vacant apartment can draw more trouble than tenants. For that reason, the use of signs must be evaluated on an individual basis. If you can use one without fear of property damage, it can produce good results. In general, however, I would advise against it.

Radio Ads. Radio advertising is too expensive for the landlord with only occasional vacancies. It is usually affordable only if you are running a busy management company. Nevertheless, if you are in a position to use radio ads, they can work very well.

By carefully selecting the time your ad will run and on what stations, you can target your market. Using the station's demographics, you can write a script to suit the listeners, and if your ad runs during the rush hour, thousands of people will hear about your rental property. If you decide to advertise on the radio, budget enough money to keep your ad running frequently. Repetition is important to success.

Print Ads. Print ads are what most landlords use to fill vacancies. They are the best choice when you are looking to generate a high volume of calls with a limited budget. They are also quick to perfect and put to work. With a phone call to the paper, you can receive tenant inquiries the next day. The simplicity and economy of this type of advertising is what makes it the most popular for many property managers.

Print ads allow you to tell the public as much, or as little, as you like about your rental unit. A prospective tenant can read the ad over and over again at his leisure and compare it to other ads surrounding it. All of these are good reasons to use print ads.

Most managers invest their advertising budget in classified ads, but display ads have their place, too. They are much more expensive than an in-column classified ad, but they can produce much faster and better results. A classified ad may get lost among all the other ads, but a well-designed display ad will stand out and attract attention. Normally, a classified ad will be all that is needed to fill your vacancy, but if you are willing to invest a little more money, a display ad should generate more calls.

When you place a classified ad, be descriptive. Long descriptive ads result in better-qualified prospects. They also reduce curiosity calls. If you don't include the rental amount in your ad, for example, many of your callers will not be interested once they find out what it is. These curiosity calls tie up your phone and rob you of valuable time. The more you put in the ad, the less wasted time you will have with unsuitable prospects.

Display ads should be open and concise, yet too many advertisers cram them full of words and clip art. A simple one, with a strong border and good open space, will be easier to read and will attract more attention. Look through the paper and notice the ads that catch your eye. By studying other people's ads, you can learn to make yours more effective.

Telemarketing Tips

Telemarketing is a numbers game. You cold-call a large number of people to generate a small number of prospects, and if you get one person out of ten calls to talk to you, you are doing okay. This form of marketing is labor-intensive. If you are not experienced in phone sales, leave telemarketing alone. The time spent dialing for tenants is usually not well rewarded.

If you do decide to use telemarketing, do some homework before picking up your phone. You can purchase directories that group people and their phone numbers by streets. If you know a certain street comprises mostly rental properties, call the people living there. If you know a street is inhabited by people who own their own condos or houses, avoid it—if they own their own property, they will not rent yours. Unless you have a large number of vacancies to fill on a regular basis, telemarketing will not be a good choice for your advertising.

Entice Them with Incentives

When all else fails, buy your tenants with incentives. In tight economies and competitive markets, incentives are sometimes needed to encourage tenants to sign up with you. They may be as simple as a free microwave oven with every apartment rented or as big as tickets for two to an exotic vacation. The value of the incentive should be determined by the value of the tenant. If you are losing a thousand dollars a month on a vacant apartment, giving away a hundred-dollar microwave oven to fill the vacancy is a bargain. When it comes to incentives, use your imagination.

If money is tight, waiving the requirement of a security deposit may fill your apartment. If a prospect is looking at five apartments that are all about the same, the savings you offer by doing so will entice the tenant to rent yours. I don't recommend waiving deposits, but in tough times it can keep your mortgage payments current.

Offering one month of free occupancy is another way to attract people watching their budget. However, this method is used often and has lost much of its pulling power. With so many landlords offering a free month's rent, you will just be a part of the crowd.

There is a way to set yourself apart with free occupancy without spending more money. Assume you are willing to offer a free month's rent. Also assume a month's rent is $800. In this scenario all of your competitors are offering a free month's rent with every lease signed. Why not change your offer to a romantic weekend for two at a flashy resort? Or, if this doesn't suit, how about two tickets to the destination of the tenant's choice with a value of up to $800? Most people will not use the $800 saved from the free rent to take a vacation, but if you are offering a free vacation, they may jump on it.

In today's market, one of the most effective incentives is allowing pets in the rental unit. I know that most landlords cringe at this idea, but pets can be your ticket to more money and fewer vacancies. People with pets consider the critters part of the family. They would no more give up their pet than they would their children. If you are one of the few landlords allowing pets, you can corner the market on some top-notch tenants.

Tenants with pets are often more responsible than those without them. With proper screening, you can come to terms that will appeal to you and the tenant. For example, you can require an additional deposit for protection against any damage a pet causes, and your lease can include strong language to control the conditions of allowing the pet.

Tenants with pets are less likely to move as often as those without them. The lack of rental property allowing pets helps to ensure that in addition to getting an extra deposit, by allowing pets you can probably charge a higher rent and still keep your units full. If you decide to allow pets, I am sure you will find filling vacancies much easier and faster.

The One-Two Punch

When you combine a strong marketing plan with effective advertising, you can deliver a knockout punch to your competition. The one-two punch of marketing and advertising can make you more successful than you know. It will be well worth your time and effort to learn all you can about sales, marketing, and advertising. If you master these skills, you should be able to minimize your vacancy rate and maximize the rate of return on your rental investments.

Chapter 5

Tenant Tactics

Tenants are a landlord's business. Without them no landlord is going to stay in the rental business for long. Successful property managers know the value of good tenants and will go to any reasonable length to keep them. It is the investor who is more infatuated with his spreadsheet than with his tenants who winds up in bankruptcy court. If watching your pennies makes your dollars grow, keeping good tenants builds a pleasing spreadsheet. Tenants are the cornerstone of your business. If you fail to recognize the importance of even the most common tenant, you will find yourself in financial trouble before you know it.

To accomplish your goal of maintaining desirable residents, you must exert some effort. In a landlord–tenant relationship, it is the little things that add up. If you ignore a good tenant's legitimate request that you repair a leaking faucet, you are creating a frustration in him that can lead to your losing him. As you read this chapter, rate your present performance. I imagine you will discover aspects of your tenant relations that can be improved.

Finding Good Tenants

The last chapter instructed you in marketing and advertising methods to use in your search for quality tenants. The procedures described there are all proven performers. In addition to what you have already learned, there are other ways to find the best available lessees. Word-of-mouth advertising and referrals are some of the best.

Current Tenants

Your present residents can be an excellent source of new tenants. If you have been keeping them happy, they will be glad to help you fill your vacancies. Let them know you need a new tenant, and they may turn one up before you can. When people are at work or meeting socially, housing is a common topic of conversation. If someone is complaining about his or her present living conditions, your tenant scout may be able to plug your building. With the right timing and this kind of referral, your vacancy may be filled expeditiously, with a remarkable inhabitant.

Military Base Bulletin Boards

If your community is home to a military base, you might capture a respectable tenant from the base's bulletin board or referral system. Military personnel are generally well disciplined and responsible. By placing your rental units on the referral system at the base, you may never have to advertise elsewhere to find acceptable tenants. Most bases assist their incoming personnel in finding suitable housing. If you are on their list, you can take advantage of the frequent personnel changes at military installations.

Corporate Referrals

With a rental property convenient to large corporations, you can capitalize on the corporate shuffle. As executives come and go, you can cash in on their housing needs. Major corporations offer all types of support to their valued employees. One of the most common services is help in finding a home. By contacting the large companies in your area, you can get on their referral list.

Being on a major corporation's referral list can eliminate your need to advertise for tenants. A side benefit is the financial qualifications of your lessee. If she is a mobile executive, she should be financially secure. Your concerns for collecting your rent should be put to ease when you rent to corporate executives through a referral service.

The Local Housing Authority

Most cities have an agency devoted to dealing with the housing needs of the local population. Such agencies can be an almost endless source of tenants—if your property meets their minimum requirements. Chapter 3 talked about subsidized rental programs. As you read there, these programs have both pros and cons. If you decide to participate in them, you can keep your building filled without much advertising.

Even if you are not interested in working with subsidized rental programs, the local housing authority can be of great help to you. In particular, it can provide invaluable information to help you establish a reasonable rental rate, and it can give you historical data to dissect for building your marketing plan. A trip to the housing authority is worth your time. You will never know what benefits you may derive from the agency unless you investigate its many services.

Real Estate Brokers

Real estate brokers can be your best friend if you are looking for short-term tenants. Brokers deal with people buying and selling houses. During these transactions, it is not uncommon for the principals to need temporary housing. If you have an established rapport with several brokers, you may never have to advertise for tenants.

Taking in short-term tenants has its advantages. Because of the frequent turnover, you can keep your rental fees at a current level. Most short-term tenants know they will have to pay a higher rent for their temporary tenancy, which allows you to collect a higher rent and enjoy a more attractive net income.

Property Management Firms

Property management firms may seem like a strange partner for the owner managing her own property, but don't rule them out. Professional management firms typically have a high volume of inquiries from qualified tenants. You can list your property with these firms on a referral basis. Yes, they probably will hassle you to let them manage your property, but they may be able to help you fill vacancies without your losing control of your property.

Full-time management companies can be flooded with calls from good tenants. In a good market, they may have more tenants than they have units to rent. While a management company would like to benefit from the earnings of managing your property, it may be willing to refer customers for commission. Put yourself in its position, and you will understand why it would do this. The following example will help you decide if property management firms can do you any good.

Assume you are a major rental management company. You have dozens of qualified rental applicants, but you are limited in what you can offer them because most of the units you manage are successfully rented. What do you do with your stable of ready, willing, and able tenants who are looking for housing? If you don't have anything to offer them, you lose their business, and in doing so, the money you spent to generate the leads has been wasted.

If you have an independent landlord to refer them to for a fee, at least you will recover some of your advertising costs. Since you have nothing available to rent to the tenant, you have nothing to lose by doing so. If the landlord signs a lease with the tenant, your firm will receive compensation for the referral.

This is a good situation for all parties. The tenant finds a place to live and is happy with you. When she is ready to relocate, she may call you again, or if she has friends looking for a rental, she may recommend you. The landlord fills a vacancy with a qualified resident. And you, as the management company, get a fee for referring the tenant to the landlord, as well as a good reputation and the possibility for repeat business from the prospect or her friends.

See how well a good relationship with a management firm can work? Chances are good that some firms will not be interested unless you give them control of your property, but if approached properly, most should be willing to work with you.

Keeping Good Tenants

By now, your mind should be swirling with a multitude of methods for filling vacancies. Well, finding good tenants is only part of the battle. Often, the most difficult part of landlording is keeping them. It does little good to find good tenants if you can not keep them. Advertising is effective, but it can get expensive. The less you have to advertise for residents because you can't keep the ones you have, the more money you will retain at the end of the year.

Most of the suggestions given in this chapter for finding tenants do not require an extensive outlay of cash. Whatever method you use to attract good people, keeping them happy will reduce your vacancy rate and your advertising expenses. The remainder of this chapter will help you reduce tenant turnover. By doing so, you will enjoy higher profits from your income property.

Start at the Beginning

The tenant–landlord relationship begins with initial contact between the two parties, which is normally made by telephone. If you are short or rude on the phone, prospective tenants may not have a continued interest in your property. Make a habit of being pleasant and friendly in all your contacts with prospective tenants, and make an effort to remember their names. People like to be called by name and will appreciate your addressing them accordingly.

First impressions are made in a matter of seconds. You may not get a second chance to alter the initial opinion recorded in a prospective tenant's mind. If on that first call there are dogs barking and children screaming in the background, your prospect's first impression of you may not be very good. If you are conducting your business from home, try to control the atmosphere to maintain a professional image.

The Second Step

If you have a successful phone conversation, the prospect will want to inspect your rental unit. Keep in mind that many good tenants have full-time jobs and thus may find it very difficult to take time off from work. Be prepared to show your units in the evening and on weekends. This is when your customer is available. If you insist on showing the property during normal business hours, you may lose someone who would be ideal.

Attempt to cater to the prospect's needs for a convenient showing. Avoid showing property when you are in a rush. If the inspection is going well, you should stick with it and close the deal. Going out to show an apartment when you must leave after twenty minutes to make a lodge meeting is not a good idea. Don't force the tenant to conform to your timetable. Remember, he is the customer and you are the vendor.

For the showing, dress appropriately and be friendly. If you give the tenant the feeling she is inconveniencing you, she will probably not stay long. Start a conversation using information you extracted in your phone interview. Talk about subjects the prospect has an interest in. If she is a golfer, talk about golf. If you don't know anything about golf, ask questions. People love it when they can give advice on a subject they know well. By mentioning that you are considering taking up golf, you could be closing the deal through casual conversation.

People want more than a comfortable place to live. They want a landlord they get along with. If you can build a basis for uncomplicated conversation, you are on your way to securing a tenant. People also appreciate someone who has an interest in their lives. By showing such an interest, you are setting yourself apart from other property managers. Inexperienced managers open the door and let the tenant roam at will. They rarely talk about anything other than the terms of the rental. While this approach will bag some prospects, your success will be much higher with a friendly, but effective, sales approach.

Making the Deal

Once the tenant wants your unit, be professional in the presentation of your paperwork. Don't shove papers at him and expect him to sign them without reading them. Treating the tenant to a cup of coffee or a snack at a nearby restaurant is a good idea for ensuring a signature on your lease. Escort the tenant to a relaxing gathering place and cut your deal in comfort.

Having all your paperwork in order will put the tenant at ease. If you present your forms in a businesslike manner, she will not feel like you are pulling a fast one. Use professionally printed forms and agreements; cheap photocopies do not induce a feeling of comfort, but rather make you look like a fly-by-night operator. If you have attractive forms, on good quality paper, the tenant will be less likely to resist signing them. Go through all of your rental policies with the tenant. Make sure there are no misunderstandings before committing yourself to a lease. When all is well, sign the deal.

After the Lease Is Signed

After the lease is signed, your work at keeping the tenant begins. You have successfully acquired a desirable resident; now it is up to you to ensure that he will stay with you. This part of your job never ends, nor is it easy. You must make a conscious effort to maintain a favorable relationship for as long as you can.

This responsibility extends from the move-in process to the move-out process. Even after your tenant leaves you, if he left on good terms, he has value to you. He can recommend your building to friends and coworkers, and you may be able to use him as a reference. The rest of this chapter will help you ensure good tenant relations indefinitely.

Communicating with Your Tenants

Communication plays an important role in successful property management. When communications between landlords and tenants are poor, relations between the two suffer. Bad communication creates confusion, and confusion creates controversy. Once you become adversarial with your tenant, your relationship may be damaged beyond repair. You can avoid most conflicts by being clear. The following examples will show how good communication skills can help you.

A Standard Rental Policy

You should establish a standard rental policy for your tenants, with the same rules for all. Your tenants will talk to each other, and if they find you have different rules for each of them, problems can arise. Once you have made your rental rules, put them in writing. Then staple them together or put them in a binder. Make duplicate copies of your original policy to give to each new tenant. Have all prospective tenants read and agree to your policy prior to signing a lease.

It is also a good idea to have the tenant sign a copy of the rental policy. If you have, then, when a question comes up, you can show the tenant the signed rental policy, proving that he accepted your policy before signing his lease. Having this type of documentation can stop many arguments before they happen.

The Lease

Have a lease prepared by your attorney, written in terms any of your tenants can understand instead of legal jargon. Make sure it dictates the terms of your agreement with the tenant in an informative and enforceable manner. If you have to go to court with your tenant, the lease will be your most effective weapon.

Your lease must include all of the terms of your rental policy. It could incorporate the rental policy, or it could refer to it as an attachment. In any event, include all pertinent facts, rules, and related language in your lease.

The Move-In List

Chapter 2 touched on the move-in checklist and how it can eliminate the possibility of some future misunderstandings. Your tenant's signature indicates acceptance of the conditions of the premises at the time she takes occupancy. The list also documents the condition of the rental unit for future reference.

When it is time for the tenant to leave, you can use the move-in checklist to assess any damage she caused. For example, if your walls look like they were sprayed with buckshot from all the pictures she hung, you can prove they were not in that condition when she moved in. By being able to prove before and after conditions, you are in a much stronger position to win any battle over a damage deposit.

When you go over the move-in checklist with your tenant, explain why and how it will be used. If she knows you will have a record to prove any damages she is responsible for, she should be a better tenant. However, the way you present yourself in this meeting is pivotal.

If you say you insist on a signed move-in checklist to protect you from destructive tenants, your new resident may feel insulted. Therefore, in your explanation, stress how the list protects both of you. Tell her that by signing a comprehensive move-in checklist, she will not be held responsible for existing damage. Explain that without the list, such damage may not be noticed until she terminates her tenancy. Telling the tenant how the move-in checklist is to her advantage should make her eager to cooperate. This is only one example of how your presentations to tenants can affect your relationship with them.

Dealing with Past-Due Rent

When a tenant is late with his rent, you must take action immediately. Too many landlords wait, hoping that the tenant's check will arrive in the next mail delivery, but this is not the proper way to run your business. If the rent is due on the first of the month, it should be in your hands no later than the tenth. If it is not, you must approach the tenant to learn the reason for the lack of payment.

Inexperienced and unsuccessful managers usually take one of two courses of action when the rent is not delivered on time. Either they do nothing or they go at the tenant with threats and rude language. Neither of these tactics is the correct method for solving your problem. If you just wait, your cash flow is affected and the situation can build into an ugly scene. If you run to the tenant like a wild person, you will damage your relationship and may wind up feeling like a fool. For all you know, there may be a very reasonable excuse for the tardy rent.

Contact the tenant in a calm and professional manner when the rent is overdue. Depending upon your normal means of communication, this may be by phone, mail, or a personal visit. Let the tenant know you have not received the rent and ask for an explanation of the circumstances. You may find that he sent the rent and it was misplaced in the mail. He may have been working out of town and overlooked his rent payment. Or he may have been on vacation and forgotten to mail his check. Maybe there has been a serious illness in his family that distracted him. It is also possible the tenant is out of work and doesn't have the money. The list of reasons could go on and on.

If the tenant makes no response to your request for payment and an explanation, get ready to take legal action. If he has good reason for being late, you may want to work with him. With a simple oversight, you will collect your rent and go on about your business. If the tenant has fallen on hard times and can't pay the rent, you must make a decision whether to work with him or evict him.

If the tenant has been a good one, with a steady payment history, consider working with him, but if this is not the first time you have had problems with him, you may wish to use this breach of the lease to get him out. In considering the possibility of accepting a partial payment or waiting for payment, remember the cost and time involved in finding a good replacement.

If you have to evict this tenant and find a new one, you are going to lose rental income. If the tenant can solve his financial problems quickly, you will be money ahead to work with him. Only you will be able to decide the right course of action. In general, if you can work with a good tenant to keep him, you will be better off in the long run.

When it comes to money, document every step you take. If the tenant gives a partial payment, draft an agreement detailing the terms for accepting the small payment. If you decide to give him an extra month to get back on his feet, draw up a written agreement describing the details. Always retain your rights to pursue any legal means available to you for the collection of unpaid monies. Also make it clear that because you are allowing an extra grace period, you are not releasing the tenant from the obligation of paying for the delinquent rent. Your attorney will be able to advise you on how to retain all of your rights to financial collections and evictions.

Routine Maintenance

All rental property will need routine maintenance from time to time, and this is an area of property management where many managers go astray. All too often they put off repairs until the last possible minute, which is detrimental to the property and to the landlord–tenant relationship. When your tenant asks for a legitimate repair or adjustment in the rental unit, respond quickly to the request.

When the tenant calls, arrange a time to get into the unit to evaluate the problem. Keep your scheduled appointment and show the tenant you care about her and your building. Thank her for bringing the deficiency to your attention. Depending upon the nature of the problem, the tenant may have saved you money by calling to report the problem.

I have seen more landlord–tenant disputes develop from ignored maintenance than from any other single cause, except for money. And when these confrontations arise, it is usually with good tenants. Bad tenants don't care about your property, and because they don't care, they won't advise you of problems hurting your investment. But good tenants, who respect you, will take an interest. When they find a problem, they will call you. If you fail to respond, they lose confidence in you. After all, it is your building—you should be concerned about its upkeep. When the tenants feel they are more concerned than you are, they become frustrated, and this frustration can build to a massive eruption. Let's look at a few examples of how your lack of interest in maintenance needs can cause hard feelings between you and your tenants.

Let's say one of your tenants calls to report a kitchen faucet with a steady drip. She gets your answering service and leaves a message. You procrastinate on returning her call because you don't like dealing with your tenants, but she continues to call and you finally get back to her. After telling you about the problem, the tenant asks when you would like to come into her home to correct the leak. You tell her you will be by the next day at noon.

The tenant comes home from work to meet you, but you get involved in other activities and don't keep your appointment. You don't even call to let her know you won't be coming by. When you don't show up, the tenant calls, but only gets your answering machine again. She gives up and goes back to work. After a few days of playing phone tag, you schedule a new time to fix the leak. This time you do show up, but you don't have the proper tools to do the job. This is another day of work wasted for the tenant. The longer it takes for you to fix the leak, the worse your relationship with her becomes. While you are putting off doing a necessary task, you are upsetting a good tenant and wasting water and money.

There is no excuse for not responding promptly to tenant complaints. If a complaint is not justified, deal with it. If it is legitimate, correct it. Don't ignore the tenant. She is calling to help you. Your attitude and actions in these cases can swing the landlord–tenant relationship in either direction. If you show an interest and fix the problem, the tenant will be happy and continue to respect you. If you don't, she may build up a resentment towards you and decide to move into another building.

I knew a landlord who put off replacing burned out light bulbs in his hallways for over two weeks. This was in large multifamily buildings in a city known for its criminal element. The tenants did not like coming home to dark hallways.

When the landlord bought the building, all the tenants were prompt in paying their rent and overall were responsible. After numerous requests to replace the light bulbs went unanswered, the tenants called the code enforcement office. It was not until the code officer contacted the landlord that the light bulbs were replaced.

This type of negligence and his poor handling of the tenants ultimately cost the landlord his buildings and his credit. His inadequacy as a property manager caused him to lose his good tenants, and when filling his vacancies, he used bad judgment and got bad tenants. In less than two years, he lost all of his rental properties and was forced to file bankruptcy. This type of disaster can strike you if you don't learn and practice good tenant tactics.

Resident Managers

When landlords own buildings with six or more apartments, the question of a resident manager often comes up. There may not be any clear-cut answer to whether or not you should have one. As with most decisions in business, there are pros and cons to be considered. Let's take a moment to look at some of them.

The Advantages

Resident managers can bring a new dimension to your property management chores. Under the proper conditions, they can handle many daily problems that arise, thus freeing you to pursue other interests without worry. Also, since resident managers live in the building they manage, they can keep a close eye on things. If a tenant is leaving bags of garbage in the hallway, the resident manager will know about it earlier than an offsite manager would. If a tenant gets rowdy on Friday night, he will be right on the spot to stop the noise. When tenants need to report something about the building, resident managers are easy to find, which can make the difference in being told of a potential problem and having it go undeclared. While tenants may not take the time to call or write an offsite manager, they will frequently talk to a resident manager, who is always close by.

A resident manager can act as a liaison between you and the tenants, which can prove very helpful. By having the tenants deal with the resident manager first, you will know what their problem is before talking to them, and you will have time to think and decide on a course of action. This one aspect alone is enough to make resident managers valuable.

When workers need access to your building, the resident manager can let them in. This saves you time and allows you to spend your efforts on more rewarding tasks. If you are trying to fill a vacancy, your resident manager can show the apartment to prospective tenants. This is another huge time-saver, but I don't recommend using resident managers in this capacity. For one thing, they may not possess the sales skills that you do when showing an apartment. For another, in some areas, anyone showing property for sale or rent must be licensed. This can cause big problems if your resident manager is not licensed for the job.

Finally, resident managers improve the security of your building. If they see suspicious people about, they can call the police. As an offsite manager, you will not know that these questionable characters are hanging around your property.

The Disadvantages

For all the good resident managers can do, they can also do some harm. And there is the question of taxes, insurance, and other employee-related expenses to consider. Most landlords give a resident manager a reduced rent in return for services. This practice is done all the time, but it can cause problems.

When you provide compensation to the resident manager, you may be creating an employee relationship. If so, you could be held responsible for workers' compensation insurance and employee taxes and expenses. These costs may be enough to outweigh the resident manager's advantages. Check with your attorney and the proper authorities before putting yourself into a potentially costly and dangerous position.

It is not uncommon for resident managers to be friends with the other tenants. While this can work to your advantage, it can also hurt you. If the manager is too friendly with the tenants, she may sometimes look the other way. And if she does not treat all tenants equally, you could be in for more trouble.

With a resident manager, you may feel the building is under control and no longer needs your personal attention. This is not true. Even with onsite help you must take an active interest in the operation of your income property. Resident managers can help you, but they cannot replace you.

Depending upon the circumstances, your resident manager may get you into legal trouble. If you have authorized her to act for you, you may be held accountable for her actions. If she violates a tenant's rights, you could be on the hook as well.

The decision to use a resident manager is one you will have to make. I have never used one. I have had tenants who kept an eye on my property, but never in an official capacity. Talk to your attorney before designating a resident manager. The repercussions from your decision to appoint one might be more than you bargained for.

The On-Site Handyman

If you have a tenant with the proper qualifications, you may be able to use him as a resident handyman. Having someone in the building to take care of minor problems can be a major advantage, but the disadvantages are similar to those of a resident manager. If you want a tenant to do your maintenance and repairs, find out what you are getting into before he starts. Check to see what you may be held responsible for before authorizing any work.

General Suggestions

There are some basic procedures that will always apply to your property management business. The remainder of this chapter deals with routine policies that should make you more productive.

Treat your tenants like respectable citizens. They are people and deserve respect as much as your banker or accountant. After all, your tenants are the people who make it possible for you to remain in the rental business. I have seen landlords who looked down on their tenants as second-class citizens. This is not only morally wrong, it is a bad business move. Tenants will pick up on your feelings and actions. If they do not feel appreciated, they will not stick around for long.

Don't ignore complaints. The longer you stall a tenant, the more enraged she will become. Take enough time to think through the situation and make a sound decision, but don't cut yourself off from your tenants. Hiding behind an answering machine is one of the worst things you can do in your dealings with them. You may not like having to face them, but avoiding them only makes things more uncomfortable when you finally meet.

Don't be afraid to stand your ground when you are in the right. As the landlord, you must remain in control. If you don't, you will not last long as a property manager. Chapter 6 tells you all about staying in control of your tenants. When you make a mistake, be willing to take responsibility for your actions, and if appropriate, apologize. It is one thing to be in control and quite another thing to be a tyrant.

When you have good tenants, surprise them with a token of your appreciation. Place a bouquet of flowers in the apartment on their scheduled move-in date. They will be thrilled to see them when they arrive. You can bet very few other landlords have ever given them flowers. After the tenants have been with you for a while, give them another showing of your appreciation, such as a discount on their December rent to help them with their holiday purchases. Use your imagination, but let your tenants know you are happy to have them in your building.

Be sensitive to your tenants' needs. If you have an elderly couple on the third floor, the steps may be an obstacle for them. When a unit becomes available on the first floor, offer it to them before you advertise it. They may not want to relocate, but they will appreciate your consideration and offer. This policy can apply to a number of situations. The key here is to be tuned in to your tenants and show them you want to make their lives easier.

Keep your building and grounds clean and well groomed. When you show the tenants you respect your property, they will be more likely to respect it too. A neat building will attract and hold a better-quality tenant than will a neglected one. Provide good lighting in and around your property. Sufficient lighting will reduce vandalism and improve your tenants' comfort level.

If you must take aggressive action against a tenant, do so in a businesslike manner—never get into a shouting match. If you exhibit improper behavior towards one tenant, the rest will know about it. Cursing and screaming is not going to resolve your differences. Follow the procedures you outlined in your rental policy to take control of the situation. Consult with your attorney and handle the matter judiciously and expediently. All the other tenants will be watching to see what happens. When they see you mean business, they may think twice before crossing you.

When the time comes to raise the rent, refer to Chapter 8. It is filled with ideas and ways for you to increase your rents without losing your tenants. Since your business is centered around rental income, Chapter 8 is mandatory reading.

Renewing leases with existing tenants can save you time and money. If you can convince them to renew, you will not have to fill vacancies, which, of course, saves time and money. This should be easy if you have done a good job managing the property. Keep track of when a tenant's lease is due for renewal, and before the due date, schedule a meeting with him. At the meeting go over any changes in the terms of your rental agreement for the next year. If you are planning a rent increase, cover the subject now.

On the outside chance that a tenant is not willing to renew, you will know it in advance. This gives you time to implement your marketing plan and advertise to find a replacement. You don't want to lose a good tenant, but if you can't hold him, you at least want as much advance notice as possible.

Summary

The summary for this chapter is simple: strive to get and keep good tenants. As simple as this may sound, expect to spend extra effort to reach your goal. Whenever possible, don't settle for less than the best. By following the suggestions in this chapter, you should have some of the most content tenants in the neighborhood.

Chapter 6

Who Is in Control?

If you have been in the rental business for long, you have probably noticed that tenants seem to have more rights than landlords. This may not be fair, but it is a fact. I have seen landlords become hostages to their tenants—not physically but financially. To avoid being the one out in the cold, you must maintain control.

If you are fair and reasonable, it would seem that your tenants should return the gesture, but they don't always do that. Have you ever had a tenant vacate your unit in the middle of the night? Has a tenant ever moved your appliances with her when she left? These are only two of many questions about problem tenants I could ask. I probably could write an entire book on the misfortunes of landlords I have known. This chapter will help you rise above this used and abused crowd.

Tenants do, and should, have rights, and as a landlord and property manager, you may not infringe upon these rights. If you do, you may find yourself in jail. At the least, you could be required to pay a heavy fine. I am not an attorney and will not attempt to tell you what you legally can and cannot do. What I will do is give you ideas to run by your lawyer. If she approves of the suggestions, feel free to use them.

What Is Control?

Control does not have to mean physical or legal dominance. A person can control people without threatening them. Respect generates the most lasting form of control. If you hold a gun to someone's head, you are in control as long as you have the gun. If you turn to leave, the other person may take control by attacking you from behind. On the other hand, if you are in control by the approval of the other person, there is little risk of being stabbed in the back. Gaining control through respect takes time, but it is the best kind to have.

As it relates to landlording, control is usually maintained with written agreements and consistent actions. Having a written rule is of little use if you fail to enforce it. Making exceptions to the rule, for chosen tenants, will erode the effectiveness of the rule for other tenants.

In all my years in real estate, I have seen many forms of control. Some worked; some didn't. My experience with managing other people's property has shown me a lot. The experience gained from running my own buildings has cost me a lot. This chapter should give you an edge. It is compiled from many years of my own hands-on field experience as both an owner and a manager.

You, The Owner

As the owner of your rental property you may have more latitude in what you are able to do than a professional management company would have. For example, as the owner of a single-family home you rent to tenants, you can be more selective in your choice of occupants than you could be with a twelve-family apartment building. However, if you own several single-family homes, you can be placed in a different class. Before you get too consumed with control, check with your attorney to see if your control measures are legal.

You, The Manager

There is a big difference between being just the landlord and being both the landlord and the property manager. With a professional manager handling your property, you have a buffer. You are not personally making representations to tenants that may result in a lawsuit. You may still be involved in a suit caused by your rental agent, but you will not have the exposure you would have as your own manager.

The law is very strict on rental management. Before you spread your shoulders and take a bad attitude, know your limitations. If you are not familiar with rental management laws attend classes, read books, and talk with your lawyer until you do understand what is required of you. Ignorance is not a suitable defense in court.

Now that you have been advised of the possible repercussions of your actions, let's consider how you can stay in control—and out of court. Going to court is a losing proposition, even when you win. It costs money—sometimes lots of it—to bring action against a tenant or to defend yourself from a suit filed against you. Nevertheless, if you do find yourself in court, the written word will rule the day. All of your actions that might result in a legal confrontation should be documented in writing. This can mean everything from a signed, written lease to a phone log.

The judicial system runs on paperwork. The more documentation you have, the less likely you are to lose your battle. There is another advantage to written agreements. They remove confusion—a major cause of conflict between tenants and their managers. If your tenants know the rules, most of them will play by them. You cannot give vague instructions and then punish tenants who couldn't read your mind.

Written documents can not only help you win court battles, they can keep you out of them. When you can produce legitimate written documentation to support your position, people will not want to wage a legal battle against you. All in all, the proper paperwork is one of your best tools for staying in control and out of court.

Forms That Can Keep You in Control

With the help of your attorney, you can maintain much of your control, at least legally, with forms. Once a basic master form is made, you can use it for all your tenants. You can either photocopy it or store it in your computer for multiple uses. Let's take a close look at what the most common forms are that owners use to stay in control of their rental property.

Tenant Application Forms

The tenant application form should be completed by every rental prospect before you decide to whom to rent your unit. It will provide you with information to be used in your approval process, such as where the tenant has lived in the past and his social security number, employer, credit references, and financial status. It may ask a number of other questions to enable you to make a sound decision on whether or not the tenant meets your criteria.

One of the most important aspects of the form will be its language giving you permission to investigate the prospect's credit history, which you cannot do without the individual's permission. Every property manager should verify the credit standing of prospective tenants. People with excellent credit ratings can turn bad, but if they have good credit at the time you check, your odds are better for collecting your rent.

If you have enough rentals to justify the expense, you should consider joining a credit reporting bureau. This will make it easy to run a credit inquiry. If you do not have the volume to support such an expense, at least call all the references given on the application. Be advised, however, that not all of them will be on the up and up. Some people give the names of family and friends.

When you call to check references, be a little sneaky. Unless the phone is answered professionally, giving a company name, do a little probing. Ask what the relationship is between the reference and the applicant before you say why you are calling. People who give false references often use them for more than rental applications. You may trip the reference up and cause her to spill the beans. If she says Joe used to work for her, but Joe gave you her name as a landlord, you have exposed Joe as a potential fraud. Look below the surface to protect yourself from the professional deadbeats sometimes encountered in the rental business.

Rental Policy

After establishing your rental policy, you should create a form detailing all the rules and regulations you plan to enforce. This might cover the ownership of pets or waterbeds. It may also refer to how many parking spaces the tenant is entitled to or who is responsible for overflowing toilets. Unless you have an agreement in writing and signed by the tenant, you will be responsible for paying the plumber and any damages incurred from the stopped-up toilet.

Many landlords require the tenant to be responsible for a repair if the problem was the tenant's fault. For example, if the toilet in your second-floor apartment overflows and floods the apartment below it, a plumber will have to fix it. Also, someone will have to clean up the mess and make restitution for any water damages. If the plumber finds a rubber ducky in the toilet, it should be the tenant's responsibility to cover the costs of damages and repairs. If the problem was caused by faulty pipes, the landlord should bear the burden.

That is just one example of how rental policy wording can give you an edge. The same principle could be applied to broken windows: if the tenant breaks the glass, she pays to repair it. The rental policy might cover any alterations to the property the tenant is, or is not, allowed to perform. How would you feel if you entered your apartment and found the living room walls painted a blaze orange?

Make sure your rental policy covers every conceivable point you can think of. Then have all prospective tenants review it before you allow them to sign a lease. It is also a good idea to have the tenant sign the rental policy; this is proof to anyone involved in settling a dispute that the tenant has seen the document.

The Lease

A lease is the next form used once a tenant passes your application screening. It is also one of the most important forms you can use to maintain control of your rental property. As with all other legal forms, leases should be prepared by an attorney. It is possible to buy generic leases in some stores, but they do not afford the benefits of a custom lease prepared by your lawyer.

The lease should be comprehensive, leaving nothing to the imagination. It should obviously dictate the terms and conditions of your rental agreement with the tenant and may incorporate it or refer to it as an attached exhibit. The amount of the rent and how it should be paid must be in the lease. Security and damage deposits should also be covered, as should the term of the rental. In general, if you can think of it, it should be included.

The Check-In Form

As I discussed earlier, check-in forms, or move-in checklists, protect you if you are compelled to retain a damage deposit when a tenant vacates your property. Have each new tenant complete one as soon as he takes occupancy, and make sure it provides a room-by-room description of items for the tenant to inspect. Walls, ceilings, cabinets, plumbing, and all related items should be described, including any appliances you provide. If the tenant finds holes in the bedroom wall, there should be a place on the form to note the deficiency. If the range or refrigerator is missing, that point, too, should be noted. Your check-in form should cover every item you will consider in evaluating the retention of a damage deposit.

The Pet Addendum

If you will be allowing some of your tenants to keep pets, you should have a pet addendum. This form can be made a part of your lease and will specify the terms and conditions of allowing pets in the property. The addendum may require the tenant to comply with rules that are above and beyond those of the standard rental policy.

Many landlords require additional damage deposits from tenants with pets. It is also not unusual for landlords to charge pet-owning tenants a higher rent than tenants without pets pay. Any rules and conditions applying to pets should be included in the pet addendum.

Other Addendums

You can create other addendums for almost any purpose. A common one is used to address the issue of water-filled furniture. People with waterbeds, for example, are often made to pay additional damage deposits or purchase insurance to protect the landlord's property and the property of other tenants. In general, you can use addendums to cement agreements on any subject.

The discussion above detailed the most common forms used to move a tenant into your rental unit. Next, we will look at some forms that are helpful after the tenants have taken occupancy.

Rent Payment Coupons. Rent payment coupons are used by many property managers to facilitate rent collection. They can be beneficial since most people are already accustomed to paying their bills from payment books or monthly statements. Coupons remind a tenant to pay his rent. They don't cost much to have printed, and anything that helps tenants pay their rent on time is worth a try.

Access Forms. If your lease is properly worded, it will allow you access to your rental unit at any time so long as the tenant is given reasonable notice. You may need such access for maintenance or to show the apartment to a prospective purchaser. Whatever reason, when you need to get into an occupied apartment, an access notice should be delivered. By creating this form you are well prepared to give formal notice of your intent to enter the premises.

Late-Rent Forms. Some people will be late in paying their rent. When they are, use late-rent forms to notify them that their rent is overdue. Such forms should be friendly but firm enough to get the tenant's attention. They should note the fact that your lease allows you to charge a late fee for past-due rent if that is the case. Don't hesitate to send these forms to tenants. The late rent form is the beginning of your paper trail for eviction. I hope you will never have to evict anyone, but if you stay in the business long enough, there will come a time when eviction is the only way to deal with a problem tenant.

Vacate Forms. The reverse side of eviction is a tenant who moves out by his own choice. Since you will want some prior notice of your tenant's departure, it is a good idea to provide him with a vacate form to notify you of his intent to leave. Your lease should cover the acceptable reasons for early termination and the notice to vacate you require. A vacate form simply makes it easy for the tenant to comply with the agreed upon terms.

Change-Order Forms. Your lease may allow for rental increases at set intervals or other changes in the lease during its time of enforcement. When a change is made during a lease's term, you should use a change order, a form describing the nature of the deviation. By having your tenant sign the change order, you have proof of her acceptance of the changes.

Not enough property managers use change orders. Too many allow changes to be made with nothing more than a verbal agreement. This is fine—until there is a problem. When a conflict arises, without a signed change order, you have little chance of defending your position in the battle.

Pay Rent or Quit Forms. When a tenant has not paid his rent in the allotted and agreed upon time, you should issue a pay rent or quit notice. This informs the tenant of your plans to pursue legal action to collect the money due you. It tells him that if he doesn't pay his rent, he must move. A pay rent or quit notice is an important form in the eviction procedure.

Perform Covenant Forms. If a tenant breaks the rules of your rental policy, you should serve her with a perform covenant notice. This will notify her of her noncompliance with your rental rules and regulations, as dictated by the signed lease and rental policy. The form will give the tenant some period of time to conform to the rules before further action is taken. It can be instrumental in the execution of eviction proceedings.

Terminate Tenancy Forms. Most leases grant the landlord the right to terminate the tenancy granted, provided he or she gives sufficient notice to the tenant prior to termination. Terminate tenancy forms will keep you within your legal rights when terminating a tenant's occupancy, in compliance with the terms of the signed lease.

Forms are very helpful in maintaining control of your rental property, but they are not a cure-all. Even so, without the proper forms and paperwork you are very likely to find yourself on the losing end of a tenant–landlord conflict; with the proper forms, acknowledged by all parties, you have a much better chance of settling disputes in or out of court.

By combining the proper use of selected forms with good management skills, you can gain and retain control of your building. If you sit in your office with a deaf ear to your tenants, no amount of forms will save you. You must take an active interest in property management. When you deal with the public, and all property managers do, you must develop people skills, and people skills are most effective when coupled with sales skills. Now that you have an idea of the basic forms to use in your property management, let's take a look at the skills you should develop and hone.

The Basic Skills

This book is filled with advice for profitably managing your rental portfolio. It covers your responsibilities from beginning to end. The skills we will discuss overlap with abilities mentioned in other sections of the book; nevertheless, they are special skills, mandatory for the property manager who wants to enjoy his or her job.

Few people enjoy tasks that involve arguments and adversarial meetings, but as a property manager, you will be performing tasks most people wouldn't consider attacking. If you went out on the street and asked a passerby to go into your building and collect past-due rent from a hard-nosed tenant, what do you think he would say? How much money would you have to offer to convince the person to knock on a door and ask for money a tenant either doesn't have or is unwilling to give up? For many people, you could not pay them enough to handle such a job. For you as a property manager, collecting late rent is an accepted part of your job.

Do you know many people with the ability to remove problem tenants, even if the tenants will have no place to go? There will probably come a time in your career when you must be coldhearted. It can be difficult to keep emotions out of your business, but to make money, sometimes you have to. There are many ways to approach the job of property manager. You can be soft-spoken and friendly, or you can be loud and abrasive. Most managers fall somewhere between these two extremes. In whatever manner you use to do it, you must remain in control.

What Not to Do

There are some rules for what you must not do when gaining or retaining control. The most important is not to violate a person's legal rights. I know I have mentioned this often, but it may surprise you how many so-called professional managers flagrantly violate the laws pertaining to property management. Don't do it; if you violate a tenant's rights, you face imprisonment and strong fines.

There are numerous other activities to avoid, but for now, let's concentrate on what you *should* do.

Getting off to a Good Start

In Chapter 5, I discussed the importance of first impressions in the establishment of good landlord–tenant relations. Creating a good first impression requires that you assume a position of control in your earliest dealings with a rental prospect. For example, if you are unorganized and hesitant on the phone, you will appear incompetent, and tenants will have little respect for an incompetent landlord. However, if you are well prepared and fluent, you come across as a person who is professional in her rental management duties. Tenants will acknowledge your business skills and see that you treat the rental of your property as a business, not an unorganized hobby.

When You Show a Vacant Unit

When you show a vacant unit, you will have the opportunity to size up your prospective tenant. The tenant will be checking you out at the same time. Many factors can influence the flow of control. Little gestures will go a long way in putting you in the driver's seat.

Don't be late for your meeting with the prospective tenant. Someone who is late for a scheduled appointment is automatically on the losing end. Being late indicates a lack of professionalism and gives the person who arrived first an edge. If you are late, the tenant will feel he has the upper hand. You should be on time and animated for the meeting.

If you do not show an enthusiastic interest in renting the property, the tenant may be less likely to rent from you, or she may try to control your negotiations. With a confident appearance, you reduce the chances of the tenant attempting to beat you down on your price.

The Presentation of Your Paperwork

As you know, the paperwork involved in the rental business can be extensive. Some tenants will be intimidated by the mass of papers requiring their signature. Many property managers lose good tenants by not presenting their paperwork in the proper manner.

If you are forceful and inconsiderate when asking a tenant to sign your forms, she may look to rent some other property where the formalities are not so daunting. Many tenants will feel that you are tying their hands and putting yourself in total control with all of your legal paperwork, and if they feel they are to be too tightly bound, they may not sign it. Yet if they do sign with these back-of-the-mind feelings, you can have management problems from the start. These tenants will feel you are taking advantage of them, and after a while these feelings will fester into resentment. You are after respect, not resentment.

If you present the forms in the right way, you can convince the tenant they are as much for their protection as for yours. Since the presentation of paperwork is so important to good tenant relations, successful management, and maintaining control, I am going to give you some examples of how you might present your legal instruments.

Getting Your Forms Signed

Most tenants will not object to filling out a rental application. They expect any good landlord to check into their past history and credit rating. However, when it comes to signing a lease, you may hit some resistance. Tenants will be expecting to sign a lease, but they may not be willing to sign yours.

A custom lease you have worked on with your attorney will favor your position. Smart tenants may catch the language in the lease that puts unusual demands upon them. For example, assume your lease holds the tenant responsible for all plumbing repairs. A clause of this nature is not normal, and it is not fair to the tenant. Landlords are expected to pay for repairs and upkeep to the rental property unless the tenant is responsible for causing the need for such capital outlays.

If you have a clause requiring the tenant to pay for the damages he causes, such as in the earlier example of a rubber ducky down a toilet, you shouldn't have much trouble getting him to sign the lease. But suppose he balks; what do you say? If you say it is your building and your rule and that the tenant can take it or leave it, he will probably leave it. This approach may cost you a good tenant and a great deal of lost time.

If you explain the reasoning behind the insertion of the clause, you can convince most tenants to accept your rule. You might say that the clause helps you keep your rents lower, that if you are forced to pay for the abuses of your tenants, you must charge a higher rent to offset the additional expenses. Further, say that the rule helps the responsible tenants and only affects those who do not respect the property. Explain that charging higher rents to cover your costs for repairs and damages problem tenants cause is a hardship for good tenants. Finally, tell the tenant that this clause will have no affect on him so long as he causes no damage. If after this type of presentation he still refuses to abide by your rules, you probably don't want him anyway. By taking the time to explain the purpose and meaning of the clause, you can gain respect from the tenant and at the same time gain control.

Convincing Your Tenant to Complete the Check-In Form

Many property managers give a new tenant a check-in form to complete, but never follow up on it. It doesn't do you any good to present the form if you do not recover a completed copy for your files. Many tenants will take the form for granted. In the hustle and bustle of moving in, the form will be left in a drawer. It will be up to you to see that you get a copy of the completed form for your files and your protection.

You could give the form to the tenant and demand she complete and return it within three days. The tenant may or may not comply. Or you could use another, more simple way to convince the tenant to get the form completed and returned. It all boils down to presentation.

Explain that you take a personal interest in all your tenants and in the condition of your rental units. Go on to explain how the completed check-in form provides two services to the tenant—yes, the tenant. First, you want to make her living conditions as comfortable as reasonably possible, and the completed form will alert you to deficiencies in the rental unit so that you can render the necessary repairs. Second, the form protects her financially, since her damage deposit is at stake for any damage done to the unit while she is responsible for it. Show the tenant that by completing the check-in form she is establishing the condition of the unit at the time of her occupancy, so that she is protected from losing her deposit for any damage caused by a previous tenant.

It will be easy to show the tenant why you need the form and how it will benefit her to complete it expediently. Once she understands that the form protects her from being blamed for damages she didn't cause, she will jump at the chance to put it on file with you.

The presentation of your paperwork can make all the difference in the world when it comes to gaining and maintaining control. By being forceful and demanding, you are less likely to see favorable results and you will not build a good relationship with your tenant. By turning your presentation around and showing her how she benefits from your paperwork, you are much more likely to gain her cooperation. With the softer approach, you win in all directions: you get the form signed, you gain respect from the tenant, you establish control, and you build a good landlord–tenant relationship.

Sales Skills

Sales skills are an invaluable asset to a property manager. You may not think of yourself as a salesman, but you should. Your job requires you to rent vacant units. You are not selling them, but you must sell tenants on renting them. The benefits of sales skills are obvious in certain aspects of your job. You see their advantages in the creation of your marketing plan. They are also valuable in showing vacancies and in probing prospects for information. For all of these parts of your job, sales ability can be easily identified as a plus.

You might not consider sales skills to be important to gaining and maintaining control. However, if you don't believe these skills are advantageous in dealing with people, you are wrong. You are not directly selling anything in this phase of your job, but you are working to maintain control. The easiest way to do this is to get people to agree with you, and the best skills available for making people agree with you are sales skills.

You do not need high-pressure sales tactics when dealing with control. In fact, subdued suggestions and careful use of the proper words will get you much closer to your goal. A skilled salesperson can imply actions and plant thoughts that will make a prospect respond in the desired manner. At the same time he or she can make the prospect think it was his idea. These subliminal messages are sent through carefully structured words and actions.

Role Playing

With an understanding friend or spouse, you can practice your sales skills through role playing. Role playing works best if you first read books on sales and managing people. After you have read the books, practice the procedures on your friend. Have your friend assume the role of the problem tenant, and you, of course, will play the landlord. Here are a few examples of how the game might be played.

Your problem tenant comes to you complaining that his kitchen faucet continually drips and keeps him awake at night. What will you say or do? Many landlords will promise to have the problem taken care of right away. For the moment, this promise appeases the tenant and he leaves feeling satisfied. However, if the plumber doesn't show up for days, the tenant comes right back, complaining with more intensity than before. If this type of situation continues, tempers flare and both the landlord and the tenant become angry at each other. The landlord still has to fix the leak, and after he does the hard feelings linger.

A better approach to this problem is to tell the tenant you will contact the plumber as soon as possible to schedule a time that is convenient with the tenant to repair the faucet. It is a good idea to place a call to the plumber while the tenant is standing in front of you. You know the leak is wasting water and will have to be fixed, so you might as well handle the problem quickly to avoid any ill will.

With this approach, the tenant sees you take action. He knows you are responding to his request and doing the best you can, as a manager, to have his problem corrected. Even if the plumber doesn't show up for days, the tenant will be angry with the plumber, not with you. This is only a slight manipulation, but it is effective. You will not be the bad guy; after all, the tenant saw you take immediate action. He cannot blame you for the actions of an undependable plumber.

How do you handle a problem tenant who comes into your office to dispute a late charge you assessed against him for past-due rent? Suppose the tenant comes in steaming mad, refusing to pay the late fee. He tells you that you are money-grabbing and selfish and flings his arms around in gestures, ranting uncontrollably.

You could answer the tenant's bizarre behavior with similar behavior, but if you did you would wind up in a shouting match that would not solve the conflict. Or you could be meek and agree to forget about the late charge, but this would cause you to lose control of the situation. If you give in once, you can be labeled as a softy whom any tenant can take advantage of.

Let the tenant go through the motions to relieve his pent-up frustration. Unless he storms out of your office, he will run out of breath at some point, and you will have an opportunity to talk. The first few words you say will influence the way the matter will be settled, so choose your words carefully.

Address the tenant in a firm voice, from a strong posture. Tell him you will be happy to discuss the matter with him in a businesslike manner if he will just settle down for a few minutes. In this way, you are telling him you are willing to talk but you are dictating the terms of the discussion. When the tenant realizes this he may feel some victory and should calm down.

Then ask the tenant to excuse you while you pull his file. Do this even if you know the details of the late charge by memory. It gives you time to think and allows time for the tenant to relax. Once you have the file, the tenant will know you are taking the matter seriously. Sit down and review it. Tell the tenant that according to your files, his rent payment was late and the late charge was assessed in accordance with the terms of the lease. Expect a brief explosion from the tenant at this point.

Give him a few moments to vent his fury and then ask him if he is ready to continue your meeting in a professional manner. By not lowering yourself to the tenant's level, you are maintaining control and wearing him down. If he is normal, it will not take long for him to realize he is being childish in his actions. Your next step should be to ask the tenant if your files are inaccurate. Ask him when his records indicate his rent was paid.

If the rent was paid late, the tenant will have to admit to breaching his rental agreement. Once you have maneuvered the tenant into this admission, you are halfway home. Next, ask him if there were extenuating circumstances that forced his rent to be late. In doing this, you are showing him compassion and defusing his anger. If he says there was no good reason for paying his rent late, ask if he remembers the clause in the lease pertaining to late payments. He should say he does, and he knows you have the file in your hands that contains the lease.

First, you got the tenant to admit to paying his rent late. Then, you had him admit he knew he would be charged a fee for doing so. Now, ask the tenant to put himself in your position. Tell him how you depend on his rent payment to make your mortgage payment. Go on to explain that you are not some rich real estate mogul, but only a working landlord whose livelihood depends on the timely payment of each tenant's rent.

By now you have the tenant thinking. Expand your speech to impress upon him that you believe in being fair and playing by the rules. Ask the tenant what he would do if he were the landlord. Ask him if he would charge a late fee to delinquent tenants when they caused him hardship in meeting his monthly obligations. By working the conversation in this direction, you can convince the tenant to pay the late charge and help him understand why you enforce the clause. Certainly, there will be tenants who will not play along the way this tenant does. There will always be people you cannot deal with, but they are the exception rather than the rule.

The old "wouldn't you agree" tactic is very effective. You might end your conversation with this problem tenant by saying, "I believe it is important to a person's character and integrity to live up to his promises, wouldn't you agree?" He will agree with you, and as soon as he does, say, "Well, when you accepted my rental policy and lease, you promised to pay late fees when your rent was not on time. Are you telling me now that you are not a man of your word?" The tenant will quickly defend his honor. At this point there is no way he can leave your office with his head up unless he pays the late fee.

What Is the Best Way to Be in Control?

Each individual must find his or her own ways to be an effective property manager. Since there is no single way that works best in gaining and maintaining control, you must experiment and find the ones that work for you. Written agreements are a given; they must be in place to ensure control. Good people skills are also necessary for prosperous management of rental property. Sales skills take the edge off the job. When you learn to work effectively with people, your job becomes easier. A positive, sincere attitude is also beneficial in dealing with the control of your building and tenants. Genuine interest in your tenants will improve your success. It is hard to sell anybody on anything if you don't believe in what you are selling. You can get away with hiding behind a smile for awhile, but if the smile is a fake, you will be exposed in the end.

Control is what you make it. If you work at improving your performance as a manager, control will come. I believe the best place to begin establishing control is with your tenants—their rent pays your bills. Don't put yourself on a pedestal—someone will knock it out from under you. Be real and be honest. There will be people you cannot agree with, but the people you do develop relationships with will make up for all the rest.

Chapter 7

Computer Basics

There are generally two emotions associated with computers—love and hate. Either you love them or you hate them. As a professional property manager, you will find computers can be a great asset to your business, so before you decide you don't want to know about computers and skip this chapter, wait. If you think you have all the computer skills you need, perhaps you are wrong. This chapter is filled with useful information on computers and software, but there is more—it is laced with ideas for using your computer in ways you may not have thought of.

When my wife bought our first computer, I wouldn't touch it. It was many years ago when that first mechanical monster came into our family. By today's standards, it would be considered more of a toy or learning tool than a real computer. However, at the time it was purchased, it was capable of amazing feats, although I would not admit it at the time.

As resistant as I was to becoming computer literate, it happened. After watching what Kimberley could do with that little gray box, I became interested, and that interest grew into fascination and from there ballooned into appreciation. Today, computers play a key role in my business endeavors. They help me in real estate, building, and, of course, writing. I can accomplish tasks easily with the computer that would be pure drudgery without it.

My point is, I was totally against computers in the beginning, but now I use one almost every day. As I have progressed in my knowledge of computers and software, I have found how beneficial they are. They can be used to make money, manage money, forecast financial needs, and educate your children, and these, of course, are only a small portion of the capabilities they offer.

Real estate investors, landlords, and property managers are all prime candidates for computer ownership. The rental business runs on numbers, and nothing handles numbers better than a computer. Computers can also prove very advantageous when purchasing, managing, and selling rental properties. If you put your market research data into the computer, you can quickly evaluate the performance and viability of any building under consideration. The paragraphs that follow will show you examples of how a computer, even an easy-to-use one, can help you make and manage your money and make your life simpler and more productive.

Buying New Buildings

Before you buy a new rental property you must evaluate it and decide on the price you are willing to pay for it. A computer provides fast, accurate information for your assessment. Think about the questions you want answered before making an offer to purchase a new property. One of the first will be about the property's income performance potential. With a little help from you, your computer can determine that profitability factor.

The computer acts as a highly organized, electronic file cabinet. When you store your market research findings in the computer's database, you are making a file you can use over and over again. The database information will be available for many uses, but for now we are interested in projecting the performance of a given building.

Let's say you update your computer with current market trends each month. By doing this, you always have fresh, accurate information for making quick, informed decisions. The ability to act quickly, without acting foolishly, is a major benefit to any investor. Your computer's files give you this option.

By pushing a few buttons, you can determine what the average rent is for a specified area of the city. You can see what the difference in value is between a two-bedroom and a three-bedroom apartment. Depending upon how much information you have fed into your computer, your electronic partner can answer all the key questions in making a buying decision.

If your data input includes comparable sale information, you can run a quick appraisal on the building you are thinking of buying. If you are a member of a multiple listing service, your computer can talk to their computer. With the use of a modem, and the proper permission code, you have access to all the service's information—information that will prove indispensable in formulating your offer to purchase a new building.

Would you like to know what a 7-percent increase in the present rents will do for the building's net income? Your computer can tell you. If you enter the pertinent information on the subject property, your computer will provide detailed reports and flowcharts to indicate the likely outcome of different scenarios. When it comes to playing the "what if" game, nothing does it better than a computer.

Preparing to Sell Your Building

Everything a computer can do for you when purchasing a building, it can do for you when selling one. With the proper information, the computer can produce numerous reports and spreadsheets to help sell your property. If you have used the computer all year, you can have reports broken down into quarters, months, or even days.

Put yourself in the position of a buyer for a moment. Suppose you are looking at two similar buildings with the serious intent to purchase one of them. The first seller's broker gives you a basic information sheet with the operating expenses and income figures lumped together. The second seller's broker provides you with reports showing the maintenance costs for the building over the last year, broken down into months and categorized. She also provides you with a number of other reports, one giving you an accurate accounting of vacancies and the time it has taken to fill them at different times of the year, another accounting for all the operating expenses in detailed breakdowns. This broker has also provided you with spreadsheets showing current rental rates and the projected affect of rental increases over the next five years.

While you as a buyer may not take any of these reports at face value, the seller with the detailed records should make a much better impression on you. Your job of sifting through each building's track record will be much easier when you have detailed information to work from. By using her computer to produce the reports and spreadsheets, the second seller has increased his odds of selling his building before the first seller sells his.

Computers and Property Management

Property management duties are considerably easier when you are computerized. There are dozens of jobs that will go faster and smoother that way. Let's look at some of the most common tasks you can tackle with your computer.

Marketing

Marketing is a part of your business you cannot take lightly. If people are not aware of your facilities, they cannot rent them. To attract tenants, you normally must advertise. Advertising can take many forms, and a computer can help you with most of them.

Direct Mail. Direct mail is an expensive but effective marketing procedure. Given the expense, making the most of each mailing is critical. If a consumer receives your mailing but trashes it on sight, you will have lost money. Certainly, a large percentage of the prospects you mail to will do just that. How can a computer help you with this?

The computer cannot guarantee success with your mailings, but it can reduce the time spent on the job and may improve the odds of your target opening the mail. If you incorporate a graphics package into your software arsenal, you can make attractive brochures and mailings. With a quality printer and the right software, you can do much to dress up your ad copy. Instead of looking like a piece of cheap junk mail, your mailing could look like an executive offering.

Most mass mailings are done from rented name lists. However, these usually contain tens of thousands of names, so a smaller list may be more desirable for you. By using database software you can create your own customized mailing list. If you have an elegant condo to rent, you may want to target professionals with incomes at set levels. If doctors and lawyers fall into this category, and they should, you can go through the phone book and enter their names, addresses, and phone numbers into your database.

Since repetition is a known producer in marketing, you will probably want to mail to these same professionals again in the future. Without a computer, you will have to write or type each address every time you do a mailing. By storing the information in the database, you only have to type it once. For subsequent mailings, you merely give a few commands to your computer and it will produce mailing labels until you tell it to stop.

Display Ads and Other Forms of Advertising. Display ads are expensive, and to be effective, they must stop the reader in her tracks. Impressive fonts and graphics are a sure way to catch the reader's attention. By preparing your ads on the computer, you will set them apart from other ads competing for the same tenants.

Fliers and classified ads can also be produced on a computer, and once they are made and saved in memory, you can call upon them at any time. This can save time, since you don't have to draw the same ad each time you need to fill a vacancy. Instead, you push a few buttons and the friendly computer does the work for you.

Tracking Your Marketing Results. Tracking the results of your marketing efforts is critical to your success. If you cannot determine where your business is coming from, you cannot refine your marketing strategies. Say you place three different ads at the same time—how do you know which ad worked the best? You tag the ads with a key phrase or word. For example, one ad will tell the caller to ask for Mr. Woodson; the second will tell her to ask for Dodge; and the third will tell her to talk with Roger. With these keys you will know which ad the caller is responding to.

Once you know which ad originated the inquiry, you can feed that information to your computer. After a while, you can run charts, graphs, or spreadsheets to determine which ads pulled the most response overall. There is a big difference between getting a lot of inquiries and getting signed leases. By keeping records of how many signed leases each ad produced, you will know which one did the best job. That will be the one that garnered the most leases with the fewest calls.

This type of tracking will enable you to refine your marketing plan. As you establish which ads result in the most leases, you can eliminate those that are not pulling their weight. This will save time and money.

Generating Paperwork

With a good word processing software package, your computer can become a paperwork factory. Once your attorney has given you copies of all your business documents, you can put them all on computer files. These documents include leases, rental applications, checklists, notices, and any other frequently used forms.

Once the forms are in the computer, it is simple to make revisions and insert names and other customized information. With your boilerplate lease in the computer, all you have to do is change the personal information for each new tenant. This makes your job easier and faster. It also increases the likelihood that you will maintain good written records.

Tenant Information

If you have a large number of tenants, keeping your files straight can be cumbersome. With a computer, you can set up a database that will manage all of your tenant information and provide fast, efficient access to all of your records. Set properly, the computer can tell you when it is time to renew leases or start eviction proceedings.

Financial Functions

When it comes to financial functions, computers are the best way to go. Whether you are forecasting income projections, producing balance sheets, preparing pro forma statements, or tracking your budget, the computer will simplify the task.

Accounting Software

With the right accounting software you may be amazed at all the power your computer gives you. The speed of computers is beyond compare when it comes to accounting and the related reports generated from your bookkeeping. Here are a few of the tasks you can accomplish.

Bookkeeping Reports. Balance sheets will be simple to produce from your accounting software. With just a few keystrokes you will have a professional form to present to loan officers. Instead of spending hours pulling together your balance sheet information, you just command the computer to produce one, and it does, giving you assets, liabilities, retained earnings, equity, and capital. All of your financial information will be put into one neat package.

A computerized income statement provides accurate information to track your earnings. It shows revenue, expenses, and income, and will segregate your revenue and expenses into itemized units. If you want to know how much you spent in maintenance materials, the income statement will tell you. It will also tell you how much you spent for subcontracted maintenance. Computerized income statements help you keep track of your income and provide support for your loan requests.

Your computer can produce a report on your trial balance in a matter of minutes. This ensures accuracy in your bookkeeping by letting you know immediately if you have made posting errors in your debits and credits. Furthermore, by running a report on the general ledger you can inspect all of your bookkeeping records. You will receive vendor names, dates, and other information as you request it.

Vendor Information. Just by asking the computer, you can have a complete vendor list providing names, addresses, and phone numbers. You can also get vendor summaries, which will allow you to see exactly how much business you have done with all your vendors and show the total of money invoiced and the status of the account. If you are past due on your payments to vendors, this report will let you know it.

Payroll and Computerized Checking. Your accounting package will handle all of your payroll needs. It will cut checks for you, post the checks to the ledger, and provide detailed reports on your employees. Once you set things up, the computer takes the pain out of doing payroll.

Paying your bills as well as your employees with computerized checks will save time. When the computer cuts a check, it automatically accounts for it in the accounting package. Thus, you do not have to make manual entries in your bookkeeping records. For writing only one check, this type of system can be more trouble than it is worth, but for payroll and monthly bills, it is a real time-saver.

Inventory. Inventory is an item many landlords fail to consider. Although you might think so, your rental properties may not be the only inventory you own. If you have been in the business for long, you probably have maintenance supplies stored somewhere. Do you buy paint when it is discounted to use the next time you have a vacant apartment? How about spare light bulbs—do you keep them around? All of these items are inventory. Your accounting package will keep track of your inventory and provide you with reports on its status.

Job Costing. When you repair, remodel, or renovate a building, it is good to know what the job cost, especially if you do the work yourself or with employees. It is easy to track a job's expense when all the labor and material are provided under a contract agreement with a contractor. It is not so easy if you use employees for the job. By utilizing the power of your accounting program, you can get a handle on all your job-related expenses.

Spreadsheet Applications

If you enjoy projecting into the future, spreadsheet programs were made for you. With spreadsheet software you have a wealth of power at your fingertips. Since they provide the most pleasure for most investors, let's examine some of the jobs you can do with these fascinating programs.

Financial Procedures

Future Values. By using your spreadsheet to figure future values, you can project what the value of your building or your cash will be at any specified time. This feature is handy for estimating the effect of annual appreciation on your building or for speculating on what the proceeds from a balloon payment will be worth when you receive them.

Depreciation. With the double-declining balance feature or the sum-of-the-year's digit function of your spreadsheet program, you can calculate accelerated depreciation. You can also use your spreadsheet to figure straight-line depreciation. If you use a constant depreciation value to figure this manually, this is the function you will use on your computer.

Meeting Future Goals. The compound-term function of your spreadsheet can tell you the requirements for meeting future financial goals. For example if you want to sell your building when it reaches a certain value, you can project an annual appreciation rate and determine how many years that will take.

Internal Rate of Return and Net Present Value. Your spreadsheet can do the math in establishing your internal rate of return, or discount rate. The internal-rate-of-return function simplifies and expedites this job. Also simplified is arriving at the net present value of your rental property. Your spreadsheet will evaluate a series of future values and assign a net present value based on a selected discount rate.

Figuring Payments. Most investors are experienced in calculating *loan payments*, but with a spreadsheet you can be assured of accurate figures. True, this is a function you can do equally well with a financial calculator; however, the spreadsheet does come in handy from time to time. Its payment function will calculate the payment amount required to amortize a loan based on the criteria you supply on the term, principal amount, and interest rate.

Other Spreadsheet Possibilities

A spreadsheet can do much more than just financial functions. The information stored in its database can be manipulated in many ways. For example, assume you have created a database of information pertaining to the known rents for 200 apartments in your area. If the database is properly defined, you can sort the information to group similar apartments.

You might sort your file so that all the one-bedroom apartments are together. You can extend the sort by street address to further define your criteria. When you have all the one-bedroom apartments sorted by street address, the computer can then average all the known rents to produce the market average in the specified area. This type of sorting and averaging is helpful in determining market rents, projecting reasonable rents for your units, and assessing a building's likely value.

In addition to serving as a database, your spreadsheet can handle many other jobs. It can perform mathematical tasks, scientific functions, statistical jobs, logical functions, and date and time requirements. The spreadsheet is a tool most investors will never give up once they have experienced its usefulness.

Database Software

Database software and your computer combine to give you an electronic filing system. To understand how, think of databases as filing cabinets and each database entry as a manila folder of information.

With paper files and metal filing cabinets you can ultimately accomplish most of the same jobs you can with a database; the difference is in the time it will take to complete the task. If you have twenty tenants, how long will it take you to determine when each tenant will have to renew his lease? With a computerized database you can have the answer in minutes.

Word Processing Software

Once you have used a computer for composing letters, reports, and so on, you will never want to use a typewriter again. With word processing software there is no need for erasing ribbons or correction tape—you can make on-screen changes in a jiffy. If spelling is not your strong suit, the software's spell checker will not only identify misspelled words but correct them. You don't even have to retype anything; simply hit a single key and the properly spelled word replaces your mistake.

If you enjoy producing a well-written document, the thesaurus that comes with many word processors will be an ally. This feature highlights a redundant word and gives you options for replacements with similar meanings. If this is not enough, you can couple grammar software with your word processor to make your old English teacher happy. Among its other grammarian duties, the grammar software available can help you correctly place commas and avoid split infinitives.

What Else Can You Do with a Computer?

There is a software package for almost any need you have. If you invest in buildings with the intent of changing their use and design, you might enjoy one of the many computer drafting programs. Computer-aided drafting (CAD) can be used to draw blueprints and furniture layouts or to meet any other drafting and design need.

If you are thinking of learning a foreign language, there are educational software programs available to tutor you. Or maybe you would just like to sit back and play eighteen holes of computer-simulated golf. Computer games are a great way to relieve stress and to regain your perspective on business.

Are You Ready to Computerize Your Business?

You now have a good overview of how computers can improve your rental business. The question is, are you ready to computerize? There is no doubt that for some investors, landlords, and managers, computers will not be an attractive addition to their lives. Computers and software take time to learn, some more time than others. If you have absolutely no interest in computers or what they can do for you, it would be a mistake to purchase one.

If you have no experience in computers, you may be wondering how long it takes to become proficient at the keyboard. You may also be asking yourself what the initial investment in the computer system might be. In the next few paragraphs, I am going to give you some answers to these justified questions.

The Learning Process

Under average conditions you will not have to go back to school to accomplish your computing goals. There are dozens of good, how-to books available for all the major software programs. However, although it is not necessary to attend structured classes, it is imperative for you to devote time to the learning process.

The time required to become computer literate will depend on you and the type of system and software you will be using. Some software programs can be put to use after only a few hours of practice; others require weeks of extensive study, but you can usually learn as you go. Since the capabilities of computers and software are so vast, you will probably never use all the features offered to you. By learning what you want, or need, to know as you go along, you can become proficient with most programs, even the most complicated, in a few days.

How Much Is a Computer System Going to Cost?

The question of how much a computer system will cost is a loaded one. Will you be buying it new or used? Do you want the mobility of a laptop, or will all of your computing be done in the office? Will you be doing work that requires a laser printer? This line of questioning could go on for pages. There are so many options when it comes to computers that there is no cut-and-dried answer to the question of expense. Even so, while I have no blanket advice, I can give you some rough examples.

Laptop and Notebook Computers. Laptops are a fast-growing breed of portable computers. Many can rival the power, speed, and performance of large desktop models. Laptops offer the advantage of mobility. You can work with them in the office, at home, on your boat, or at your investment property. And since they can run for hours on batteries, there is no need for electricity in many instances. There are a multitude of advantages to laptops for the property manager on the move, but these advantages don't come without compromise.

A laptop's built-in monitor is not as large as a desktop monitor, but this doesn't mean it is no good. The quality of the monitor will depend on the price you are willing to pay for the laptop and the features it offers. It is possible to get laptops with monitors equal in quality to desktop units.

Less expensive laptops don't have hard drives, although this is also true of inexpensive desktop computers. Depending on the nature of your work, a computer that uses floppy disks may very well be all you need, but if you want a hard drive in a laptop, you can have one. Don't let the diminutive size of laptops fool you: they are regularly shipped with 40-MB hard drives, and much larger drives are available.

The keyboard on some laptops will be awkward to use compared to a full-sized computer keyboard, but again, it doesn't have to be. The laptop I use the most has a full-size keyboard and a numeric keypad. How about speed? Well, the speed of the laptop is determined by the price you pay. My primary laptop has a speed of 20 megahertz, which is very fast. My first laptop had a speed of less than 5 megahertz. Speed is not critical for most applications. If you are doing a lot of graphic work or drafting, a fast machine is necessary, but for basic business procedures, a slower machine will be fine.

Now for the big question: what do these laptops cost? The used computer market is unpredictable, so my estimates are based on new equipment. Also, where you buy your gear will have an impact on the price. If you go to the local computer store, you will probably pay more than if you order from a mail-order company. In general list prices are rarely paid for computers; there is usually a big difference between the suggested retail price and the price on the street. On average, laptops start in the $500 range and go up close to $10,000.

If you are buying your first laptop, a good machine that will suit all your normal needs will cost around $1,000. This will give you the computer and the built-in monitor, but you will still need to buy software and a printer.

Notebook computers are the newest entry into the competitive computer market. Most of them look like laptops, and their prices are similar, but they are smaller and weigh less. They also offer fewer features. Notebooks can perform many functions, but I cannot see buying one for your first and only computer.

Transportable Computers. Transportable computers are a larger, heavier version of the laptop computer. They are portable, but many of them are so heavy you will wish they came equipped with wheels. Transportables offer the options of a larger monitor, detachable keyboards, and more high-tech goodies. However, most laptops can be connected to an external monitor, just like the type used by full-sized computers, and many laptops will allow you to plug in a detached keyboard.

For the average user, I believe a laptop is the better investment. Plus, if you decide you don't like it, there will be a larger market of interested buyers for a used laptop than for a used transportable. Unless you have specialized needs, I don't think a transportable will make your best first computer. Prices for transportables start in the neighborhood of $1,500.

Desktop Computers. Desktop computers offer the most bang for your buck, as long as you don't want portability. As technology improves, prices on computers decline. Today you can get a new desktop computer, with a monitor, for under $1,000. When it comes to speed, hard drives, and expansion options, desktops have the edge and offer the best value. The used computer market is glutted with desktops, as everyone is racing out to buy laptops. You can capitalize on this glut and buy used desktops at previously unheard-of prices.

Monitors. Your computer will not be of much value without a monitor—it always helps to see what you are doing. Monitors come in different qualities and must be matched to the video card in your computer. The list of possible monitors includes monochrome, CGA, EGA, and VGA.

Monochrome monitors do not display color, but are fine for most business applications as they relate to property management. CGA, EGA, and VGA monitors produce color images, but they differ in the quality of the image and the number of colors displayed. A CGA monitor will be fine for normal business use, but if you will be staring at the screen for hours at a time, as I do, a VGA monitor is the only way to go.

Monochrome monitors are available for less than $100, but many of today's computers are not equipped to work with them. CGA monitors cost in the $200 range. EGA monitors fill the middle ground and are not as common as CGA and VGA monitors. In my opinion, if you are going to step up from a CGA monitor, go for a VGA. VGA monitors cost in the $300–$500 range.

Printers. The odds are good you will want to print reports and letters from the information in your computer. To do this, you will need a printer, but what type? The type of printer you choose will depend on your desires and applications, but a good dot-matrix printer is the best choice for most applications when price is a consideration.

Dot-matrix printers are fast; they can spit out a letter before you can get a cup of coffee, and they can run in draft or near-letter-quality mode. For the average landlord and manager, a dot-matrix printer is the logical choice. It is relatively inexpensive and gets the job done quickly, and though the quality of text will not compare with that of a laser or letter-quality printer, it is fine for most jobs. One thing to keep in mind: if you will be printing spreadsheets with a large number of horizontal columns, you may want to invest in a printer with an extended carriage. Dot-matrix printers start under $200 and go up from there. Expect to spend around $300 for a printer you will use regularly and about $500 if you want it to print in color.

Letter-quality printers produce excellent text that looks like it just came off the typewriter, but they take a long time to print. If you are printing a four-page lease, plan some activities to spend your time on while you wait for it to finish. Letter-quality printers are good if you are only doing light printing, but you will appreciate more the speed of a dot-matrix printer, even if you do give up a little quality in the text. Letter-quality printers can be purchased in the $200 range. They are the only printer discussed that does not produce graphic images.

Jet printers are the middlemen, bridging the gap between high-quality dot-matrix printers and laser printers. Their prices, in the $800 range, will open your eyes. Jet printers basically spray ink on paper to create text and graphics. They are a good choice if you need color graphics with better quality than a dot-matrix printer can produce, but I don't see where they are worth the extra money for average duties.

Laser printers are the cream of the crop, the most envied type of printer on the showroom floor. With the ability to produce between four and eight pages of perfect text in a minute, these devices are meant to work, and you can't beat them when it comes to graphics. If you want color images, you may have to mortgage your home to afford a laser with color capability. However, for the average user, a standard laser that prints superb text in black ink is all that is required. These printers start at prices under $1,000, and for around $1,300 you can get a top-name model with more options than you are likely to ever use.

Modems and Mouses. Modems allow your computer to talk to another computer over the telephone lines. They are advantageous if you are tied into a credit reporting bureau or a multiple listing service, but they are not necessary for standard procedures. Modems can be mounted inside most computers or they can be an independent, external device. Buying one could cost you less than $150.

The mouse is a pointing device. It allows you to move about the screen and give commands to the computer without using the keyboard. Unless you are using drawing or drafting programs, you will not need a mouse. Even so, it is handy and inexpensive. Prices start at under $30.

Now You Know the Basics

At this point you know the basics of computers. Now, it will be up to you to decide if you will benefit from computerizing your business, and the chances are good that you will. If you decide to set up a computer system, do your homework before you buy. Have no doubts that the one you choose is the right one. If you invest your time and money wisely in a computer, it should come back to you many times over.

Chapter 8

Increase Your Rents without Losing Your Tenants

Increasing rental income is always a primary interest for successful owners of income property. The more income you receive, the more successful you are. Many rental expenses remain the same during the ownership of a building. If costs remain unchanged, increased income will put more profit in your pocket. This is obvious, although many investors learn a hard lesson from this concept.

Novice investors buy a building, immediately raise the rents, and project their future profits. Do you think their profit projections prevail? On the contrary, more often than not, their projections take a dive into deep red ink. Cold greed rarely produces a profit. These same investors could have seen significant income increases and reduced vacancies with an organized business plan. Do you know when and how to successfully raise your rents?

The average investor has no idea of the potential repercussions from the simplest act. This is because investors typically know money and investments better than they know people. Investment skills are important, but without people skills, you become engulfed in trouble, fast. As I have said before, a well-rounded investor will be skilled in, among other areas, sales, public relations, legal matters, and marketing. Beyond this, he or she should be familiar with the banking industry, have a working knowledge of building and fire codes, and be connected to a strong network of real estate professionals—investment brokers, attorneys, certified public accountants, maintenance services, mortgage brokers, and so on.

Many of these contacts are discussed in detail throughout this book. All of them offer the investor an angle for increasing the bottom line of a financial statement. After all, making money is what income property is all about. What follows is advice on the numerous ways to increase rental income—without negative side effects. Indiscriminately increasing rents can result in a loss of income. Your spreadsheet may show a 7-percent increase as a profit, but if your tenants revolt and move, your increase results in an income loss.

Change-of-Ownership Rental Increases and How to Handle Them

The first chance real estate investors have to raise rents is when they take possession of a new property. Inexperienced landlords tend to immediately raise the rents with a change of ownership, but although this is a good opportunity, the timing and method of the increase are critical to success. It is not enough to randomly pick an increase figure and send a notice to the tenants. Frequently, the result will be a mass exodus and a significant negative cash flow.

A large negative cash flow is the last thing you want when taking over a new building. At best, you lose money; at worst, you lose the property. Perhaps you noticed that the current rents were below present market rates when you evaluated the purchase of the building. This knowledge is valuable, but it doesn't justify an immediate increase. For all you know, the prior landlord raised the rents before putting the property up for sale.

If the tenants have had an increase in their rent within the last six months, your increase could force them to move, and any time you have a vacant rental unit, you lose money. Along with the lost rent there is the expense of cleaning the unit, advertising for tenants, and, in particular, your time spent interviewing prospects. If your time is worth money, showing apartments can be very expensive. Using a property management firm is one solution to this dilemma, but it is not without its problems.

Professional Property Managers

Property management firms generally charge an annual fee equal to a percentage of the gross rental income—a rule-of-thumb figure is 10 percent. On a large building, this can amount to serious money. Moreover, many companies charge extra to oversee maintenance work and fill vacancies. This latter charge, called a rent-up fee, varies in amount, but it is never cheap. In many areas, it is equal to one month's rent.

If you like playing with numbers, run a spreadsheet on your annual losses from rent-up fees. I think the numbers will show you the importance of avoiding vacancies. If you move fast on increases as the greediest landlord in the rental business, you will lose your shirt with vacant apartments. Instead, use ways to increase the rents with a change of ownership that don't alienate existing tenants. Doing so will result in stronger net worth and fewer headaches.

A Letter of Introduction Breaks the Ice

When you first acquire the building, send the tenants a letter of introduction explaining that their home has been placed in your hands and that you hope to develop a good relationship with each of them. An acknowledgment of their importance to your building's operation will go a long way. Don't treat the tenants like rental slaves.

Stress your interest in meeting with them to hear their likes and dislikes about their living quarters. Tell them you view them as partners in your rental business, since without them, your business would wind up in the bankruptcy courts. In your letter, schedule a time to meet with each tenant. The residents will be nervous about rental increases and changes in the tenancy rules. Be aware of this expected fear and approach them with a consoling demeanor.

The first meeting with your new tenants will reveal much about them and your recently acquired investment. It should be nonconfrontational, with the intent of gathering vital information. Since the tenants know you are coming, they will try to make their apartments as neat as possible. They should be on their best behavior and a little intimidated. All of this works in your favor.

Read the Room

When you enter the apartment, if it is a mess, you know the occupants may not be the type of tenants you want. Size up the unit. Are there any unpleasant odors? Is there evidence of property abuse? What is the thermostat set at? Check out the furniture and personal property. Does the tenant appear to be a transient or a settled, mature individual? The more you notice from reading the room, the better your chances are of making solid decisions.

Within the first ten minutes, the tenant will probably inquire about any rental increase. Don't skirt this issue, but address it in a noncommittal way. Explain that you have just purchased the building and are not aware of the current market rents for the area. Tell the tenant you will assess the property, the tenants, and the market conditions before making any decisions.

Change the subject by asking for feedback on the tenants' living conditions, and take notes as she talks. When the tenant sees you doing this, she will begin to respect you. Most landlords have little interest in their tenants' opinions. By exhibiting an interest, you will be paving the way to raising the rents successfully.

When the interview questions are complete, allow the tenant to ask you questions. In most cases, there won't be many. She will be reserved and unlikely to pose questions about your plans or abilities. The mere fact that you are willing to hear her out will make an impact. Your purpose in this meeting is to gather data and gain control. If the tenant does complain or make any requests, listen and take notes.

Evaluate the Written Word

After your initial meetings with tenants, you will have a good idea who the desirable ones are. Review the notes you took and note the expense involved in responding to any complaints or requests. Also carefully examine existing leases or rental agreements. When do the agreements expire and how does the recent sale affect the leases? Are there provisions in the leases for the new owner to cancel them? Are the present rents at the same amount found in the lease?

Draw as much information from the existing leases as possible for your planning purposes. Start a file on each tenant and put all applicable notes there. When you have accomplished this, contact the local housing authority. They can provide you with invaluable information. Request all available data pertaining to historical rental information for the last three years.

Once you have this information, start a spreadsheet to dissect it. Using only the information pertaining to properties in the same general location of your building, create a breakdown according to the number of bedrooms in each unit. Ideally, comparisons should be made with buildings housing a similar number of apartments. A two-bedroom apartment in a duplex should bring a higher rent than the same apartment found in a twelve-unit complex. Also note who is responsible for utility expenses. If the tenants pay, their rent will probably be lower. Find the most comparable information available to determine your rental income ceiling.

When this stage of your evaluation is complete, turn to the local newspaper. Look through the classified section for price and availability of rental property. Again, keep your comparisons fair and comparable. Use only examples from similar apartments in the same general area. Are pets allowed, and if so, is additional rent charged for the privilege? What amenities are included in the rent for comparable properties? The more information you compile, the better your chances are of getting the most out of your property.

With your spreadsheet complete, you can draw an accurate conclusion about your present rental income status. Are your rents below the current market amounts? How does your property compare with other buildings for parking, utilities, and condition? Assuming your building is equal to the ones studied, you can evaluate your maximum rental increase, and if you are at or above market rates, there is still a chance you can raise your rents.

They Won't Want to Move

If you found the tenants to be happy in your meeting, they will not want to move. Therefore, if the surrounding apartments are charging $600 per month and your tenants are paying $600, can you charge $620? You probably can. It will not be worth the cost and inconvenience for the tenant to move. Would you go through the hassles of moving to save $20 a month?

If you decide to raise the rents, don't send a letter notifying the tenants of the increase. Instead, arrange to meet with them again. This meeting will be an excellent opportunity to have the tenants execute a new lease and to acknowledge any changes in policy. It is common for there to be changes in the rental rules when property is transferred. They may pertain to parking, storage, or any number of other items, and they should be in writing, acknowledged, and accepted by the tenant's signature. Meet with the tenants separately, starting with the least desirable. He will be your testing ground.

When you advise the tenant of the increase, he may say that it is unwarranted and he will move. If this happens, show him a detailed outline of your rental comparison findings. If he sees that moving will save him no more than $20 a month, his attitude may change. You can help expedite this change by pointing out the costs and inconvenience of moving. If you have justification to retain the tenant's security deposit, you have even more leverage. Don't, however, abuse this power and come off looking like a villain.

Tenant–landlord relations are important. Before being too bullish, explain to the tenant why you are raising the rent. If you are going to make repairs or improvements to the building, tell her of these plans. Be diplomatic and try to make the tenant understand that the increased rent will improve her living conditions. In most cases, this approach will enable you to raise the rent without the risk of losing her.

Monitor tenant reactions as you work your way from the least desirable to the most desirable. If you are catching heavy flak from all the tenants, back off on the increase. Don't miss this opportunity to increase your cash flow, however. By following this approach, you will almost always be able to see some increase in your income.

The above recommendations were slanted toward dealing with existing tenants. You learned how to safely test and raise your existing rents with minimum risk. Now, you will learn to maximize the building's overall income. The most obvious way to do this is by working the monthly rents upward, but this is not the only way to make more money with your investment.

Breaking Out of the Pack

In order to get maximum monthly rents, you must set yourself apart from the competition. What will your building allow you to offer prospective tenants? Do your apartments have more bedrooms or bathrooms than other units on the market? Are the rooms in your units larger than average? Total square footage is a consideration when setting rental income figures; larger apartments should be worth a little more than their smaller competition. The number of bedrooms also has a great deal of influence on value; an additional bedroom puts your unit in a whole different category and allows for substantially higher rent. If you can offer more than one bathroom, you should expect a higher rent as well.

These factors are routine and recognized by most investors, but in many cases, you have little control over them. The building either has good features or it doesn't. Nevertheless, if you want to maximize your rental income, explore all of the possibilities. Don't overlook the obvious, but never fail to look below the surface. It is the hidden value of a building—the dormant opportunities— that offers the highest rate of return. Here are some examples of dormant opportunities.

Pets

Do buildings in your area allow pets? Do you allow pets? If you don't, you should consider changing your policy. People with pets are frequently more responsible and less likely to move. This is especially true of older tenants. Pets are generally discouraged in apartment buildings and rental homes, so this is an opening for the aggressive entrepreneur to capitalize on.

Take some time to make a comprehensive policy regarding pets. Require an additional security deposit whose amount is determined by the type of pet and the possible damage it could cause. In addition to the deposit, charge an extra monthly fee. This can be justified by the increased risk of loss on your part. The amount will vary with geographic locations, but $25 to $50 a month shouldn't be unreasonable.

Consider what this new policy does for you. The additional deposit protects you from property damage, and allowing pets expands your base of qualified tenants and reduces your vacancies. Also, if you average the monthly rental increase, the amount is $37.50, which, with a twelve-unit apartment building, translates into an annual income increase of $5,400. This alone should be reason enough to allow pets, but if you still are not convinced, consider the other gains. The money saved from lower vacancies and the decreased downtime will increase your net annual income. This simple policy change can make your investment grow rapidly and without undue risk.

Waterbeds

Most landlords frown on waterbeds, so when competing advertisements say, "No waterbeds allowed," yours should say, "Waterbeds welcome." Why should you incur the risk of flooded apartments when other landlords refuse to? Because you can make more money and not increase your risk. You can require the tenant to enter into a written agreement for the privilege of having a waterbed, and you can require her to provide insurance coverage for any damage. Such liability policies will protect you for any reasonable amount you deem necessary.

Storage

If your building has facilities for storage, you can charge extra for it. I am not talking about chicken-wire enclosures in the basement—those are more of a fire hazard than an asset. I mean that if your building has provisions for lockable, secure storage, it is valuable. Does your property have garages? Are you charging additional rent for the garage space? If you aren't, you should be. Also consider a change in use for the garage. Look for the highest and best use of all your assets.

Assume you are charging $60 a month for your garage, and that the garage dimensions are 24 feet by 24 feet, for a total of 576 square feet. This means that at $60 a month, you are receiving a little over ten cents per square foot for your space. Now consider if you divided the garage into nine independent, 50-square-foot storage cubicles, which is adequate exterior storage for most tenants. You can easily charge $25 a month or more for each of them, which amounts to $225 a month instead of the $60 you had been collecting for the same garage. The cost of the conversion is minimal, and the rate of return is excellent. Moreover, this secured storage area increases the desirability of your rental units. You win two ways. You make more money, and more tenants want to live in your building.

Parking

In some cities, parking is a problem for renters. If this is true in your location, you may be able to charge extra for your parking space. Compare the rents in other buildings and their parking arrangements and then adjust your fees accordingly. If your property doesn't have sufficient parking space, look at your options. Can you fill in a section of the lot and create space? Could you convert some of the lawn into a parking area? Use your creative ability to increase your income when parking pays.

Coin-Operated Laundries

What else can you do to increase your building's income? Are your apartments equipped with private laundry facilities? Do you offer a laundry room for tenants to share? Are you presently using coin-operated laundry equipment? In buildings without private laundry hookups, coin-operated machines in a common laundry room can add thousands to your rental income. Installing the plumbing and electrical connections for them is not going to break your bank. This add-on investment should pay for itself in short order.

Keys to a prosperous laundry room include good lighting and security, as well as clean conditions and regular maintenance on the machines. Laundry rooms can be placed in the basement of many buildings. If there is no plumbing at floor level, a relatively inexpensive pump system can be installed that uses a holding tank and a float-controlled effluent pump. When the washing machines discharge into the holding basin, the excess water is pumped up to the building's main plumbing drain.

If you don't have a basement, consider remodeling a small section of the building. Adding a laundry room to the exterior is another way to overcome space problems. Project your planned earnings from the machines and evaluate your situation. If the installation cost isn't too great, a laundry room should be a moneymaker.

Consider these numbers. In a twelve-unit building, you have twelve families, most of them with children. At a minimum, each family will need to clean three loads of clothes each week. If your machines are set to collect $3.25 for every load of clothes washed and dried, how much money do you make a year? You earn $6,084 yearly in additional income. Of course, operating costs must be accounted for. There will be water and electrical usage from the operation of the machines, and there will undoubtedly be some maintenance required. Also, not all families will use your facilities, and some will do many more than three loads of clothes each week. Many factors will affect your actual return, but the numbers work. Coin-operated laundries offer strong potential for enhancing your net worth.

If you have, or create, a laundry room, consider adding some entertainment. Vending machines and arcade games will produce well in a laundry area. They provide the tenants with snacks and entertainment while they wait for their clothes. Be pragmatic in this consideration, however; you don't want a laundry room the majority of your tenants will avoid because of its game-room atmosphere. Forego the arcade equipment if you feel it will draw an undesirable crowd.

Weekly versus Monthly

Do you collect your rents weekly or monthly? In many cities, rents are collected on a weekly basis for several reasons. One is to ensure that the tenant never gets too far behind in rent payments. If the rent is due weekly, you can take eviction actions much sooner than you could with a monthly rental agreement. Also, you do not have as much money owed to you at the time of default. Your chances of controlling the situation, before extensive losses are incurred, improve.

Another reason for a weekly rental agreement is increased income. Let's assume rents in your area average $600 a month. If you tell a prospective tenant you will accept weekly payments, he normally multiplies that amount by four to determine what an equivalent monthly rent would be. This is a natural reaction, but it is not an accurate way to calculate the gross annual rent. A weekly rent of $150 does not equal a monthly rent of $600 because there are fifty-two weeks in the year. Instead, the annual rent would be $7,800, or $650 a month. This is a common tactic for city-based landlords. With it they reduce their exposure and increase their income.

Making the Most from Your Single-Family Rental

Many of these suggestions have been based on multifamily housing. Now, you will learn how to make the most out of your single-family rental property. The principles already discussed, in the main, apply to landlording any type of residential property. However, some of the suggestions have no place in a single-family rental—for example, building a laundry or game room.

The easiest way to increase profits with single-family rentals is through a rent-to-buy program. Such a program nets the best tenants, the highest income, the least headaches, and some outstanding opportunities. The world is full of people hoping to own their own home someday, but many cannot afford the required down payment and closing costs. These home seekers make excellent tenants and can send your rate of return off the charts.

How can you get a piece of this high-profit action? If you own a single-family rental, all you have to do is adjust your attitude toward finding a tenant. Instead of running a classified ad for monthly tenants, advertise your property as a rent-to-own home. The principle here is simple, but the execution requires thought and planning. In particular, beware of due-on-sale clauses in your mortgage agreement, which I will expand on later in this section.

Assume your rental property has a current market value of $85,000, and allow a reasonable amount for its annual appreciation. Depending on location, this amount may be anywhere between 5 and 15 percent, and in boom times, it can be even higher. This example uses a rate of 7 percent. Before placing your ad, decide what you are willing to sell the home for in one year. If the house is worth $85,000 now and will appreciate by 7 percent annually, the market value in a year will be $90,950.

In a rent-to-own arrangement, part of the tenant's rent is applied, in some manner, to the purchase of the home. For example, if you have been renting out your home on a monthly basis for $925 per month, you can advertise it on a rent-to-own plan for a monthly rent of $1,200. State in the ad that $400 of that will be applied to the tenant's option to purchase. The key phrase is, "applied to the tenant's option to purchase."

When you get an interested party, offer him the deal with an agreed upon sale price of $92,450, explaining that this figure is based on an estimate of the home's value in a year's time. Maintain a solid lease agreement and security deposit arrangement with the tenant, but do not make the amount applied to the purchase price part of the lease. Instead, create an option agreement for it to avoid the due-on-sale clause that is found in most modern mortgages.

Due-on-Sale Clauses

If you clearly state that the rent will be applied to the purchase of the home, your agreement with the tenant could be construed as an installment-sale contract, and you could trigger the due-on-sale clause. Due-on-sale clauses prevent an owner from financing her property to a new owner without satisfying the present mortgage note. Some older mortgages don't contain such clauses, but you shouldn't take unnecessary chances.

If you trigger the due-on-sale clause, the lender can force you to pay the note in full, upon demand, and if you are unable to do so, it may take steps to gain possession of the property. This risk is too great to approach with a casual attitude. Talk with your attorney before using the rent-to-own plan. In most cases, if the rental rebate is applied to an option, you are safe.

Structuring the Deal

The mechanics of the deal work like this. The tenant signs a standard lease and agrees to pay the $1,200 per month in rent. At the same time, you and the tenant enter into an option-to-purchase agreement that offers the tenant the right to buy the property in one year for an amount of $87,650. This number is arrived at from the agreed upon sale price less the equivalent of $400 per month.

Structuring the deal this way does many things for you. First, you receive an increased monthly cash flow of $275. This is the difference between the $1,200 being paid and the $925 you have been collecting. Second, you have a tenant who intends to buy your property, and since she expects to own it in a year, she will treat it as her own. Third, your rental agreement is the same one you have always used. So far, nothing has changed, except your increased income.

Your worst-case scenario is that the tenant will actually buy your property at the end of the year, but if you allow the $400-per-month rebate, you have not lost a cent. The projected value of the home at the end of the year is $90,950, and you agreed on a sale price of $92,450. A reduction of $4,800 leaves you with a sales price of $87,650. Are you thinking you lost $3,300? Well, you didn't. Remember, you collected $1,200 for twelve months instead of your original $925—this additional rent equals $3,300. Keep in mind, this is your worst-case scenario.

In most cases, the tenant will not be able to exercise the option to purchase. She will not have accumulated enough money for the required down payment and closing costs by the end of the year, and thus you will have increased your annual income by $3,300 without giving up anything. At the same time, you had a perfect tenant in your rental property who cared for the home as if it were her own. How much better can it get?

At this point, you can renegotiate with the tenant or solicit a new one. If you renegotiate, increase the sales price by the annual appreciation figure and follow the same deal you made originally. The keys to this plan are simple. Don't trigger a due-on-sale clause, and don't allow the rebate to apply to the down payment or closing costs. If the tenant does buy the property, you obtained the price you wanted and can purchase other investment property.

The tenant will be likely to accept your deal because of the option rebate. She sees $400 per month of her rental expense being applied to the investment of a home. This perception is true, but it doesn't work quite the way most tenants think it does. What is the downside? As far as I know, there is none if the deal is done right. However, this is a complicated deal to structure and should be handled by your attorney.

In Closing

I am sure there are other ways to increase your building's income, but the ones I have given here are some of the best. Be creative and use your entrepreneurial skills to add to the list. Different locations and buildings offer various opportunities, so work on it until you find the procedure best suited for your situation. In your search for the best methods to increase income, remember that reducing expenses can be more effective than increasing income.

This book is filled with useful tips on controlling your operating expenses. A dollar saved is worth more than a dollar earned because you don't pay additional taxes on it. For true financial freedom, you must learn to balance savings with increased income. Being a professional landlord can be highly rewarding when the proper principles are applied. The most important rule to follow when managing rental property is to treat your endeavors as a business, not a hobby.

Chapter 9

Collecting Rents

Collecting rent is what the landlording business is all about. When you buy rental property, your main motivation is the income you will get from the rent you collect. However, rent collection is also one aspect of owning and managing rental property that many people hate. They love having the rental income, but they despise having to get it. If you are going to be successful in this business, you must be successful in getting your money.

This chapter deals with the details of collecting rent, suggesting ways to make your rental collections easier and ideas for making your tenants want to pay their rent. Its abundant examples should prove very helpful to you. Even if you have been landlording for years, the methods compiled here may teach you a few new tricks. Now, let's get on with the business of collecting your rental income.

Why Landlords Dislike Collecting Their Rental Income and What They Can Do about It

Since people enter the rental business to collect rent, why do so many dislike doing it? How do you feel about it? There are countless reasons landlords don't look forward to collecting their rent. When rent checks arrive in the mail, they are all happy, but when they must exert effort to collect past-due rent, many are weak. They don't want to confront their tenants; in some cases they are afraid to approach them. To survive in the rental game you must get around these fears and dislikes. You must take control and collect the money due you.

If you don't like chasing after past-due rent, you must develop a plan to avoid being put in that situation. Many elements contribute to the success of landlords who are not forced to go after their rent. These successful landlords have learned to motivate their tenants to pay their rent on time. They have also learned to see problems developing in their early stages. When you can catch a problem early, you can often solve it before it becomes a burden.

By implementing procedural techniques, you can reduce the frequency with which you must hunt down tenants for your rent. With knowledge and experience, you can use salesmanship to win the late-rent battle. When you are up against a tough tenant, there are ways to strengthen your position while weakening hers. Thorough screening of tenants is one way, and there are many other tips and techniques to help you given here. If you master these skills, you will not have to worry about your dislike for chasing rent checks; they will come to you.

As a property manager, you will have to find the methods that work best for you in collecting rent. Not all of the following ideas will suit your temperament or circumstances, but many of them will. Whichever ones you choose, all of them are proven performers, used by all types of landlords. Some of them are not well known; others are common knowledge. By the end of this chapter, you will have all the ammunition you need to collect your rent. With the proper organization and use, these methods will make your life easier and your bank balance fatter.

Your Lease Is the Backbone

Your lease is the backbone of your rental business. It dictates the terms and conditions of your agreement with a tenant. Many of the suggestions in this chapter will only be effective if they are properly addressed in your lease, so before you sign up a new tenant, be sure your lease protects you and gives you the needed control over him. When you are ready to draft a lease, include in it notes on all the procedures you intend to use in your collection of rental income. Then have your attorney review your notes and draw up the formal documents. Once you are operating with the right lease, your job of collecting the rent will be much easier.

Communication

Clear communication will solve more rent-related problems than any other single maneuver. When the communication channel is open between you and your tenant, you may never have a problem collecting your rent. When communication breaks down, trouble begins. Go over the terms of your lease and rental policy with the tenant when you rent your unit. Make sure she understands your terms and conditions. By getting all the cards on the table early, you can avoid many future hostilities.

Don't avoid a subject because it makes you uncomfortable to talk about it. If you are going to have a clash with a tenant, have it before you sign the lease and move her in. If the tenant doesn't like your terms for rent collection, find a different tenant. Putting a bad tenant in your building is one of the worst sins you can commit as a property manager.

You are in business to make money. The tenant knows this, and you know it. Explain to the tenant that you depend on prompt rental payments to meet your mortgage obligations. Make her understand that if she is delinquent in her rent, it puts all of the other tenants, as well as you, in jeopardy. If you impress upon the tenant that you need her rent payment to make your mortgage payment, she may not resent you.

Many tenants assume all landlords are rich. They think you need the money just for your golf game or new luxury car. If you show the tenant that you are just an average person, working for a living as a landlord, he will be more apt to pay his rent on time. Make it clear that you cannot tolerate tardy rent payments. Explain that your credit, your future, and your family are at stake. If you let the tenant know how serious you are about collecting the rent promptly, he should be willing to cooperate.

If the tenant has intentions of not paying his rent, you might scare him off with a hard-line stance. If this is the case, you have saved yourself time, money, and grief. Don't be afraid to spook a tenant, but don't come off looking like a dictator. If you present your rental policy in a diplomatic manner, good tenants will play by the rules and bad tenants will deserve what they get. Keep the communication lines open at all times. If you stop talking with your tenants, you are headed for trouble.

Screening Tenants

The first step in making rental collections easy is doing a complete screening of all prospective tenants. You cannot look over a rental application and decide right then to rent to the applicant. You must check references, credit ratings, job stability, and all other pertinent facts. If you place many tenants, you will do well to join a credit reporting bureau. As a rental business, you can do so for a set annual fee. Then you will pay a nominal fee for each credit report you request. The cost of these services is a bargain if you consider that weeding out one bad tenant will more than pay for a year's worth of reports.

Setting the Rental Interval

It is up to you to set your rental intervals. Most landlords choose to collect their rent on a monthly basis, the industry standard, but that is not the only way to do business. You can set your interval to be anything you and your tenant agree upon. You could even collect rent on a daily basis, although this would be much too time-consuming. Many landlords set their rental intervals on a weekly basis, and they have some good reasons for doing this. We discussed these reasons in Chapter 9.

Picking a Due Date

Just as you can choose any rent interval you like, you can also pick a due date that suits you. Your tenants will have to agree to your date, of course, but that shouldn't be a problem. Standard procedure calls for rent to be due on the first day of each month, and many landlords allow a grace period of five to ten days beyond that. With this arrangement, you may not see your rent until the tenth of the month, and if you have a mortgage payment due on the first of the month, waiting until the tenth for your rent can create some stress. There is a way to avoid this.

It is true that rent is traditionally due on the first of the month, but there is no reason you can't break with tradition. Tenants will be willing to work with whatever schedule you establish if they are motivated. Imagine you set your rental due date as the twenty-fifth. What will this do for you? For one thing, you should have your rent in plenty of time to pay your first-of-the-month mortgage payment. Even if you allow a grace period, you will still have your money five days earlier than if the rent was due on the first.

If a tenant moves into your building on the first of the month you may have to prorate the first month's rent. This is because his old residence was most likely on a first-of-the-month cycle. All you have to do is deduct the rent from the twenty-fifth of the previous month to the time the tenant takes possession. Thereafter his rent will always be due on the twenty-fifth. It may take a little getting used to, but collecting your rent due at the end of each month will provide a more consistent cash flow for making your mortgage payments.

Collection Methods

By Mail. The most convenient way of collecting your rent is by mail. This way is also easier for the tenants because they don't have to arrange to meet with you to deliver the check. Collecting by mail is good only if the tenants pay on time, however. To encourage this, many landlords give their tenants preaddressed, stamped envelopes, which makes it a little easier for them to put a check in the mail.

In Person. Collecting the rent in person is another effective way to improve your percentage of on-time rent. When you are standing in front of the tenant it is much harder for her to deny paying you. You also avoid the excuse of checks being lost in the mail. On the other hand, personal collection takes time away from your other work. You can't be generating new income when you are going door to door to collect rent. The fact that you are forfeiting the opportunity to make more money by collecting money already owed you is a loss or an overhead expense.

One good aspect of collecting the rent in person is your regular contact with the tenants in your building. You see them frequently and have a chance to develop a relationship. When handled properly these meetings can be turned to your advantage; by keeping the tenants happy you avoid vacancies. Often, all it takes is a personal interest in a tenant's job, children, living conditions, or favorite sport. If you spend a few extra minutes in conversation when collecting the rents, you can be a person, not just a cold, greedy landlord. This type of interaction is invaluable to the tenant–landlord relationship.

When you pick up the rent personally, you get to see your building on a routine basis. This is good because going from unit to unit allows you to spot-check the apartments for damage or abuse. Also, while you are in the building you can inspect your common areas for any items that may need attention. If a smoke detector is missing, you will know about it before the code enforcement office puts you on notice.

There are some drawbacks to face-to-face rental collections besides the time they take away from other income-generating activities. For example, tenants who love to gossip will try to tie you up for hours, and you cannot afford this loss of time. Spend enough time with the tenant to maintain good relations, but don't get trapped into losing half your day. Also, some tenants will be chronic complainers. They would never go to the trouble of writing a letter of complaint, but when you are standing in their doorway, they will go on and on about whatever is bothering them.

Hand-Delivered. Some property managers insist that tenants personally deliver their rent to the rental office, but if you run your business from your home, I doubt you will want a string of people lining up at your door. Most managers, in fact, don't want their tenants to know their home addresses. If you have an office outside of your home, you might want tenants to deliver their rent there, but I wouldn't. You have no control over when they will be coming, which can disrupt your normal business day.

Tenants will not be anxious to deliver their rent unless the rental office is located in the rental building or complex. If they have to drive across town, they will be more likely to put the task off until they are on that side of town already. This can delay your rent collection. I believe the mail is the most desirable way to collect your rent, but if mail collection is not effective, I think going to the tenants to collect the rent is the next-best choice. There are few occasions when I would want a tenant to bring the rent to my office.

Sending Monthly Statements

Should you send your tenants monthly statements to remind them to make their rent payment? Well, it couldn't hurt, but you shouldn't have to do it. When tenants sign your lease they know your rental terms, and they know when the rent is due. If they are responsible, reminders to meet their obligations shouldn't be necessary. Even so, while you shouldn't have to send out statements, your rent collection may be more successful if you do.

Some property managers give their tenants coupon books to pay their rent with. Since people are used to coupons for their car and installment loans, having them for their rent makes sense. The added expense of having coupon books printed is minimal when compared to the cost of other forms of rent collection. Whether you mail out monthly statements or issue coupon books, your rent will be more likely to arrive on time with these methods.

It is also effective to use both coupon books and monthly statements. Some people will put the coupon book in a desk drawer and forget about it, but receiving a statement in the mail will jog their memory. Enclosing a self-addressed, stamped envelope with your statements is another way to expedite the mailing of rent checks. If all the tenant has to do is stick a check in the provided envelope and mail it, she will do so promptly. If she must go to the post office to buy a stamp, your rent payment may be delayed. The easier you make it for your tenants to pay their rent, the better off you will be.

Offering Discounts

Should you offer rental discounts to tenants who pay their rent on time? Many landlords believe you should, but I disagree. I don't believe you should reward people for doing what they are supposed to do. My tenants receive a discount if they pay their rent early, but not if it is only paid when due.

In fact, I believe that offering a discount for rent received on the due date encourages late payments. Many tenants think that once they miss their discount, it doesn't matter when they pay. This defeats the purpose of a discount program. With my method the attitude is different. The tenant who pays his rent on time pays full price, but is not charged a late fee. The tenant who pays early avoids late fees and benefits from a 10-percent discount. The tenant who pays late is charged a late fee and put into the collection grinder. By maintaining my strong position and treating all tenants the same, this policy has served me well. If you start making exceptions, you erode your policy and lose control.

Should You Offer a Grace Period?

A majority of property managers allow their tenants a grace period on their rent, although some hard-nosed managers are standing on the doorstep of a past-due tenant when the clock ticks one minute past midnight. I believe grace periods should be allowed but under controlled circumstances. I see no reason to allow a ten-day grace period; five days is plenty of time to compensate for a holiday or slow mail service.

The longer your grace period, the longer you go without cash or the ability to take action. If you allow a ten-day grace period, you can easily overlook the past-due rent. Manipulative tenants will use that time to extend the use of their money, knowing they won't be in default until the grace period is over. Chances are they will only pay the rent at that point, if you are lucky.

Some tenants will assume their rent is not due until the end of the grace period and that if the rent is later than that, you will give them a warning. If you don't enforce the rules of your lease with authority, you will lose control. Tenants will see you as a softy and will bleed you to the end. You may not have any intention of evicting a tenant who is late with his rent for the first time, but you should start the paperwork for eviction to protect yourself.

Every eviction for nonpayment of rent starts with a first time, so the first time the rent is late, get your paperwork in order. If you wait, by the time you realize eviction is inevitable, you will have lost substantial income. Starting the paperwork doesn't mean you must evict the tenant, but it does give you the option.

Late Fees

Tenants expect your lease to have a late-fee clause. Anyone who has had credit is aware of late fees, since they are a common element in installment loans and charge card accounts. Are late fees effective? They help, but they are not a cure-all. Hard-line bad tenants will not care if you charge a late fee; they are not going to pay it anyway. And good tenants will not resist it because they will be paying their rent on time. Late fees will help borderline tenants to pay the rent when it is due.

If your lease calls for late fees, collect them. If you don't, tenants will soon ignore them. Paper threats that are not followed up on are worthless. There is no point in putting a rule in the lease if you are not going to enforce it.

Friendly Reminders

Do friendly reminders work? They work for oversights. Even good tenants can be going through a rough period in their life and forget to pay the rent. They have no intention of robbing you of your money, but have just let the rent payment slip their mind. For these tenants friendly reminders are effective.

It doesn't cost much to send out reminders, and they can bring your rent in earlier. Mail them as soon as the due date has passed. Don't wait until the end of the grace period—by that time you should be sending out not friendly reminders, but legal notices.

Calling the Tenant

Many management companies employ collection specialists for the sole purpose of calling tenants and collecting rents. A phone call can replace a mailed friendly reminder; it is certainly more difficult for a tenant to ignore. Be prepared for excuses when you make collection calls, however. A few will be legitimate, but most will be ludicrous.

It will be up to you to decide when your tenants need temporary relief from their rental responsibilities, but don't be too generous. Even if you feel bad for your tenant, protect yourself. Start the required paperwork to allow yourself all legal options in removing the tenant if events turn bad.

Paying the Tenant a Visit

If you are willing to make a personal visit to the tenant, your collection percentages will improve. Friendly reminders are fine and phone calls work, but it is hard to beat a face-to-face meeting. When you are looking the tenant in the eye, he can't lie to you. Your physical presence can be all it takes to make the tenant produce a rent check.

Don't use this meeting to make macho threats. Your tenant has rights, and you had better know them and not violate them. If you verbally abuse her, you may find yourself under arrest. Be diplomatic; show concern for the tenant and her reason for not paying. If you can't collect with kindness, rely on the legal system. Our judicial system may leave a lot to be desired, but it is your only reasonable option when you cannot collect through amicable means.

Standing Firm

Don't turn into a jellyfish when you collect your rents. You own the building, and you have a contractual agreement with the tenant. If the tenant breaches that agreement, there is no reason for you to stray from the printed word. Follow the terms of your lease to the letter. If you step backward, the tenant may bowl you over. It is imperative for you to retain control.

It is not unusual for people in a rental community to talk. They talk in the hall, the laundry room, and in other places. If word gets around that you let the tenant in 3-A get away without paying his late fees, you may have numerous late payments in future months. Your demeanor in and around your rental properties will set the pace for your success. If you present the image of a fair but firm landlord, you should do fine.

Cash, Check, or Charge?

In what form will you collect your rent? Will you accept cash, checks, or charge cards? Personal checks are an accepted practice and the most common form of payment, but they are not the only option. Your rent may come as a money order or bank check. Progressive property managers even accept major credit cards for rental payments. Cash is also legal tender, but it can cause problems. Your lease should spell out the acceptable forms for rental payments.

Personal checks are good for many reasons. They can be replaced if they are lost or stolen. Your tenant can stop payment on a missing check and issue a new one. Personal checks can also be sent through the mail without fear, and they provide physical proof of rental payments. This can come in handy in legal disputes and tax audits. The only bad side of personal checks is the fact that they can bounce.

Money orders are as good as cash, maybe better. When you have a money order in hand, you know you have your rent money—unlike a personal check, a money order doesn't bounce. Money orders also provide the proof of your rental collections. With a photocopy of a money order you can prove the date the rent was paid and the amount. For tenants without checking accounts, money orders are a good way to pay the rent.

Bank checks work on a similar principle. They are typically collected funds that protect you from overdrawn bank accounts. A bank check can be copied to provide physical proof and documentation of your rental transaction. Bank checks and money orders are two of the best ways to ensure your rent payment has been made with viable funds.

Credit cards seem to be here to stay. You can charge dinner and clothes on credit cards. Why not make it three out of three—food, clothing, and shelter? Many management firms will accept plastic to pay the rent. As the owner of a rental business you can probably arrange to accept credit cards too.

Should you accept them? Credit cards provide you with two big advantages. One, if a tenant pays her rent with a credit card, you know the transaction is safe—once you have called for authorization the money is as good as in your bank account. Two, by accepting credit cards you can remove many of the excuses for past-due rent. When the tenant pleads poverty, offer to let him charge the rent to his credit card. If they are able to charge their rent, tenants are not as likely to make you wait for your payment.

Be advised that the use of credit cards is not without its price. As a credit-card vendor you will be charged a fee for the privilege, normally a set percentage of the cost of the sale. Before you sign up for credit card services, read the agreement. If it leaves you in doubt, have your attorney review it. The fees charged are usually fair and are a small price to pay for collecting your rent on time.

For many reasons it is bad business to accept cash for rental payments. When a tenant pays with cash it is hard to document the payment. If you accept cash, fill out a receipt for it including the date and a description of what the payment is for, and have the tenant sign it. You cannot refuse cash since it is legal tender, but you should discourage it.

If it is known that you collect your rent in cash, you could become the victim of crime. This is especially true if you go door-to-door when collecting. Some seedy character may wait until you have picked up all the money and then relieve you of it. How the crook gets the money can be left to your imagination.

He may hit you over the head, shoot you, cut you, or use some more creative method. Cash collections are not a good idea.

Another possibility with cash collections is becoming the victim of a scam. If you collect the rent on a regular schedule, you increase the odds of being taken by a con man. Let me tell you a story to emphasize my point.

In a certain city, rent is often collected on a weekly basis and often paid in cash. The city has numerous multifamily buildings sitting next to each other, and many of these buildings are owned by a small group of landlords. Con men got the names of these owners from the Registry of Deeds and watched them for several weeks to learn their habits and cycles. Once they knew the days and times when the landlords collected their rent, they went from building to building at those times, taking the tenants' rents and telling them that their landlord had hired them to do so.

The tenants assumed that since these men knew their landlords' names it was okay to give them the rent money. By the time the landlords got to their buildings, the bogus managers had already run off with the cash—a great deal of it. Of course, it wasn't long before the scam operation was exposed, but by that time it was too late. This type of scam could happen to you.

Bad Check Charges. If your lease contains the proper language, you can penalize tenants for bouncing their rent checks. A bad check can cost you money. If you bounce your own check because of the tenant's bad one, your bank will charge you a fee, putting a crunch on your cash flow. By the time the tenant makes good on the bad check, your mortgage payment may be late. If your lease calls for a steep penalty fee on all bad checks, the tenant may think twice before giving you worthless paper.

Past-Due Promises

Past-due promises don't pay your bills. Nevertheless, as a past-due rent collector you will collect many more promises than checks, many of which will never be kept. Novice landlords lose a lot of money accepting past-due promises. If you are going to accept them, at least put a time limit on them. Never accept a tenant's promise to "send the rent as soon as I can." This type of promise will force you into the poorhouse.

Pin the promises down. If a tenant claims she will send you a check within the next week, ask for a specific date on which you can expect it, and if the payment doesn't arrive, take assertive action to collect. If the tenant promises a payment in two weeks, ask her to sign a promissory note for it. This will help you if you go to court—if the tenant tries to lie, the note may call her hand.

Separating Lies from Excuses

There are times when even your best tenants will need your understanding. Perhaps they have had a bad bout with an illness and need some time to catch up financially. When a tenant gives you his reason for being late with the rent, you must decide what to do. Is it a legitimate excuse, or does it sound like a lie? It is not as difficult to sift through the excuses and lies as you may think.

If the tenant is telling the truth, he will be willing to cooperate with you. The earlier advice about asking for a promissory note is a good example. The tenant will not mind signing a note for the owed money if he intends to pay. On the other hand, if he is lying, he will not want his signature on any written agreements.

Research can go a long way in telling excuses from lies. When your tenant says she has been laid off from her job but will be going back in two weeks, do you believe her? If you have a long rental history with the tenant, you may feel confident that she is telling the truth. If you have doubts, ask if you can call her employer to confirm the date set for her return to work. If she allows you to call the employer, you will know she has a reasonable excuse for being late. If she hedges, she is probably lying.

With these methods you can quickly identify troublesome tenants. If you are unable to get satisfactory answers to your questions, start legal proceedings. The longer you put off the legal process, the longer you will have to go without income.

Beware of Harassment

As a landlord you must be aware of the laws pertaining to your business and avoid harassing your tenants for late rent. It can get very frustrating when you know a tenant is hiding behind an answering machine, but your legal actions are limited. For example, you cannot go to the tenant's apartment in the middle of the night to accost him about the rent. There are many laws protecting tenants. If you don't educate yourself in these legal matters, you will be the one on the wrong side of the judge.

Keep Solid Records

Good records are instrumental to any business. They are especially valuable if you become engaged in a legal battle. Document your actions. Make photocopies of rental payments. Keep a phone diary of the dates you call your tenants, and even if they are not home, write down the date and time you attempted to contact them. Use return-receipt mail when you mail legal notices, and save the signed receipts. The more you document during your dealings, the better off you will be in court.

Start a paper trail when tenants are in default of your lease. There will be reams of paperwork between the nonpayment of rent and the eviction. If you don't handle the process correctly, you can lose your case on a technicality. Laws vary from location to location, but they all dictate specific requirements for how you carry out your legal options.

If you are new to the property management business, seek the advice of a good lawyer and have her handle your first case involving a bad tenant. If you pay attention to the schedule of events, you may be able to take care of your own legal notices, filings, and responsibilities in the future. Don't attempt to play lawyer, however. When it comes to drafting legal documents, hire a professional. If you insist on preparing your own documents, at least have an attorney review and approve them.

Partial Payments. Be careful in accepting partial payments. In some circumstances, doing so can weaken your legal position. Your attorney can instruct you in ways to accept partial payments without deteriorating your legal stance. If you decide to take partial payments, make sure you are not making a bad situation worse.

Reassuring Words

This chapter has presented a host of ways to make collecting your rent easier. Study them and decide which will suit your circumstances best. If you develop a solid plan for collecting your rents, the job will go much smoother. One of the most important things to remember is follow-through. Once you have a plan, follow through with it; it does little good to draft a plan and ignore it. Collecting rent is a key element to your business. Learn how to do it right and you should prosper.

Chapter 10

Building a Winning Spreadsheet for Your Banker

Bankers are essential to the successful operation of most businesses. The property management business is no exception. Whether you are remodeling an existing building or buying a new one, the chances are good you will seek financial assistance, and when you do, you must present a persuasive proposal. Simply walking in and requesting a loan for ambiguous reasons rarely works.

Seasoned lenders look for key elements in loan requests. If the right information is available to the banker, she is more likely to grant your loan. Inadequate information is a major cause of loan rejections. The style in which you present your proposal can influence a banker's decision as well. Your personal attitude and demeanor can have much to do with the success or failure of your loan request.

Bankers know numbers and like to see them well laid out, so in most cases, you will want your proposal to be concise and easy to understand. However, there may be times when clouding the spreadsheet with complicated information can work to your advantage.

To maximize your borrowing power, you must learn to manipulate your lender. Find out what he reacts to and how he reacts. This will take some time, but once you know the right buttons to push, getting your loan approved can be easy. The manipulation can be as simple as knowing what types of loans different lenders like to make. While one loan officer may be generous with improvement loans, she may be stingy with acquisition loans. It will be up to you to get inside your banker's head and find the path to success.

If you know how to create a winning spreadsheet, you increase your odds of acceptance for loan requests. The process of building a salable proposal is not difficult, but you must know how it is done. This chapter is going to teach you how to package and present information to improve your chances of being approved for a loan. With the tips and guidelines given here, you will be able to prepare winning spreadsheets for your lenders.

Should You Borrow Where You Bank?

Should you attempt to borrow money from the bank where you keep your money? Logic would say yes, but your present bank may not be as liberal as others. In the old days people tried to keep all their dealings with one financial institution. Today many investors find it is wiser to spread their business out among several. To determine where to borrow money, you must ask questions and do research.

All banks will welcome your savings account, but they are not all so willing to lend you money. Just because you have your accounts with a particular bank, you cannot assume that bank will be aggressive in its lending policy. Some banks like to lend money for automobiles and home improvement but not for rental property. Others will be happy to lend on rental property up to four units in size, but may not even consider a loan for larger buildings. Still others prefer dealing in large multifamily property. Construction and rehab loans are loved by some banks for their short terms and high rates of return. Other lenders are afraid of such loans because of the risks involved. Finding the right lender for your type of loan is the first step toward getting your loan request approved.

Finding the Right Lending Institution

The right lender is critical to your success in finding suitable financing. There are banks, savings and loans, credit unions, and private investors to choose from, and these are not the only ones available, although they are the ones most often used. Mortgage bankers and mortgage brokers are also on the list of most popular lenders. When you are planning for financing, you should investigate all the options available to you.

Not all lenders are the same. We have already discussed how different lenders prefer different types of loans, but there are other differences. Some lenders sell their loans in the secondary market and so must meet predetermined criteria in their loan packages. Such lenders can be inflexible to your needs; if your request does not fit the mold of a secondary-market loan, you will be denied. Banks that hold portfolio loans, however, can make any type of loan they wish to. If you are seeking creative financing, portfolio lenders are what you want.

Loan officers also come in different configurations. Many are on the payroll of the lending institution and get a steady paycheck whether you get your loan or not. They may be nervous about losing their job by making bad loans and so are likely to be the hardest to deal with. Loan originators who are paid a commission will generally work harder to get your loan approved. If you get your loan, they get a commission check. This monetary incentive motivates them to be more aggressive.

Commissioned mortgage brokers add a new dimension to the search for financing. They are not tied to a single loan source, but work with a stable of lenders to place all types of loans. Thus, they can often get a loan approved when others have failed. There are fees involved when using mortgage brokers, but they can be well worth the cost if they make your deal come together.

With so many choices, how will you find the right lender for your loan? You can narrow the field by asking questions and doing some research. The first questions are those you must ask yourself pertaining to the type of loan you want, the interest rate and points you are willing to pay, and the terms that will be acceptable. Once you know what you want, start asking the lenders questions to determine which one is right for your loan request. Your research will be used to identify liberal lenders and build your winning spreadsheet.

Banks

Banks are normally the first place people think of when planning to borrow money; they are a logical and often good source of financing for various projects and purchases. Commercial banks may be able to accommodate all of your banking and borrowing needs. Most will issue financing for owner-occupied and non-owner-occupied buildings. Choosing a lender that works with non–owner-occupied loans is important for the many investors who don't live in their rental properties.

Banks are also capable of providing financing for acquisitions, construction, renovations, repairs, and refinancing. An aggressive bank will offer portfolio loans. With all their ability, banks may be your best source of financing. They have the tools to make your financing plans work, if they are willing to use them. Not all banks are willing to exercise the full extent of their lending power, and this reluctance can force you to expand your financing search.

Savings and Loans

For a long time, savings and loans were the place to go for construction financing and creative financing. With their liberal, aggressive style they over-shadowed more conservative banks when it came to specialized lending. However, today many savings and loans are in financial trouble or have failed. With their current problems they are not the oasis they once were to entrepreneurs.

Credit Unions

If you belong to a credit union, check with it for your financing needs. A credit union operates differently from most banks. It may approve your loan request when a commercial bank would deny it. If you are seeking financing for buildings with more than four units, credit unions may not be willing to help you. Some will not even consider lending money for commercial-grade rental properties.

Other Sources

Mortgage bankers specialize in mortgage loans. If you are buying a new property or refinancing an existing one, these lenders can be very helpful since the bulk of their business comprises these two loan types. Generally, they will not be your best source for rehab money or construction loans, but they love long-term take-out loans.

Mortgage brokers are freelancers. They work with you to find financing at any of their numerous sources, including insurance companies, banks, or private investors. Once they secure and close your loan, mortgage brokers are typically paid a commission equal to a percentage of the loan. However, some charge an up-front fee and others a flat-rate fee instead.

Dealing with mortgage brokers can get complicated. Up-front fees are dangerous because you pay them without any guarantee of receiving loan approval. Most mortgage brokers don't have the authority to approve loans; they simply place them with a willing lender. The big advantage to mortgage brokers is that since they work with so many lenders, they are often able to do in a day what it could take you weeks to do. Their variety of lenders also makes it possible for them to place loans that might otherwise be denied.

Private investors are responsible for much of the money used in real estate transactions. Normally, their money is channeled through commercial financial institutions, but some investors will lend money directly to borrowers. The interest rates for private money are often higher, but the flexibility for approval is usually greater. There are risks involved when you deal with the private sector. Individuals are not regulated in the same way commercial lenders are, which can lead to a no-holds-barred loan agreement. If you are playing in a game with no rules, you can get hurt. Be careful when you borrow money on the street.

Choosing the Best Loan Officer

After deciding which type of lending institution best suits your needs, you will have to find the best loan officer. As not all financial institutions are the same, neither are all loan officers. Some are very conservative, while others are aggressively liberal. Some will want to see a complex strategic plan for how the money will be used and repaid. Others will only want to see the bottom line of what you want and how it will be secured. Lenders paid on a commission basis should be more willing to stretch the ratios and bend the rules than those receiving a payroll check each week.

How will you know which loan officers are most likely to approve your loan? Check with your friends and fellow investors, or ask real estate brokers for the names of friendly bankers. Start with those working on a commission basis. There is an easy way to distinguish commission from noncommission loan officers. Call one and say that you want to apply for a loan. Ask if he will meet you at your home or office. If he is willing to leave his office to come to yours, he is probably on commission. If he refuses to abandon his desk, he is most likely on the institution's payroll.

Many other factors influence lenders in their decisions on loan requests. Inexperienced loan originators may not have the savvy to understand your loan proposal. If you have a detailed plan with extensive math and formulas, they may say no just because they don't understand your projection methods. On the other hand, a new loan officer might go out of her way to get your loan approved to generate customers. There is no way to know what a loan officer is going to do until you know her.

Loan officers with years of tenure may be reluctant to approve any but the most desirable loans for the bank. With only a few years until retirement, they will not want to lose their position by making high-risk approvals. Even so, seasoned loan officers have the experience needed to read between the lines, and they can often sense a good deal that may not look good on paper. It will be up to you to evaluate loan officers on their own merit. Find the ones you have confidence in and give them a try. Until you run some loan requests in front of various loan officers, you will not be able to identify the best ones to work with.

Putting Your Proposal Together

Once you have a good idea of which lending institution and loan officer you will be working with, you are ready to start putting your loan package together. Allow adequate time for this process. Building a winning spreadsheet can take days to accomplish, and the time will be directly related to the research needed and the manner in which you present your proposal.

If you have the power of a computer and suitable software, structuring a viable loan package will go a little quicker. With the computer you can play the "what-if" game to hone the edge of your spreadsheet. Computers allow this type of testing to be done in a matter of minutes, but if you are working with a pen and paper, your time invested will be considerably more.

Your contacts in and around your business will have bearing on how quickly you can formulate a successful plan. With good working relationships with brokers and appraisers, your research will not take as long. Knowing other investors who are willing to share information can also expedite the process of running your numbers, and having a contact in the local housing authority can produce needed statistics in record time.

Defining Your Desires

Before you start drafting your plan, define your desires. Knowing exactly what you want and what you are willing to settle for can save you untold hours later. If you know your plan will not work with anything higher than a 10-percent interest rate, you can rule out many lenders with a quick phone call. If you are sure the only way your request will fly is with a portfolio loan, you can narrow the field of lenders even more.

Don't just think of ideas and desires—write them down. Otherwise, in the heat of negotiation you may forget important aspects of your plan. After you have determined all of your desires and potential compromises, you are ready to move on to the next step. This is deciding what it will take to convince your lender to make the loan.

Think Like a Banker

You obviously believe in your plan or you would not be pursuing it. By removing your emotions and thinking like a banker, you can find flaws in it in time to fix them. Remain unbiased in your scrutiny. Ask yourself the questions you envision a banker will ask. How long will it take you to repay the loan? Will the loan increase your net cash flow? Will the purpose of your loan improve your financial position or damage it? Continue with this line of questioning until you cannot think of any other questions to ask.

Imagine that an investor is asking you to lend your money for the same purpose as the one you want a loan for. Would you agree to do it? If you answer no, why not? Find as many flaws in your plan as possible. It is much better for you to find them than it is for the banker to find them. If you walk in with a shaky plan, the banker will have a bad first impression of the deal. Then it will be very hard to sell him on an amended proposal.

Pulling Information Together

If you think your reason for borrowing money is bulletproof, pull your supporting information together. This information will come from a multitude of sources, starting with your personal financial statement. If this document is not strong enough, the rest of your efforts will be wasted.

After preparing your financial statement, you will need to gather tax returns and information on credit-card debts and installment loans. Also include information on all your real estate loans. If you have been divorced, a copy of your divorce decree will be helpful. In general, gather all the information available to make it easy for the loan officer to evaluate your loan request.

The remainder of your information gathering will be centered on the purpose for your loan, which you will want to make as attractive as you can for the loan officer. If you are borrowing money to add a coin-operated laundry to your building, compile data to prove the potential earnings you can expect from your investment, and include details on how the laundry will increase your cash flow and your property's value. This information may be obtained from appraisers, brokers, other investors, and many other sources.

Even interviews with your tenants could prove your point. For example, if you have twelve tenants, ask each of them how often they do laundry and if they would use a coin-operated laundry if one were installed in the building. Record the responses and run the numbers. If they are good, ask the tenants to write a brief letter documenting their response to your survey. These letters will help to build a strong case when you sit down with the loan officer. If she can see that your tenants are willing to use your new facilities, she will be more inclined to give serious consideration to your loan request. By running the numbers you can show the loan officer the expected revenue. All of this type of documentation will make obtaining financing easier.

Let's say you want a loan to convert an unused attic into living space, which could require a large sum of money. To justify such a loan you will need strong evidence that the venture is worthwhile. This means you will need to complete a market study showing the demand for housing and the amount of money tenants are willing to pay for rental units. By investigating existing units comparable to those you plan to create, you can determine what you are likely to receive in increased revenue.

Getting prices from contractors will give you the numbers needed to estimate the cost of your project. Looking through historical data will produce the numbers needed to project the operating expenses for the new units. When you have all of your numbers together, you will begin to see the overall picture. You will see what the project should cost and what it should mean to you in terms of cash flow and property value. Then you can further project the time needed to break even on the investment. By doing all of this planning before you talk to the loan officer, you are building a strong case.

In some instances, your research may prove to you that your plans are not as good as you thought. This saves you the embarrassment of taking a bad plan to the banker. If the numbers work, however, you will be prepared to make an impressive presentation to the loan officer, and if you convince him that the plan will work, he will be inclined to lend you the money you need.

Packaging Your Proposal

How you package your loan request can influence the lender's decision. If you go in with papers sticking out of your briefcase and coffee stains on your spreadsheet, the loan officer will be impressed, but not favorably. In the banking world, neatness counts. Bankers appreciate a well-organized and complete loan package. It makes their job easier and makes you appear more professional.

Have your documents laid out in chronological order. There is nothing worse than losing your place or searching for an elusive report in the middle of a loan application meeting. Placing your papers in a presentation binder is a good way to keep them in order and to give a good impression. Have your exhibits labeled so that the loan officer can quickly identify them. You don't want her picking up your paperwork and not knowing what she is looking at.

Preparing to Meet Your Lender

Preparing to meet your lender is the next step in making a successful loan application. Know your proposal inside and out before meeting with the loan officer. This way you won't have to rummage through your papers to answer the lender's questions, making it appear that you are not well prepared to execute your plans. Commit your proposal to memory, and if possible, have a friend or spouse act as a loan officer so you can practice your presentation. Besides giving you the chance to rehearse, this role playing will expose any of the proposal's flaws.

Work all the bugs out of your proposal and presentation before you meet with the banker, so that when you sit down together you will be calm, confident, and convincing. Your presentation will have a significant affect on the lender's opinion of your proposal. If you ramble back and forth and have trouble defining your needs and desires, the lender will not have confidence in you or your plan. Once you are prepared, call your lender and make an appointment for a loan application.

Making a Formal Loan Application

Formal loan applications can take on many different looks depending on the lender you are dealing with. Some lenders want piles of paperwork. Others prefer to hear a verbal presentation, before they see anything in writing. Normally, the process will involve an oral discussion, followed by a written application. It is during the face-to-face talk that you have the opportunity to convince your lender to say yes.

If you have prepared well for your meeting, you can change the mind of even a doubting loan officer. There will be few situations when a concise plan, delivered in a confident manner, will not convince her to lean in your direction. Loan officers are used to meeting people for all types of loans under all kinds of circumstances. The majority of these loan applicants are not well prepared or organized. With the right presentation, the lender will pay close attention to your plans. As she mentally compares your presentation to the haphazard requests she is accustomed to getting, your ideas will sound great.

Your paperwork and numbers will have to substantiate what you tell the banker. If you have a winning spreadsheet to cement a successful talk, you all but have the loan. Let's look at right and wrong versions of two loan proposals. Put yourself in the loan officer's chair as you read each request, and formulate an approval or denial for the loan. I think you will quickly see what a difference the concept and approach of your proposal can make.

Example 1—The Wrong Way

In this example, the investor, Joe, is applying for a $6,000 loan to add a coin-operated laundry facility in the basement of his building, which has twelve, two-bedroom rental units. The rental units do not have provisions for individual laundry equipment, so Joe's tenants must take their dirty clothes to a laundromat down the street.

Joe's reason for installing the laundry room is to increase cash flow and the property's value. Because his tenants must leave the site to do their laundry, he is convinced he will make more money after the facilities are installed.

When Joe asks you, the loan officer, for a loan, he tells you all about his plan, but only in the detail described above. He has quotes from contractors to prove the approximate cost of the improvements, but this is his only factual information other than the description of his building. Are you willing to lend Joe $6,000? Do you need more information to make a sound decision? Well, if you lend Joe the money based on the sketchy details he has provided, you probably won't be a loan officer for long.

Joe has failed to provide enough information for you to make a clear evaluation of his loan request. Like many other landlords, he knows what he is thinking, but he doesn't do a good job of putting his thoughts together to explain his plan to someone else. This type of loan request will either be denied or countered with a request for additional information.

Now let's see how Mike asked for the same amount of money for the same improvement.

Example 1—The Right Way

Like Joe, Mike wants to borrow $6,000 to install a laundry room in his building. His reason for doing so is to increase cash flow and the property's value. Mike has decided this improvement is worthwhile because his tenants must leave the site to do their laundry. He is convinced he will make more money after the facilities are installed. Here are the highlights of Mike's proposal:

1. There are twelve apartments in the building. Two are occupied by single men; eight by a husband, wife, and child; and two by husbands and wives. There are twenty-two adults and eight children living in the building. None of these people do laundry with personal equipment. They all go to the corner laundromat to clean their clothes.

2. There are affidavits in the loan-request package from each responsible tenant requesting the installation of coin-operated laundry facilities in the building.

All residents have included an estimate of their weekly spending habits for cleaning their clothes. Based on the numbers they have provided, they collectively spend around $40 per week at the laundromat.

3. Mike has indicated that he wishes to install four washing machines and six dryers (more dryers are necessary since it takes longer to dry clothes than it does to wash them). With this number of units, one-third of all the tenants could do laundry at the same time, which is adequate to keep tenants from becoming frustrated by a lack of available machines. If they are always made to wait for a machine, they will go to the laundromat down the street.

4. Mike has requested $6,000 to create his laundry room. This amount includes all expenses incurred to build an operational laundry as described. According to the income amounts estimated from the tenants' affidavits, it will take just under three years to recover the cost of the investment. After the loan is repaid, Mike's cash flow will increase by approximately $2,000 per year.

5. Mike is asking for a five-year loan. He wants the additional two years to allow for vacancies, operating expenses, maintenance, and repairs. He is certain the coin-operated machines will pay for themselves in less than the requested five years.

6. Mike has included three quotes from reputable contractors for the costs to provide the laundry facilities. According to the contractors' quotes, the job can be done for $5,300. Mike is asking for a loan approval in the amount of $6,000 to guard against cost overruns, but he does not expect to borrow more than the actual cost of the job.

7. Mike points out that his building has twelve units and is considered a commercial income property. Since the assessment of this type of building is based largely on its income performance, the increased cash flow will increase the property's value. According to the documented projections Mike has put together, the $6,000 investment will probably be recovered in the third or fourth year, but no later than the fifth year. After this time, all income from the laundry, except that used for operating expenses, maintenance, and repairs, will be profit.

Mike projects that the $2,000 of additional profit will translate into an additional property value of nearly $19,000. He arrived at this figure by running numbers on his spreadsheet, which is a part of his loan-request package. He shows that the income from the laundry will amount to about $166 per month. With current interest rates at 10 percent, $166 will carry the payment for a thirty-year, amortized loan in the amount of nearly $19,000. Even if 20 percent of the income is lost to vacancies and maintenance, there is still about $132 per month to generate increased value. This amounts to an equity gain of about $15,000.

Mike has all of his facts and figures neatly arranged and protected in a binder. He hands it to you for a decision. Do you think you will give Mike the loan for the laundry room? Mike has made his proposal clear and has supported it with documented facts, so there is no reason why you shouldn't. Your file is well documented to verify your reasoning in approving the loan. You get a good loan, and Mike gets the laundry room he wants.

The Comparison of Right and Wrong

Joe did not provide much information, and the information he did provide was not substantiated with facts and figures. There were no contingencies planned or shown for cost overruns, vacancies, or other unforeseen obstacles, nor did he disclose how many washers and dryers he planned to install. He said he wanted to increase his cash flow and property value, but he didn't provide any projections for these factors. All in all, Joe did not present a winning proposal.

When Mike made his loan request, he was well prepared. He had statements from his tenants to support his feelings that a coin-operated laundry would be a successful investment. He had numbers to project his increased income. He allowed for unforeseen problems in the cost of the job and the time it might take to recover his investment. He knew how many machines he needed to get the job done without going overboard. And he provided a winning spreadsheet to document the value of the investment to his building. In general, Mike made a proposal that was too good to deny.

Example 2—The Wrong Way

Lisa comes to you with a request for $35,000 to remodel her four-unit building. She tells you the existing kitchens and bathrooms are old and need to be renovated to attract better tenants and a higher rental income. She points out that the building needs minor repairs and extensive cosmetic work to improve its condition and appearance. She lays out her plans and even shows you samples of the wallpaper she plans to use in the job. Her proposal includes cost quotes from several reputable contractors.

Lisa has talked to all of her tenants, and they think it would be great to get their apartments upgraded. However, she didn't ask if they would be willing and able to pay a higher rent after the improvements are made. Lisa's plans call for replacing the plumbing fixtures in all the bathrooms and kitchens. She intends to cover most of the walls with wallpaper, and new floor coverings are targeted for the floors.

Lisa is sure she can get more rent for the units once the improvements are made, but she has not compiled evidence to support her opinion. Lisa is also certain her property's value will skyrocket with the proposed improvements. She thinks she can recover her investment in ten years—sooner if she sells the building. All she needs is your approval to start the work. What do you think, will you lend her the money?

Lisa's project may be viable, but she has not provided enough information for you to make an informed decision. The improvements she has planned make sense, except, perhaps, the wallpaper, but what effect will they have on the building? It is doubtful her cash flow will increase enough to carry the debt service of the loan, but without projections, you have no way of knowing one way or the other at the time of her application. If you were to make a decision

on the spot, it would probably be a denial. Lisa will have to gather more information and generate projections before you can give her the answer she wants.

Example 2—The Right Way

Kim comes to you for a $35,000 loan to remodel her four-unit building. She
tells you that the existing kitchens and bathrooms are old and need to be renovated to attract better tenants and a higher rental income. She points out that
the building needs minor repairs and extensive cosmetic improvements to improve its condition and appearance. Her proposal includes cost quotes from
several reputable contractors. She also has detailed plans and specifications in
her loan-request package.

Kim has talked to all of her tenants, and they think it would be great to get
their apartments upgraded. They have all agreed to a monthly rental increase of
$50 if the improvements are made. Kim's plans call for replacing the lavatories
and toilets in all the bathrooms, and she plans to have the existing bathtubs
refinished, so they will appear new. In the kitchens, she is going to have new
cabinet doors and drawer faces installed, which will give the appearance of all
new cabinets at a fraction of the cost. She intends to paint the walls and ceilings
a lighter color to make the units appear larger. The new floor coverings she has
targeted for the floors will meet government standards for loans, but will not be
fancy.

There are many miscellaneous minor repairs to be made, and there will be
cosmetic work done throughout the units. Kim will also be replacing outdated
light fixtures, installing new doorknobs, and making other small but noticeable
improvements. All of her improvements are aimed at making the rental units
modern and attractive at a minimal expense.

Kim expects to receive more rent for the units once they are done. Based on
the statements from her tenants, she is assured of an increased monthly income
of $200. This is not enough to carry the debt service of the loan—it will take about
$376 to make the payments on a $35,000 loan at 10 percent interest amortized for
fifteen years—but Kim believes that as the units become vacant she can obtain
an even higher rent than the existing tenants are willing to pay.

By interviewing the local housing authority and compiling historical data on
comparable properties, Kim has proven on her spreadsheet that she should be
able to command a total monthly rent increase of $300 once the improvements
are made. This still is not enough to make the payments, but her financial
statement shows cash reserves and a strong discretionary income that could be
used to meet the difference between the increased income and the payment.

Kim has also run a spreadsheet showing the results of taking a seven-year
balloon mortgage with the monthly payments amortized on a thirty-year basis.
At 10 percent interest, the payments on the $35,000 will be about $307. The
projected income will make these payments, and she can refinance or sell the
building to pay the balloon payment when it matures. Further, Kim has run the
numbers on a seven-year balloon with interest-only payments until the term
expires. These payments will amount to a monthly debt service of approximately
$291. She has investigated all the angles and wishes to take the loan as a seven-

year balloon at 10 percent interest with the monthly payments amortized for thirty years.

To be sure her improvements are a wise investment, Kim has had a before-and-after appraisal done by a certified, bank-approved appraisal firm. She plans to act as her own general contractor, so the $35,000 she invests in her property will yield an equity gain of $7,000. When the improvements are done, apart from the additional net equity, Kim will have a building with a new look and a higher income. This will make the property more desirable to tenants and purchasers. The renovations may draw a higher value than the conservative appraisal, but almost certainly no less. If she chooses to sell the property, there should be more than adequate equity to satisfy all debts and show a profit.

Kim has given you a financial statement and all supporting data to confirm her solid financial position and experience as an investor and property manager. As part of her package, there are several spreadsheets showing different scenarios, all of which produce winning results. The findings of her market research and documentation of her sources of information are enclosed for your review.

The decision is now yours. Will you approve Kim's loan or deny it? Well, the profit potential is not outstanding, but the proposal is solid and well thought out. Kim has done extensive research and compiled the information in an easily understood manner. She has proven her investment will return a profit, barring local economic disasters. The numbers have been run and the projections have been made. Kim has demonstrated a strong knowledge of the rental business.

Further, she has made wise decisions in the type of improvements she plans to make. The before-and-after appraisal supports Kim's belief in increased value. Her careful study of various types of loans shows her intent to repay the debt, and she has contingency plans built in to account for her balloon note. Can you find a reason not to grant this loan? If you are in the business of making renovation loans, this is a good one. It may not produce the strongest return of all rehab loans, but it is a safe bet to take.

The Winning Pitch

Now you have seen what a difference a well-prepared loan package can make. The more factual information you supply, packaged and presented professionally, the better your chances of having your loan approved.

Chapter 11

Putting a Price on Your Accommodations

Your net income from your rental units will be largely determined by the amount of rent you charge for them. If you price your apartments too high, you will be plagued with vacancies. If you price them too low, you will have plenty of tenants but not enough money. Finding the optimum price for your accommodations will take a little doing. You will have to research market conditions.

Part of your research will be on the prices being offered by competitive buildings. The supply of apartments available for rent will also influence your findings. Demand is always a factor. If local unemployment is high and people are moving away to find work, you will not enjoy high rental figures.

Determining the value of your rental units is not a one-time job. Every year you must assess the rate of increase you will pass on to your tenants. When a unit is vacated, you must determine its current market rent; renting it for the same amount the previous tenant was paying could be a mistake.

If you used a management company in the past, they probably advised you on obtainable rents. Now, as your own manager, you are on your own. Don't despair, however. This chapter will help you master the skills needed to find the perfect price for your property. By the time you complete it, you will know enough to peg a price that will make you and your tenants happy.

How Much Money Do You Need?

If you already own a rental property, it may be a little late to figure out how much income you need to break even. Even so, if you don't know what your cash needs are, find out now. It will be counterproductive to set a rental figure that will not allow you to keep your property. You should have determined your minimum income needs when you were debating whether or not to purchase it. Once you own it, you are at the mercy of the market. Let's run through an example to show you how to project your minimum cash needs.

The first step in projecting your breakeven point is gathering information on your operating expenses and debt service. You can use a computer to create a spreadsheet, or you can get by with a legal pad and pencil. It is not important how you lay out your figures, but it is important not to overlook any expenses.

Start with the mortgage. For the sake of example, we will say the building's monthly payment is fixed at $3,000 per month. Next, add in real estate taxes, say, $2,800. Now, enter the cost of insurance coverage, including hazard, liability, loss-of-rents, and any other coverage directly related to the property. This building's annual insurance premiums are $5,200. So far, we have a total annual need of $44,000.

Now we must tally up all remaining operating costs. Our sample building has twelve three-bedroom units. The landlord pays the heating and cooling expenses and also provides water and sewer services, including hot water. The tenants pays their own electrical bills, but the landlord pays for electricity in the common areas. The landlord also provides snow removal and trash pickup. Altogether, the landlord's operating expenses for the building have an annual total of $37,700.

When we add our two known subtotals we come up with an annual need of $81,700, but we are not done yet. The landlord will incur other costs to keep her building going. There will be advertising expenses to keep the building full, as well as legal fees and accounting fees. Office supplies, postage, long-distance phone calls, and printing expenses will continue to raise her cost of doing business. The potential list of these often forgotten expenses could go on and on. For our example, the landlord's hidden expenses come to $4,500 a year. We still have not factored in the cost of routine maintenance, and we are already at an annual total operating expense of $86,200.

Maintenance costs are often projected as a percentage of the rental income. In this case, the building was sold with good maintenance records and the owner knows the building should have an annual maintenance expense of $2,700. That brings our current total to $88,900. Being a smart investor, however, the landlord adds 5 percent of the known expenses to the total to offset items that may have been overlooked. Thus, our sample building is now projected to need an annual income of $93,345.

If our imaginary investor wants to break even, she must charge about $650 per month for each of her twelve units, a figure arrived at by dividing the $93,345 by twelve units paying equal monthly rents. However, this is a false reading of the breakeven point. There is no compensating factor for vacant apartments, yet it is a very lucky investor whose vacant apartments never cause lost income.

Banks normally use a figure equal to 10 percent of the gross income to represent the money lost to vacant apartments. In our example, this would be in the neighborhood of $9,500. When we add this to our original total for projected annual expenses, we get $105,845, and when we divide $105,845 by twelve units, we arrive at a figure of about $715 for a breakeven, monthly rental amount. Any amount the investor can charge above the $715 should result in a profit.

* * *

This is not a complete picture—for that you would have to factor in deprecia-tion and a host of other factors—but it should give you an idea of how to determine your cash needs. Using this outline as a guide, you should be able to work the numbers on your property to build a projection worksheet with accept-able estimates.

Just Because You Need It You Can't Always Get It

Knowing how much money you need to break even doesn't mean you can get it. Market conditions and your abilities as a property manager will have bearing on what you can expect in rental income. If the going price for a three-bedroom apartment is $650, you will have a rough time getting $800 for yours. It is not enough to set your rent at a figure you like. You must market your units at a figure acceptable to the public.

Many investors stumble when building pro forma statements including the rents they would like to charge. It is easy to plug numbers into a spreadsheet; it is not always so easy to achieve rent to match those numbers. Novice investors often go astray on this point. They buy a building based on hypothetical rental figures that usually came off the top of their heads when they rated the building for acquisition. After closing on the property, they find they cannot get the rents they had planned on, and this reality often leads to negative cash flow and loss of the building. If these same investors had done their homework, they could have avoided financial problems. They would have known before they pur-chased the property whether or not it would pay for itself.

This same advice applies to investors who make capital improvements to their property. If they don't compile accurate income projections before investing their improvement money, they can be extremely disappointed with the return on their investment. Whether you are buying, renovating, or renting rental property, you must conduct a complete market evaluation to maximize your income. What follows is a look at how to go about doing that.

How Does Your Building Stack up against the Competition?

How does your building compare with the competition? The answer carries a lot of weight in the determination of how much you can charge for your rental units. First, you must look at all the angles. How many bedrooms do the competi-tive units have? Are appliances included in your competitor's apartments? Do the competing landlords pay the heating and cooling expenses for their tenants? These are only a few of the questions you must answer before you can answer the primary question. Since competitive properties are such a large factor in setting your rental amounts, let's examine how certain features affect market rates.

Location and Physical Condition. Location may be the single most important element in establishing the rent you charge. People will pay a premium to live where they want to. A two-bedroom condo in an undesirable location may be worth only half the value of the same condo in a good one. You cannot take location for granted. Again, as you build your comparative spreadsheet, the value of various locations will become apparent.

The physical condition of a rental property also has much to do with its value. If you own the worst building on the street, you cannot expect to get the same rent your competitors do. But owning the best building on the street doesn't mean you can command a significantly higher rent either. Exotic wallpaper, fancy doors, ornate trim, and other superfluous garnishes will not convince the average tenant to pay a much higher rent than he would for an adequate unit. Ideally, your building will be on the upper end of the middle ground. This will provide you with strong rental income without the expense of flashy fixtures.

Bedrooms. The number of bedrooms a rental unit has is a key factor in its rental value. A one-bedroom apartment is not worth as much as a two-bedroom apartment; two bedrooms are not as valuable as three-bedrooms. Look at the number of bedrooms your units have and compare them to the competition's. If your competitors are charging a rent of $700 for their three-bedroom units, you will not be able to charge the same amount for one-bedroom units. Make adjustments for the number of bedrooms when you build a spreadsheet showing the features of competitive properties.

Appliances. If, unlike your competitors, you supply appliances, you should be able to charge a higher rent. However, since most landlords do supply appliances, you will be on the low end of the rental spectrum if you don't. For many tenants, a rental unit without kitchen appliances is useless since they don't have their own. By not supplying your tenants with a range and refrigerator, you narrow your prospective market considerably.

Heating and Cooling. In many old buildings unequipped with individual zones and thermostats for each rental unit, the landlord pays the tenants' heating and cooling expenses. You must know who pays these expenses when you compare your building to a competitor's. In Maine a landlord who pays for a tenant's heat can charge a much higher rent than one whose tenant is responsible for her own heat.

Keep in mind that such a difference can cloud your judgment if you look only at the amount of rent being charged by other landlords. If you skim through the paper and see that two-bedroom apartments are renting for $600, you may assume you can rent your two-bedroom units for the same price. However, if the landlords of the other buildings are paying the utilities and you are not, your monthly rent may have to be lowered by over a hundred dollars. In reverse, if you see rents advertised at $500 a month that don't include utilities, and you do, you would be making a huge mistake to rent your units at that price. When making your comparisons you must compare all aspects of each property.

Parking and Amenities. Parking space can be a valuable asset. If it is hard to come by in your area, pay attention to the parking status of competitive buildings. Tenants who have to pay a monthly fee at a parking garage will not pay as much in rent for their apartment as they would for one with parking included. On-site parking is convenient and will demand a higher rent in many cities.

Amenities, too, play a role in the value of a rental unit. If you have a large complex, there could be many amenities to investigate before setting your rental fees. Swimming pools, tennis courts, and fitness rooms are only a few possibilities. Their value will influence the value of your rental units.

There are many other considerations in a comparison of your property and your competitors'. Look at your competitors' advertisements to see what features and benefits they are pitching. Listen to the comments of prospective tenants. When a tenant declines your unit, ask him why. Keep notes and see if a pattern develops. In time, you will learn what your building has going against it. You can then upgrade the building or adjust your rental fee to offset the objections.

How Is the Market Demand?

The supply of rental units has a strong influence on rental values. If the market is glutted, rental values will drop. Assess the supply of comparable apartments before setting a price on yours. When supply is greater than demand, you will have to make concessions. As the cycle turns and demand outpaces supply, you can increase your rents.

The market demand for rental property can be affected by numerous factors. Unemployment can devastate demand. If people are forced to move away from your area to find work, they will not be renting your apartments. On the other hand, if new businesses are moving into your area, the demand for housing will increase.

I have seen apartments that once rented for $550 a month going for under $300. The cause of this dramatic drop? High unemployment and low job expectations meant people could not afford the prices paid a year earlier. Landlords were thus forced to rent cheap or not rent at all. Remember, though, while it is better to earn some money than no money, the decision to lower rents is not without its complications. Once you rent your units at a low rate, it is difficult to raise that rate in large increments. Before setting your rents, do adequate research. It is much easier to lower your rents than it is to raise them.

How Do Interest Rates Affect You?

Interest rates affect the demand for rental housing. When they are low, people buy their own homes, leaving apartments empty. When they are high, people put off buying homes and stay put. High interest rates can help you keep your rental properties full. By using interest rates as a rental barometer, you can navigate your path through the investment landscape.

Many smart landlords sell their buildings when rates are low because they can cash in on the equity they have gained. But when interest rates go up, they hang on to them. Interest rates have a direct effect on the value of multifamily properties having more than four units. When rates are low, so is debt service. A low debt service should mean an increased net income for successful landlords. This higher income makes their property more valuable.

When rates are high, the value of investment property drops. This is due to the higher debt service and lower net income higher interest rates bring with them. As you gain experience, you will be able to predict when to sell and when to keep your rental investments.

Reading Classified Ads

Most landlords find tenants for their buildings with classified advertising. To determine a fair rent for your units, read your competitors' ads. They will give you a broad insight into the current market conditions. Not only will you be able to see how many apartments are available; since many landlords put the price for their units in their ads, you will also know what they hope to rent their units for. Finding the same ad week after week will indicate to you that the price being asked is too high.

You can learn much from the classifieds. If you read the help-wanted ads regularly, you can predict the need for rental housing and how prices are likely to run. When there are more jobs than there are people to fill them, you have a strong rental market. The people who are working are likely to keep working, and new people will probably move to your area to fill available positions. This means you will have more tenants to choose from.

If the advertisements for labor are few and far between, you should think twice before raising your rents. A weak job market creates a soft rental market. Cut out some of these ads and put them into a file. If you see a company repeatedly running ads for jobs, maybe you should seek permission to put a notice on its bulletin board. The notice will make new employees aware of your building and may reduce your vacancy rates.

By cutting out ads for competitive buildings, you can build a strong database of information that will help you set the rates for your rental units. You will also be able to see which ads are working and which ones aren't. If the ad is only in the paper a few times, it is a good one. If it shows up for weeks, it isn't doing its job.

You will have to carry your research a little further to see why some ads work and some don't. The ad that only lasted a day or so may mean the advertiser rents his units too cheaply. A long-running ad could indicate that the requested rent is too high. Moreover, these ongoing ads might indicate that the advertised rental is in a bad location or in bad condition.

Going Undercover

Reading newspapers will give you an idea of what the competition is offering, but to be sure of what you are up against, you must see for yourself. The easiest way to do this is to go undercover as a prospective tenant. Call about the ads placed by your competitors, and arrange to be shown their vacant units. After a few showings you will know what real tenants will be comparing your property to, and this information will be invaluable in deciding how much you can charge.

As you make the rounds of various apartments, take notes. Pay attention to detail and look for items that make the opposing apartments better, or worse, than yours. Once you have adequate information, it will be time to put it to good use in a comparative spreadsheet.

Building a Comparative Spreadsheet

A comparative spreadsheet is one of the best ways to compare your property to the other properties available to prospective tenants. Design it with columns for each aspect of your property that will affect its value for a tenant. Headings might include location, number of bedrooms, parking, utilities, and amenities.

When your spreadsheet template is done, fill it with your research information. Look at it to see what the rent for an average two-bedroom apartment is. Then compare the features of that apartment with those in your rental property. With a little comparison work, you can identify prices you can reasonably ask for.

Base Your Projections on Solid Numbers

The projections for your rental income must be based on solid numbers. Pulling figures out of thin air will serve no purpose. If you follow the suggestions I have given here, it will be easy to arrive at viable rental figures for your building. Putting a price on your accommodations is not difficult if you do the proper research and comparison.

Chapter 12

Property Maintenance

When you manage your own property, you are responsible for your building's maintenance needs. If you don't have any experience in the maintenance and repair of real estate, this responsibility can be a burden. When your tenants call in the middle of the night to report a broken water pipe or some other crisis, you must know what to do. It may mean calling a professional or your maintenance person. It may mean going out to solve the problem yourself. Before you are faced with such calls, you should have a plan for handling after-hours' emergencies.

Even when there are no emergencies, routine maintenance will be required to keep your rental property in good repair. This may involve cleaning the heating system or cutting the lawn, but in any case, ignoring routine maintenance will lead to more tenant calls and lost money. It is up to you, as your own manager, to schedule, coordinate, and inspect all the work done on your property.

Many investors know money, but often know nothing about maintenance and repairs. The property maintenance aspect of the rental business can be the most difficult to learn. It can also be the most costly if you rely on experience as your teacher. This chapter will cover the most common requirements for the maintenance and repair of rental properties. It is up to you whether you perform the work yourself or hire others to do it for you. Most important, you will learn what to look for and what to expect from your property in its repair and maintenance needs.

Whether you have a single-family house or a twelve-unit building, many of the repair and maintenance procedures will be the same. Once you understand the principles involved, you can apply them to all your rental units. The sections that follow focus on the areas of your property where attention may be needed—for example, the outside, the hallway, the basement, the roof, and the rental unit interiors.

Some Initial Considerations

You must decide how you will arrange for the upkeep of your property and how much you will do yourself. For example, many landlords who are unable to perform technical work inside their buildings are quite capable of keeping up the exterior. While you may not know how to solder copper pipes or clean your heating system, you are probably more than qualified to cut the grass. The question is, should you? It may be more beneficial to hire a company to take care of it. If you can be making deals while they are doing your lawn, you will probably be money ahead.

Some investors enjoy doing the exterior work around their properties. It gives them a chance to take a break from the stress of fighting their day-to-day battles and provides needed exercise. How much you decide to do depends on your situation.

If you hire independent contractors to do your maintenance and repair work for you, are you qualified to supervise and coordinate them? When you contract someone to do a job, you must tell him what to do, when to do it, and, to some extent, how to do it. If you have no idea what the subcontractor should do, you are at his mercy. This is a bad position to be in.

Learn something about a job before you hire people to do it. Read books and research the work until you can talk intelligently about it. Showing the contractor that you have a basic understanding of the job will help to avoid ripoffs. Also, make all your arrangements and agreements in writing. It is easy to become lazy about the required paperwork when working with contractors, but if your property ever has a mechanic's lien placed against it and you have to defend your position in court, a written agreement will be the key to victory. No matter how well you know the subcontractor, don't get sloppy on your paperwork.

Knowing when to schedule regular maintenance is mandatory for a property manager. If you fail to keep the building running smoothly, your repair bills will get out of hand. If you don't know what to do or when to do it, seek help from books, seminars, or consultations with professionals. For example, ask a few heating contractors how often to have your heating system cleaned and tuned up. Don't rely on the advice of just one. Ask three and compare their answers. By doing this type of research, you can avoid many major repairs with simple maintenance.

Have you allowed enough money for maintenance in your operating budget? Many landlords don't, largely because of a lack of experience. It is hard for the average person to look at his water heater and know if it is going to have to be replaced within the next year. You can solve this puzzle by spending a little money on a professional inspection of your property.

There are companies that specialize in inspecting and evaluating the condition of buildings. They often provide a detailed report that covers everything from the foundation to the roof. By paying a few hundred dollars for a thorough, professional inspection, you have a strong basis for setting your maintenance and repair budget. You may not like finding out that your roof will need to be replaced within the next two years, but it is better to know about it beforehand.

With advance warning you can begin to prepare for the costs involved to replace the roof before it starts to leak.

Let's take a tour of an average rental property and see what you are likely to encounter with its upkeep.

The Grounds

The lawns and grounds of your property include all of its exterior features that are not a part of the building. These can include lawn, parking area, driveway, sidewalks, landscaping, security lights, and drainage systems. Depending on your rental policy, garbage disposal, snow removal, and other exterior services can also fall into this category.

Keeping the exterior of your property in good repair improves it appearance, value, and performance. If the exterior is neat and clean, it will attract more tenants, and these tenants will customarily be of a better quality than those housed in neglected properties. Furthermore, existing tenants will remain happier if their rental unit is pleasant to come home to. No one wants to wade through puddles of standing water to get to the door. Neither do tenants enjoy coming home to a building where there is garbage scattered around the lawn.

A well-kept building will be more impressive to an appraiser than a run-down one. Your interest in your property should be reflected in a higher appraised value. All of these factors are motivation for you to maintain your lawns and grounds.

The Lawn and Shrubbery

If your property has a lawn, don't underestimate the effect it has on people. A shaggy, unkempt lawn is not conducive to a good relationship with your tenants. If they see that you don't take care of the lawn, they may not take care of your rental unit. Keep the grass cut and the leaves raked. A manicured lawn goes a long way to making a good impression on all who view your property.

Drainage problems in your yard can create bad feelings and hurt your building. Standing water in the lawn will not make the tenants happy, the puddles are a nuisance to walk around, and they encourage insects. If the drainage problems are near the foundation of the building, they can create other problems. Your basement could flood, or mold could grow in a crawlspace and cause health problems. The moisture from poor drainage may make the paint peel off the building. In some cases, it can be responsible for foundation damage. If you have drainage problems, they should be corrected.

If your property has landscaping features, keep them looking nice. Trim hedges and foundation shrubs to keep them below your first-floor windows. If the building looks overrun by wild bushes, people will not want to live in it. Dense greenery can also contribute to crime; if your shrubs are too tall and bushy, burglars or vandals can hide behind them.

Driveways and Parking Areas

Your tenants use your driveways and parking areas every day. If these areas fall into poor repair, the tenants will become unhappy, and the more you allow them to go unattended, the higher the cost of eventual repairs. For example, if your paved driveway has cracks or holes in it, winter freezing can make them larger. In graveled drives, insufficient gravel will lead to erosion. In both cases, repairing the driving surface will cost much more than maintaining it. By sealing paved areas and resurfacing graveled areas you can preserve your investment without costly repairs.

Security Lights

Tenants feel more comfortable when your property has security lights. If you have these lights, keep them in working order. Burned-out bulbs discourage your tenants and encourage the criminal element. Protect your lights from rocks with impact-resistant covers. If kids know they can't break the lights, they won't throw rocks at them, and by discouraging rock throwing, you reduce the number of broken windows in your building.

Garbage Control and Removal

Garbage or trash scattered around your building is unhealthy and ugly. Have your lease make the tenants responsible for their refuse, and if necessary, provide metal containers for their use. Putting the trash cans in an enclosed area will shield them from view. In tough neighborhoods, you can issue each tenant a key for access to the enclosure.

Snow and Ice Removal

In cold climates, snow removal is a part of every property manager's job. If you expect to get snow in the winter, make arrangements for its removal by fall. Tenants who cannot get their cars out of your parking lot cannot get to work. And tenants who cannot get to work cannot pay their rent. It is in your best interest to provide fast and efficient snow removal.

If your exterior walkways and steps are covered in ice, you are in danger of a potential lawsuit. If someone falls on the ice, you may find yourself in deep financial trouble. Make arrangements to clear ice before it becomes a problem. The small investment of sand or ice-removing chemicals is much easier to take than the cost of a lengthy legal battle.

Dead Trees

Dead trees often go unnoticed—until they fall. When they fall, they can land on your building, a tenant's car, or even the tenant herself. Obviously, this can cause severe damage with potentially expensive consequences. Inspect the trees and limbs around your property. When you see a hazardous situation, don't wait to fix it—act quickly to avoid damages or injuries. Normally, you should call a professional to handle the situation.

Exterior Maintenance

The exterior of your building is exposed to weather, and inclement weather has a way of deteriorating its condition. To guard against substantial damage from the elements, you must be willing to provide routine exterior maintenance. This maintenance may encompass the roof, siding, paint, trim, doors, windows, porches, and other similar items.

The Roof and Chimney

If you allow the roof of your building to go bad, you will have angry tenants and damaged property. Water damage from a leaking roof can do serious structural harm that can progress to dangerous levels before you know it exists. If your attic is heavily insulated, it can take months for the water to stain ceilings, but in the meantime you could have rafters rotting or water entering electrical boxes.

Many factors influence the life of a roof. Exposure to extreme heat can reduce its useful years. The type of roofing used will also make a difference. Your untrained eye may not be able to tell if your roof is bad. Have it inspected by a professional, who will tell you how long you can expect it to last. When the time comes to repair or replace your roof, don't procrastinate.

If your property has a chimney, expect to give it some attention from time to time. The mortar joints on the masonry work may occasionally need to be pointed up and the flashing around the chimney should be inspected periodically for leaks. Depending upon the device connected to it, the chimney should be cleaned annually or on a regular, recommended basis.

The Siding and Exterior Trim

Siding and trim that are not properly maintained will rot. When that happens, you may not be able to match the new materials with the existing materials, which will result either in great expense to replace more than you need to or in a mismatched building.

By inspecting your siding and trim at regular intervals, you can catch problems in their early stages. If you detect rot early, you can make simple repairs. One key to the preservation of your siding and trim is a good paint job. Having the proper flashing, caulking, and weather protection is another way to ensure their long life.

Vinyl or aluminum siding may need to be washed periodically to remove mold and mildew buildup. A good scrub with a power-wash machine will get the job done. Check your yellow pages for a contractor who specializes in power washing.

Moisture that collects around your exterior walls, near the foundation, can shorten the life of your paint job. If you have a habitual problem with cracking and peeling paint, check for a high moisture content. A severe problem may mean the wood in your exterior walls and plates is rotting. Keeping your paint in good shape will help to protect your investment while making it more attractive.

Outside Windows and Doors

Outside windows and doors can cost you a lot of money when they are not up to par. If you are responsible for heating and cooling your building, they can drain your bank account, especially in older buildings.

In addition to energy losses, windows and doors are prime candidates for rotting wood. The exterior trim around them will rot quickly if it is not protected. Then the water gathering in windows will work its way into your walls. Door jambs and trim can also fall prey to rot. It is important that all these surfaces be properly caulked and painted.

Porches, Balconies, and Rails

Landlords frequently ignore porches and rails. This is a mistake. If your porch or railing is in bad repair, an injury could result. Someone could fall off a balcony because of a rotted railing, and then you would be in trouble. The same could be true for an injury due to faulty porch flooring.

Old buildings are famous for bad porches, balconies, and rails, but many landlords prefer to look the other way instead of replacing or repairing them. While thousands of landlords get away with their shaky rails and porches, however, you may not be so lucky. There is no reason to jeopardize your assets, or your tenants' health, by ignoring a dangerous situation. Inspect your railings, porches, and balconies. If they need repair or replacement, have the job done.

If these structures are in good repair, keep them that way. Routine maintenance with paint and frequent inspections can prevent the need for large sums of money spent on replacements. They can also reduce the risks of lawsuits and injuries.

Fire Escapes

If your building is required to have a fire escape, be sure it does. You should also be certain it is in good working order. Never wait until human lives are in danger to discover that your fire escape is useless. If the fire inspector finds fault with your fire escape, you may be facing a heavy fine.

Interior Common Areas

Common areas are those shared by your tenants. A hallway is considered a common area, as is a laundry room or basement. Common areas are often used on a daily basis. They are also the most likely part of the interior of your building to suffer from vandalism. If your building is not equipped with a security door, people off the street can wander in. Some may be looking for a warm place to spend a cold night. Others may be there to steal what they can and vandalize what they can't.

The condition of your common areas will affect all of your tenants. None of them will appreciate missing or burned out light bulbs or stolen smoke detectors or fire extinguishers. Nor will they be happy with bags of garbage left sitting in the hall with the smell permeating the entire building, attracting rodents and other undesirable animals. All of these problems exist in many multifamily rentals. You can solve some of them by installing a security door.

Hallways and Security Doors

The halls in your building will take a lot of abuse. The hall walls will be damaged when people move furniture in and out of the building. The floors will be subjected to heavy use in all kinds of weather and particularly suffer from water and melting snow. Without security doors, outsiders are likely to visit your hallways. When they do, damage is likely to occur.

Inspect your halls frequently. Test the lights to be sure they work. Test the smoke detectors to see that they are operating properly. If you find garbage in the hall, clean it up and find out who is responsible for the mess. When you find the guilty party, insist that he not dirty your halls again. Keep your halls well lighted and free of clutter. When the code enforcement officer pays your building a visit, the hallways will be one of the first areas she looks at.

If your property does not have security doors on the exits, you should consider installing them. By restricting access to the building to authorized tenants, you reduce many maintenance headaches. After installing security doors, you can look to your tenants when problems occur in the common areas, such as missing light bulbs, fire extingushers, or smoke detectors. This is not to say that an outsider couldn't be responsible for the trouble, but the odds are greatly reduced when good security doors are installed.

Security doors also please the tenants, who will be happy to know they are the only ones likely to be in the building. None of your tenants will enjoy leaving their apartment only to trip over someone sleeping in the hall. With good exterior lighting and security doors, you can attract tenants who might have gone to another building if yours had not been so well equipped.

The Basement and the Laundry Room

Many landlords use the basement of their building as a common area, housing a laundry room or storage facilities. If it is not used this way, it should be locked to prevent prowling tenants from entering. There are usually many ways for people to get hurt in basements. By restricting access, you reduce your chances of a lawsuit.

If the basement is a common area, make sure it is up to snuff. The stairs must be sturdy and equipped with a railing, and both stairs and basement must be adequately lighted. Install partition walls to limit access to the intended common area. All of your mechanical equipment and noncommon areas should be behind locked doors to prevent unauthorized entry.

Your basement may be equipped with a sump pump to remove water below the basement floor. If the pump fails, your basement can flood, so check it monthly to reduce that risk.

Laundry rooms that are open to your tenants are a potential trouble spot. If the tenants abuse your equipment, the repair bills can add up quickly. Inspect your laundry equipment on a regular basis. If you find a washer or dryer that is not working, repair it. A tenant who becomes frustrated with a broken machine may abuse it. By keeping your equipment in working condition, you lower your tenants' stress levels.

Inspect the hoses on your washing machines frequently. Those can become worn and break, and when that happens, unless the valve controlling the water to the hose is cut off, it will release a steady stream of water. Regular inspections of the hoses can reduce the chance of an unwanted flood. If the hoses appear cracked or tender, replace them.

The Attic and the Crawl Space

Most likely you do not regularly venture into your crawl space or attic. For that reason, you must make a note to inspect them occasionally.

There should be little need for maintenance in your building's attic, but still, there are a few things you should check on from time to time, including roof leaks and insect damage. If the roof plywood has turned black, you more than likely have a moisture problem. If you notice small piles of sawdust in the attic, you may have an insect infestation. Wood-eating insects can destroy your building, so arrange for a professional pest inspection at least once a year. Such inspections are often done without charge.

While you are in the attic, check to see that it is ventilated. There should be gable vents, soffit vents, or a ridge vent to circulate air. A healthy attic needs proper ventilation.

If you have a crawl space foundation, inspect it at least twice a year. Look for standing water, which can cause mold, mildew, rot, and peeling paint. Insect activity can also be a problem in the crawl space. When you arrange your annual pest inspection, the inspector will check there as well as the attic.

Most crawl space foundations are equipped with air vents mounted in the walls. It is important for the crawl space to receive proper ventilation because cold air blowing on any plumbing pipes there can freeze them. Protect your pipes from drafts. Insulation or even a heat tape may be necessary to prevent frozen plumbing.

Inside the Rental Units

The interior of your rental units is where most routine maintenance will be required. This is where your tenants live and where most problems occur. Plumbing or electrical system problems are only the beginning; appliances, walls, ceilings, floors, doors, and other components of the rental unit all need your attention.

Plumbing Problems

Plumbing problems are probably the most frequent cause of panicked calls from a tenant to a landlord. If you plan to manage your own property, be prepared for problems ranging from dripping faucets to flooding toilets. Since some of the calls will be emergencies, either be prepared to play plumber yourself or have a regular plumber you can depend on.

Plumbers can be an independent lot. They are expensive and usually busy, so plan ahead. Establish a relationship with a dependable plumber before you need one. If you wait until you need a plumber to find one, you may not be able to. Plumbing emergencies know no boundaries. They may occur in the middle of the night or on a weekend. If you need a plumber after normal business hours, you can expect a hefty bill.

If you have numerous rental units, you may not have as much trouble finding and keeping a plumber. When you give them steady business, plumbers respond to your calls. One way to hedge your odds is to learn basic plumbing principles. If you are not handy, find and keep a good plumber within easy reach.

Most landlords have lease provisions that hold the tenant responsible for plumbing problems she creates, just as she is responsible for repairs and damages if her child breaks a window. By including the proper language in your lease, you can reduce your out-of-pocket expenses on plumbing calls.

The routine maintenance of a unit's plumbing, however, is your responsibility. If the toilet's flush valve is bad, causing the toilet to run constantly, repair or replace it. If you are paying the water bill, you will see a noticeable increase in it from the wasted water. The same is true for dripping faucets. It is a good idea to inspect a unit's plumbing at least twice a year. Tenants may not care if their bathtub faucet is dripping, but your water bill will force you to pay the price for the drip. Include a clause in your lease to allow you to inspect the interior plumbing on a regular basis.

The Interior Electrical System and Appliances

Bad plumbing can be messy and costly. Faulty wiring can be deadly. Inspect a rental unit's electrical system at the same time you inspect the plumbing. If the unit has its own fuse panel, check the fuses to see that they are the proper size. A tenant trying to fix a blown fuse may replace it with one that is wrong for the circuit, and an oversized fuse could lead to a fire. Make provisions in your lease to prevent tenants from creating electrical safety hazards. If you see extension cords running all over the unit, insist that they be removed.

Any electrical appliances you supply should be inspected as warranted. Keep them in good working order to avoid expensive repair bills or premature replacement.

Other Interior Maintenance

Windows and doors that stick can annoy your tenants. Doorbells that don't work are also a nuisance, and cabinet drawers that are hard to operate can send a tenant into a tailspin. These may be little things but they can add up to make a hostile tenant. By going through your units on a regular basis, you can control the small complaints.

Working with Independent Contractors

Most landlords retain independent contractors to perform at least some part of their property maintenance; many subcontract all of their maintenance and repair work. Independent contractors are often the most cost-effective way to handle building maintenance. Given wages, taxes, and employee benefits, it rarely pays to keep a maintenance person on the payroll.

When you arrange for independent contractors to do your work, you are the general contractor. If your property is being managed by a professional management firm, they act as the general contractor and probably charge extra for their services. Many landlords resent these additional charges, but once you start doing your own general contracting, you will understand why management companies have them.

Being a general contractor is not easy. First, you must find reputable subcontractors, and after you find them, you must learn to control them. A general contractor must be well organized, firm, in control, and confident, and these qualities are not always easy to come by, especially when you have a burly plumber staring you down. Subcontractors can be quite intimidating if you are a general contracting novice.

As the general contractor, you assume final responsibility for the subcontractor's work. If he or she fails to perform, it is up to you to enforce your rules. To stay in control you need strong written agreements. With them, you will have disputes; without them, you will have lots of disputes. A written agreement gives you some power over your subcontractors. They have lien rights and may not hesitate to take you to court. If you can settle your disputes out of court you are money ahead. Let's look more closely at how you should prepare for working with subcontractors.

Finding Your Subcontractors

It will be easy to find names and phone numbers of subcontractors. The hard part will be finding good, dependable ones. No one advertises that they are incompetent and unreliable, so you should consider advertisements only as a place to start, not the end of your search. After generating a list of subs, you must qualify them and weed out the bad ones.

Finding subcontractors by way of referrals makes your job easier. If a friend has had good luck with a particular sub it stands to reason that you can expect similar results. Look for all your subcontractors before you need them, since the best will have regular customers who keep them busy. Check the references they supply, and check with any agency that would have knowledge of legitimate complaints lodged by customers. Do enough homework to reduce your risk of getting less than you expect from your subcontractors.

The Contractor's Paperwork

As a property manager and general contractor, you will do best when all of your agreements are in writing. Verbal contracts are legal, but they are usually unenforceable. Also, if there is a deviation from the original contract, you should insist on having a written change order executed. When you pay your subcontractors for services rendered, have them sign a lien waiver preventing them from placing mechanic's and materialman's liens against your property. This is important because once a subcontractor has started work on your building, he or she has lien rights.

Too many property managers learn the importance of well-documented agreements through bad experiences. You, however, have the opportunity to learn from this book. If you follow good business principles in your dealings with subcontractors, you eliminate many risks.

Certificates of Insurance. Obtain certificates of insurance from all of your independent contractors before they work for you. If you fail to keep a subcontractor's certificate of insurance on file, your insurance company may penalize you at the end of the year, charging you additional money for allowing uninsured contractors to do your work.

Getting Bids

If the work you need done will be expensive, you should solicit bids from several subcontractors. This can be an inconvenience, but it can also save you a lot of money. When you put your job out to bid, keep all of the bid packages identical. If the contractors do not bid on exactly the same work, the prices you get will be meaningless. Furthermore, beware of substitution clauses in the subcontractor's quote or estimate. If you specify a particular brand of an item, see to it that the contractor bids with that item.

It is common for contractors to put in an "or equal" clause to avoid providing specified materials. When you see this clause in a quote, be suspicious. Substituting materials can make a huge difference in the cost of a job. Be certain the prices you are getting are based on the materials you want. Also scrutinize the quote for omissions. Some sly contractors will purposely forget to include an aspect of the job to make their quote more attractive. When you are just starting out as a property manager you are an easy target of such unscrupulous behavior.

Letting Contractors in the Rental Units

If your subcontractors are going to be working in occupied rental units, be careful. Even if they don't do anything wrong, some tenants may make accusations. To protect yourself, see that your subcontractors are bonded, and, if possible, have the tenant present while the work is being done. If the tenant can't be there, you should be there instead.

Be Prepared to Make Calls at Night

Many of the best subcontractors do not have large businesses. They work alone or with just a small crew, without fancy offices or full-time secretaries. When you call during the day, you are likely to reach an answering service. Since these subcontractors are in the field during the day and return calls at night, you will have trouble connecting with the best of them if you are unwilling to talk business after hours. It may be inconvenient to have to deal with night calls, but it can save you money. Because these small subcontractors have low overhead, their prices are often better than those of larger companies.

The Wind-Up

This chapter has probably changed the way you look at property maintenance. Many landlords believe they can handle their routine maintenance with ease. By now you should realize there is much more to maintenance and repairs than meets the eye. As long as you tread carefully in this area of your business, you should do all right. If you jump in with your eyes closed, you will soon regret it.

Chapter 13

Capital Improvements

There is much to think about when you consider improving your rental property. Nonessential improvements require you to evaluate their financial feasibility. Making the right improvements can improve your cash flow and the property's value. Making the wrong ones can drain your bank account without providing any financial rewards.

Many investors fall into a trap when it comes to capital improvements. They are convinced their efforts will be profitable, but if the improvements don't prove viable, they may lose money, and lots of it. This chapter is all about improvements to your investment property. It exposes hidden treasures and flagrant flops. Before you spend money on capital improvements, study this chapter carefully.

What Are Capital Improvements?

For the purposes of this chapter, capital improvements are those that will cost more than five hundred dollars. Normally, such improvements are not mandatory. They can include exterior painting and new siding, as well as extensive remodeling to the kitchens and bathrooms. Having a new roof installed is a capital improvement, even though it may or may not be essential. The same goes for the replacement of a heating system and other similar situations.

When a landlord makes a capital improvement to his building, it is usually in an attempt to generate a stronger cash flow or a higher appraised value. The intent is good, but the result is not always what he had hoped for. To be successful with major improvements you must research market conditions and plan carefully. It is easy to dump several thousand dollars into a property without any noticeable increase in income or value. When this happens you have spent your money with little chance of seeing a return on it. This is bad business and can cause you serious financial distress. To eliminate the risk of losing big money, invest some of your time in research before going ahead.

What Type of Research Is Needed?

There are a few angles to look at when it comes to large improvement investments. Much of your research will depend on the reasons for the improvement you are contemplating. If you are planning to increase cash flow, you must research market conditions and demand. If you are hoping to increase your property's value, you must assume the role of an appraiser or hire a professional. If you want better cash flow and a higher property value, you must combine your research duties.

With any type of improvement you must assess the cost. This research requires soliciting bids from contractors, as well as projecting for your improvement's performance. This part of your homework will be speculation, based on as much available data as you can find. By the time you are done with your planning, you should know within a reasonable margin of error how effective your improvement will be in meeting its goal.

Setting Realistic Goals

When you project the rate of return from your improvements, set realistic goals. If you remodel your rental units to give them a modern appearance, you should be able to obtain a higher rent. However, you will not be able to collect more rent than the market will bear. Projecting your increased income based on a percentage of your improvement investment could turn out to be sorrowfully disappointing. You may be able to project your equity gain as a percentage of the improvement expense, but not the income performance.

It is easy to get caught up in the excitement of punching numbers into the computer and grinning at their results on your spreadsheet. But if these numbers are not realistic, there will be little joy after the improvements are made. Some improvements may even cause your cash flow or property value to decrease. The key to reaching realistic goals is basing them on accurate information. Personal opinions are not worth much in business. You may love the idea of painting your building pink and blue, but an appraiser will probably have a different opinion. From a business standpoint, the appraiser's opinion is the one that counts. You must base your decisions, projections, and goals on factual information.

The Two Basic Reasons for Capital Improvements

The two basic reasons for capital improvements are to increase cash flow and to increase a property's value. Ideally, your improvements should fill both of these desires. Those that increase a property's value also create better cash flow, although those that increase cash flow may not show a significant impact on your property's value. When you plan your improvements, you also must decide what you want them to do. Then you must predict how well they will do it. Let's look at some specific examples of each type of improvement.

Cash-Flow Improvements

The primary objective of cash-flow improvements is to generate higher rents. Since many rental properties are appraised according to formulas based on building income, these improvements often increase a property's value as well. For income properties with less than five rental units, the results will not be as favorable as they are for larger buildings. Most buildings with four or fewer units are appraised with the comparable-sale method, which does not allow as much opportunity for increased cash flow to determine their value. We will get into the differences in appraisals a little later on.

The effectiveness of cash-flow improvements will be determined by three basic factors: the present condition of your property, the condition of competitive properties, and market demand. If your apartments are dingy and dark, a fresh coat of paint can make a big difference in the amount of rent tenants are willing to pay for them. On the other hand, if the apartment's paint is satisfactory, freshening it or changing the color may have no effect at all.

Suppose all the apartment buildings in your area have painted wood siding. They are all in good condition and attractive. Your building is comparable to the competitive properties in its present condition, but you decide that installing vinyl siding on your property will make it easier to maintain. You further believe that by adding vinyl siding, you can recover the cost in increased rents.

This is not likely. As long as all the available rental units are clean and neat, tenants will not care if their building has vinyl or painted wood siding. That means your new vinyl siding will not convince them to pay a higher price to live in your building.

If the surrounding, competitive properties are all equipped with appliances, adding appliances to your units should command a higher rent. In contrast, if none of the local landlords supply appliances, adding appliances might cause the increased rent to price you out of the market. No matter how nice your rental units are, if people can't afford them, you will not see any additional income.

By being the only landlord to offer appliances, you should attract more tenants. This will reduce your vacancy rate, but may do nothing for your rental figures. You must be careful not to overimprove your building to a point where tenants will not, or cannot, pay the increased rent to offset the cost of the improvement.

Increased-Value Improvements

Improvements made to increase a property's value can influence the building's cash flow, but they may not. For example, building a garage for your tenants should increase your property's value. There could also be an equity gain from the construction if you act as the general contractor or build the garage yourself. However, if your building is already producing rents at the upper end of the market demand, you may not be able to raise the rents to cover the cost of your improvement. As I said, you could accumulate equity with this type of improvement, but you will have to spend liquid cash to do it. Even if you build the garage yourself, you will have cash invested that you cannot extract from it. These improvements can cause you to lose your rental property.

Almost any increased-value improvement that is worthwhile will increase your cash flow. However, if it will not boost your net income from an up-and-going building, don't do it. Increased-value improvements are most effective for rehabbing old, rundown properties, because they allow you to build substantial equity. Buildings that have been abandoned, damaged by fire, or that have not had routine maintenance for years are the best bets.

Now that you understand the difference between the two types of improvements, we will look at specific examples of the various upgrades.

Replacing Your Roof

Unless your roof is leaking, don't replace it. The only reasons for replacement are to prevent leaks or to improve a particularly ugly roof's appearance. If your roof is a mismatched, multicolor eyesore, replacing it might be worthwhile. If the roof is leaking and cannot be repaired, replacing it will be mandatory.

Tenants will not be willing to pay a higher rent to live in a building with a new roof. As long as the existing roof doesn't leak and isn't a beacon of ugliness, they will not care if it is new or not. An appraiser may allow a little extra value for a new roof, but not enough to cover the cost of the job. In general, don't invest money in roof replacements unless you are forced to.

New Paint Jobs and Gutters

The paint on your building should be kept in good condition. Replace it if it is cracking and peeling; leave it alone if it is in good shape. Moreover, a white building will produce as much rent as a brown one, so unless you have a horrendous paint job now, repainting your building to change its color will be a waste of money. Tenants will not pay extra for the new paint, and appraisers will not adjust their reports much because of it.

Installing gutters on your property will not be very cost-effective. Appraisers may allow some extra value for them but not much, and prospective tenants are not likely to have them on their list of must-have items when searching for an apartment. Gutters can solve basement flooding, ice buildups on walkways, and other water-related problems, but while they are beneficial, they do little for your cash flow or appraised value.

Adding Porches and Decks

Depending on the property and its location, adding porches and decks can increase your cash flow and your property's value. It can also set your building apart from the competition and attract more tenants. You will not experience a huge equity profit by adding these features, but you shouldn't lose any money either.

Of the two investments, decks should produce a better rate of return than porches. They are less expensive to build, and they still add a touch of difference to your building. Tenants will enjoy having a deck for cooking out and entertaining. They may be willing to pay extra for that privilege.

From the appraiser's point of view, decks and porches add value. When you combine increased desirability, increased value, and increased cash flow, you have a winning improvement. This is not to say that adding decks or porches to all buildings will be successful. In this and all the examples, you must factor in regional differences, market conditions, and your own situation. There is no hard and fast rule to lock onto, only averages and historical data to point you in the right direction. The final outcome will be decided through your research.

New Siding

Many landlords consider installing vinyl siding when the time comes to paint their existing wood siding. This is a reasonable consideration, since vinyl siding does reduce long-term maintenance cost. However, installing vinyl over perfectly good wood siding is not likely to produce positive results.

Your appraisal report will show a higher value with new vinyl siding, but it will not be enough to compensate for all the money you have spent. Tenants won't care what kind of siding the property has. Your return on your investment will come mostly from reduced maintenance expenses. If you plan to keep the building for many years, consider vinyl siding when the time comes to paint the wood siding, but if you plan to sell in the next few years, painting is probably the best choice. You will have to weigh the expenses and make your own decision.

Improving Your Parking Area

Paving your parking area will improve the appearance of your property. It will also increase your property value to some extent, although it probably won't increase your cash flow. Tenants will normally accept a well-kept graveled parking lot as easily as a paved one. Unless there are personal reasons such as snow removal to consider, save your money for a more profitable improvement, such as increasing your parking area's size.

Parking space can be very valuable in cities. If you can alter the grounds of your property to create additional parking, you may be well rewarded. Tenants might welcome a higher rent in return for the benefit of convenient parking, and appraisers will be generous if the additional parking space is something competitive buildings don't have.

Again, we are back to a personal evaluation. If you have adequate parking for all your rental units, it would be silly to replace your lawn with gravel or pavement. But if your tenants are paying a monthly fee to keep their cars at an off-premises lot, you should cash in by creating your own additional space. The value of parking will vary greatly between locations. It is much easier to find parking in Brunswick, Maine, than in Boston, Massachusetts.

On-Site Play Areas and Fencing

If you cater to families with children, building an on-site playground could keep your units full while your competitor's are empty. The cost of a simple play area is not enormous, but the results include happy tenants, stronger cash flow, and a lower vacancy rate. The playground will not do much for your appraised value, but the other redeeming qualities make it worth considering.

There is a downside to having your own playground. This is the liability factor. If a child is injured on the playground, you may be held accountable. Before you invest in a playground, talk with your attorney and insurance company. The risks may be more than you can afford to gamble.

Installing a fence around the perimeter of your property can serve many functions. For one, it can act as a kiddy corral. For another, it will give tenants with pets a safe exercise area. Also, even a small fence will discourage outsiders from running through your lawn and abusing your building. For all its benefits, however, your fence investment will be hard to recover. Some tenants may pay more to live in a unit with a fenced yard, but they are a minority. Appraisal reports will not show enough equity gain to pay for the fencing. The choice is yours, but fencing is rarely a good investment.

New Windows and Exterior Doors

If you own an old building, you might be considering replacing the windows. This is an expensive proposition, but it can pay for itself in reduced heating and cooling costs. If your windows are drafty and poorly insulated, new windows can make a notable difference in your utility bills. The public is aware of energy costs and the value of tight, well-insulated windows. Tenants who expect to pay for their own utilities may inspect the windows of a property before agreeing to rent it. If your building has new energy-efficient windows, tenants may rent in yours instead of the next landlord's. Even so, they may not be willing to pay a higher rent for your unit solely on that basis.

If you do a sales job on the tenants, you may be able to justify your higher rent. But if their net out-of-pocket expenses will be the same in yours as in someone else's building, you will need more than new windows to get a signed lease. When your building is appraised, the new windows will make a difference in the property's value. It is doubtful, however, that the appraisal will reflect a high enough gain to offset the expense.

The biggest advantages to replacement windows will be reduced operating expenses. Your utility costs will be lower, and, if the windows are vinyl-clad, so too will your maintenance costs. If you are hoping to pay for the windows with higher rents, however, don't hold your breath, and I doubt that you will recover your investment from a higher appraisal. You will recover some of your window investment, but probably not all of it.

If you are hoping new windows will make your building more appealing to a potential buyer, they will. A savvy buyer will notice the windows and appreciate their value. She may not be willing to pay the long dollar for them, but if she can get your building at a reasonable price, the windows may be the thing that makes the deal. Remember, though, while many improvements can increase the desirability of your property to potential purchasers, they may not bring you a higher sales price. It will be unlikely that you sell the property for more than its appraised value.

As with windows, the replacement of exterior doors can give you energy savings and possibly increased security. The value of the investment is also similar.

Adding Security Features

Security doors, lights, alarms, and related equipment can produce a stronger income. Depending on the building's location, the increased security may convince tenants to pay a higher rent for your units. In locations with a high crime rate, such features enhance your property's ability to pull and hold tenants. Equity gain, on the other hand, will be minimal with security equipment unless it is normal for the area.

On average, beefed-up security is not a good investment in terms of direct return. When you assess your situation, you may find there is no need for increased security. Then again, it may give you the marketing tool you need to reduce your vacancy rate. Know the pros and cons before buying a security system.

Interior Painting and Flooring

Most landlords expect to paint their rental units each time they become vacant. This is routine maintenance. It is important to keep the walls and ceilings of your building attractive and bright, but it is not necessary to go through the entire building, painting all the walls and ceilings, just to change the color. Unless there are extenuating circumstances, there should be no reason to paint the interior of your rental units except between tenants. If some tenants have been with you for many years, it might be a nice gesture to give them a fresh coat of paint, but this is the exception rather than the rule.

Hallways will need to be painted more often than the rental units, because they take a lot of abuse and they are the first thing people see of your building's interior. Hallways create the first impression of your building's condition. While you may not recover the cost of regular painting in increased rent or property value, you will enjoy a more stable tenancy record. Plan to paint your halls as often as needed and your apartments between occupants. Confine your painting expenses to necessities rather than desires.

Like paint, floor coverings need to be replaced periodically as part of routine maintenance, but look carefully before you start. Often, a good cleaning will make a world of difference in the appearance of carpet and vinyl floors. Sanding wood floors and adding a new sealant can make them look new again.

Weigh your decision to replace flooring carefully. New floors will enable you to rent or sell your building faster, and they will have some positive impact on the property's value. Nevertheless, the cost can be prohibitive and the rate of return poor. There are many grades of carpeting, carpet pads, and vinyl flooring to choose from, and with conscientious shopping, you can save money on your purchases. Selecting the proper grades will be a matter of money and use. You will want a heavy grade for your halls, which will have to endure much more traffic than your bedrooms.

Be careful. With so many grades and choices, it is easy to spend more on flooring than you can recover. Also remember that it only takes one bad tenant to ruin your investment. It is hard to raise the rent only because you have new flooring. Appraisers expect rental property to have satisfactory floor coverings, and they will not raise your appraisal dramatically because yours is newly installed. Be sensible with the money you spend on flooring—it can be tough to recover your investment.

Light Fixtures and Appliances

Most landlords never think about their light fixtures. They are so used to seeing them that they accept them for what they are. Tenants and appraisers, however, may see them in a different light, so to speak. Light fixtures can date your building. Outdated ones can make it look old. Take a look at your units and see if the fixtures are old and dingy looking. Do they impress you as ancient artifacts? If so, consider budgeting a little money to selectively upgrade them. Doing so can make your property more desirable.

In making capital investments, landlords often overlook the little items that expose the building for what it is. Giving your property a modern facelift is good, but follow through with the job. If you are transforming an old building into a modern one, don't forget the light fixtures. You may not see a cash-on-cash return for your investment, but the overall effect will be good.

If you supply your tenants with appliances, you must keep them in good repair. With regular maintenance, appliances can last for many years, although sometimes they last so long they should be replaced simply because, like light fixtures, they can tell the age of your building. How often do you see harvest gold and avocado green appliances today? If your washing machine has a handle and rollers on it, consider replacing it. Appliances influence tenant opinions. Battered appliances tell the tenants the rest of the building is probably beat too.

You won't see much equity gain or increased cash flow from replacing appliances, so choosing a time to replace them is up to you. As long as they function properly and are not too old, you can leave them alone. However, if you are making improvements to change the image of your units, appliances could be high on your to-do list. Tenants use their appliances frequently. They will appreciate modern ones, but probably will not pay a lot more for them. As long as your appliances work, an appraiser will not deflate your property value by much. Most of the benefits you derive from appliance replacements will not be noticeable, but they do exist.

Window Treatments

Window treatments may not seem like a capital improvement, but if you have several large, multifamily buildings, outfitting them with window treatments can cost thousands of dollars. Some landlords provide window treatments for their tenants and others don't. If you don't, maybe you should.

Window treatments allow you to control the appearance of your rental units from the outside. When units are vacant, window treatments can reduce break-ins and vandalism. From the street, your apartments will appear occupied even when they aren't. If you don't provide window treatments, your tenants may elect to hang bed sheets on the windows, which degrades your property and hurts the first impressions of prospective tenants. These two reasons alone justify your window treatments expense.

The value of window treatments is difficult to assess. They may allow you to achieve a slightly higher rent, but the extra income will be minimal. And although an appraiser may assign them additional value, you can't count on it. If you decide to invest in window treatments, accept the fact that you will not be able to track your rate of return. The venture should draw more tenants, reduce losses to theft and vandalism, and lessen tenant turnover, but whether it will pay off or not is hard to tell.

Large-Scale Projects

Large-scale projects involve heavy investments in remodeling, rehab, and additions. Some examples are building private storage areas, adding a coin-operated laundry, remodeling all of your kitchens or bathrooms, and adding bedrooms or entire rental units. These large-scale projects can make you—and they can break you. When you talk big projects, you are talking big money, and when there is big money involved, there are big risks. Here are some examples of big-league projects and their effects on your building.

Private Storage Areas

Private storage areas have become a thriving business. They vary in size to accommodate everything from small possessions to vintage automobiles. The price a person pays for these storage facilities is nothing to laugh about. Some serious money is being made by the owners of private storage businesses.

As a landlord, you are in an ideal position to get a piece of the storage pie. As more and more people are forced to remain tenants longer, the need for storage grows. Most people don't need a garage to house an antique car, but they do need a place for Christmas decorations, outgrown toys, abandoned exercise equipment, and a myriad of other things. You can let your tenants go down the street and rent a storage cubicle, or you can provide them with an on-site storage area for an additional rental fee. This is a tremendous opportunity for you to increase your cash flow.

Whether you convert your building's basement into storage areas or build a new facility, the rewards can be great, but if your mind is racing with thoughts of chicken-wire, forget it! People will pay handsomely for secure storage, but they won't for old-fashioned wire enclosures. If you want to make money from storage rental, you will have to spend money on the development of a suitable facility.

Consider that you may be able to rent your storage units for $35 to $100 a month, and the idea becomes very interesting. How would your building's net income look if you factored in this type of additional income? Give this idea a lot of thought. I think you will like it more as you run the numbers.

Laundry Facilities

Are your rental units equipped with individual laundry facilities? Do you have a laundry room your tenants can share? Tenants must wash their clothes somewhere. If you are not providing free laundry facilities, many of them are spending money each week at the local laundromat. By creating a coin-operated laundry room, you can cash in on their dirty clothes.

Why let the business down the street take your tenants' money when you could be taking it and at the same time making their laundry duties much more convenient at the same price? You would be providing them with a service and making money while doing so.

Coin-operated laundries can produce exceptional net income, and in commercial-grade, residential properties, increased income translates into increased property value. Your initial investment may be steep, but the payoff should more than outweigh the expense.

Bath and Kitchen Remodeling

Bathrooms and kitchens are the two rooms that influence many people's decision to rent or not to rent. If they are modern, clean, well appointed, and desirable, you are well on your way to renting your unit.

Recently remodeled kitchens and bathrooms can demand a higher rent and favorably influence your building's appraised value. They can often reduce your vacancy rate and at the same time help you eliminate many of your repair calls because of their new equipment.

The costs of major remodeling can be intimidating, so you will have to evaluate your decision to take on a large project carefully. However, if your research shows promise, these two rooms are where you should direct your remodeling efforts.

Bedrooms

The value of a residential rental unit is often established by the number of bedrooms it contains. Typically, a three-bedroom apartment will rent for more than a two-bedroom. If you can make conversions to your existing units to create more bedrooms, you should be able to generate more cash. Old buildings, frequently spacious in their room sizes, are particularly good for bedroom conversions. You must be creative to add a bedroom to an existing apartment without adding additional space. In the conversion procedure you must make do with what you have. We will talk about adding space a little later.

Walk through your buildings and look for wasted space. Is there a dining room that could be converted to a bedroom? Could you gain that extra bedroom by dividing the apartment into a different layout? Is there an attached, covered porch that could be converted? Would it be possible to combine a closet with some wasted hall space?

If you can find a way to make a new bedroom without ruining the rest of the rental unit, go for it! But be aware of building codes pertaining to this type of remodeling. If you must have an emergency egress window, some locations will not be suitable for your new bedroom. If your building is served by a septic system, make sure you will be able to add the bedroom without a system upgrade. When you get into expanding septic systems, you can run up a tall bill quickly.

Adding New Units

If your lot is large enough, you may be able to add new units to your existing building. The expense of such a project will be considerable, but you already have the land. Before you go ahead, you will have to check zoning regulations and other local laws that may affect your plans. Also, although additional units will give you the opportunity to make more money, be sure the market demand will support them. If the market is glutted with vacant units, adding more to your building could be a financial flop.

Rehab Work

Many investors make their living by rehabbing rental properties. They buy buildings in need of major work and make their money in the improvements. If they do the work themselves, these investors can make a year's income on a single building. If they only act as the general contractor, they still may make more than most people do in a year. Much of their earnings will depend on the extent of the work done to the property. Logically, the more they do, the more they make.

By using low-interest loans and grants, landlords who do rehabbing and remodeling can take an abandoned building and turn it into a money machine. However, this is not light work. It requires experience, dedication, and hard labor to be successful in the rehab business. It also requires a strong credit rating and a willing lender, since the money required for large rehab projects is formidable.

When done properly, rehabbed buildings can make the owner large sums of money. They can produce excellent rental income and can often be sold for a tidy profit. Many times they can be refinanced to extract cash while producing income and tax benefits. As you get further into your landlording career, you may find rehab work worth investigating, but don't attempt it until you are well prepared. If you don't know what you are getting into, rehab work can spell the end of your real estate career.

How Big a Gamble Are Capital Improvements?

Capital improvements are a gamble, but you can hedge your bets. With enough research, you can remove most of the risks they carry with them. For example, let's say you are thinking about remodeling all of your bathrooms and kitchens. This project is going to be expensive, and you have no idea if you will see a fair equity return for the money you invest. What should you do?

You could flip a coin for the answer, but there is a better way to decide. Hire a professional appraiser to give you a before-and-after opinion of value. Have her appraise your property in its present condition. Then provide her with a detailed set of plans and specifications for the proposed improvements and ask for a value on the property if these improvements are made.

Appraisers are accustomed to working with plans and specifications to obtain a value. This is what they do when they appraise new construction projects. Your appraiser will be able to give you an accurate assessment of what affect your proposed improvements will have on your building. When you receive her report, you will see how much more your building will be worth after the work is completed.

At that point you can compare the increased value to the quoted costs for doing the work. If you plan to have contractors perform the work, they will be happy to give you free quotes. Just make sure they are firm quotes and not estimates. By comparing the quotes with the appraisal report, you will quickly be able to determine the feasibility of the project.

If your equity gain will be marginal or unsatisfactory, abort the project. All you will have lost is a little time and the cost of the appraisal. However, if the figures show a hefty gain and you can afford to do the job, go ahead. By getting a before-and-after appraisal, you have eliminated much of the unknown. You know how much the job will cost and how much it will increase the value of your property. With this information you are able to make an informed decision.

By following this type of progression, you take much of the gamble out of capital improvements. On the other hand, if you jump into an improvement without sufficient information, you may lose your shirt. Learning to play the rental game is not particularly perilous—if you take your time and watch your step.

Chapter 14

Low-Interest Loans
and Grants

How would you like to receive thousands of dollars as a gift to improve your rental property? Suppose you could obtain improvement money for your building without ever having to pay it back—would that interest you? Can you imagine being able to borrow rehab money with interest only a fraction of the going rate?

Well, all of this is possible, and there are no strings attached. You don't have to worry about big men in long, black limousines coming to break your kneecaps. You don't have to surrender your soul. All you have to do to enjoy the benefits of low-interest loans and grants is to work with Uncle Sam. No, you don't have to join the military. I am talking about the numerous government programs available to help landlords improve the quality of their rental properties.

If you want to receive money to invest in your rental property, you must investigate these programs. They make it possible to improve your property when it would be impossible otherwise. Why would the government do this? To revitalize neighborhoods.

There is major money to be made in working with these programs. This chapter is going to show you how. By the time you finish, you will have the knowledge to become a more affluent landlord. Low-interest loans and grants can give you the edge you need to become wealthy.

First, let's examine the various programs.

Community Development Block Grants (Entitlement)

Community Development Block Grants are given to entitled communities to apply to a vast array of community development activities. Such activities include neighborhood revitalization, economic development, and other improvements. These grants are designed to prevent and eliminate slums. Among other activities, they may be used for the rehabilitation of residential properties. At least 60 percent of their funds must be used to benefit low-income and moderate-income citizens.

In 1989, over $2 billion was allocated to over 700 cities and more than 100 urban counties. Think of what you could have done with a share of this money. There are also Community Development Block Grants for states and small cities. This type falls in the "nonentitlement" category. Since 1982, more than $6 billion has been awarded through these grants.

Rental Rehabilitation

The Rental Rehabilitation program is ideally suited to landlords of residential properties. Designed to encourage the rehabilitation of rental property through grants, it also offers rental subsidies to aid lower-income tenants.

These grants are awarded to selected communities with populations over 50,000 people. On average, a landlord may obtain between $5,000 and $8,500 per unit to rehab her building. The amount of money received cannot exceed one-half the total cost of approved rehab expenses. An average minimum of $600 per unit is required to ensure that enough work will be done to warrant the use of these funds.

There are limitations on the type of improvements you may use this money for. Approved are the upgrade of substandard conditions, repair of major systems that may fail if not repaired, essential improvements, and some energy-related work. Alterations to allow handicapped people access to the rental units are also acceptable.

Once you have used these funds and completed the work, you must rent between 70 and 100 percent of the units to low-income families. Moreover, your rents must be set at market rates and may not be limited by rent controls. These grants may not be used in neighborhoods where the average income exceeds 80 percent of the area's median. If rents in your neighborhood are likely to escalate more rapidly than in the general rental market, you may not be able to take part in this program.

There are three things to be considered before these funds will be awarded to an area: the income of tenants, the age of existing rental units, and the living conditions of existing rental properties. This last aspect is weighted double in the decision formula. Its specific areas of concern are plumbing facilities, kitchen facilities, overcrowding within the properties, and the cost of rents. In 1989, this program dispersed $150 million.

Consider the possibilities available with this type of program. A savvy investor can use the grant money to pay for up to one-half of all her approved expenses in renovating her building. Plumbing and kitchen facilities are high on the program's priority list. Kitchens and bathrooms are also high on the priority lists of perspective tenants. Consider your options with this plan. What follows is an illustration of how you can increase your net worth, very quickly, with the use of these funds.

How the Process Works

Imagine that you own an eight-unit apartment building that is qualified to receive rental rehabilitation funding for the improvement of its bathrooms and kitchens. Your building is in a location that can support the increased invest-ment, and having had a before-and-after appraisal done, you know what to expect in increased equity from your improvements. Let's see what happens.

First, you arrange for an improvement loan with your regular banker, who is comfortable enough with your plans and your before-and-after appraisal to approve the loan. Also, working with your local housing authority, you have made arrangements to receive rental rehabilitation grant funds for your project.

The cost of renovating the kitchens and bathrooms in all your units is esti-mated to be $80,000. You borrow $40,000 from your banker and receive the other $40,000 from the rehab program, which breaks down into $5,000 per unit—the low-end average of funds allowed. The work is completed, and the property is appraised. The final appraisal supports the numbers originally generated from the before-and-after appraisal, which was done from plans and specifications for the improvements.

Your $80,000 investment caused the building to gain $80,000 in value, and of that $80,000, none came out of your pocket. The bank lent you $40,000 based on the increased value resulting from the improvements, as supported by the appraisal. The Rental Rehabilitation program gave you $40,000 to match the funds you put into the job. By renovating the kitchens and baths, you increased your property's value by $80,000, with no out-of-pocket cash. This in itself wouldn't be bad, but it gets better.

Of the $80,000 invested, you are only responsible for repayment of the $40,000 borrowed from the bank. The rehab money was a grant and does not have to be repaid, so in effect, you have just been given $40,000. If you had acted as your own general contractor, you could realistically have pocketed an additional $16,000, which represents the typical general contractor's 20 percent of a job's cost. Then you would have earned $56,000 in net equity. In all probabil-ity, you could have paid yourself the $16,000 in cash for your time in running the job.

Think about this. You might have generated a $16,000 cash income for yourself and still have been left with $40,000 in net equity. If you put your mind to it, you can devise many ways to profit from the Rental Rehabilitation program. For example, if you had done some of the physical labor yourself, you could have made even more money.

Some Disadvantages

There are reasons not to take advantage of this program. If the building you are rehabbing will not support the increased value in its sale price, you could be throwing your portion of the money away. It would be ridiculous to invest large sums of money in a building that shows no promise. Improving a building in a slum, for example, will not make it worth much more unless the majority of the neighborhood is revitalized.

You must temper your spending with good judgment. Greed can drive you out of the landlording business. If you are not careful, your quest for paper profits will be your undoing. Spend these grant funds as if they were your own hard-earned money instead of a gift. If you do, you should be able to make better decisions and investments.

Rehabilitation Loans

The Rehabilitation Loans program is available to aid in the financing of real estate renovations. These loans may be made to anyone who can demonstrate the ability to repay. Special consideration is given to applicants with low or moderate income.

Rehabilitation loans are available for single-family and multifamily housing, mixed-use properties, and nonresidential real estate. They are meant to reduce the destruction of basically sound buildings and may be used for insulation and weatherization projects, as well as for bringing properties into compliance with building codes and standard living conditions.

A loan from the Rehabilitation Loan program must not exceed $33,500 per dwelling unit, or $100,000 for nonresidential properties, and of course, loan amounts may be less. As a borrower of these funds, you may have up to twenty years to repay. The interest rate will be set at a Treasury bond rate for multifamily properties and moderate-income homeowners, but low-income borrowers will repay the loan at an interest rate of only 3 percent. In 1988, this program lent approximately $102 million.

Manufactured Home Parks

The Manufactured Home Parks program provides federal mortgage insurance to finance the construction or rehabilitation of manufactured home parks. While at first glance, this may not seem to be a program for landlords, it can be. You might consider investing in a manufactured home park, and if you do, you become the landlord of all the lots. This program is normally thought of as serving builders and developers, but there is room for landlords in the program as well.

To qualify, a manufactured home park must have a minimum of five lots, its location must be approved by HUD, and market conditions must show a demand for this type of housing. Mortgage amounts cannot exceed $9,000 per lot, but if your area is considered to be high-cost, they may be increased to $15,750.

HUD insures mortgages made by private lending institutions for building or rehabbing manufactured home parks. The lender originating the loan must be approved by the Federal Housing Authority (FHA). Through September of 1988, over 66,000 lots were insured with values exceeding $200 million.

Multifamily Rental Housing

The Multifamily Rental Housing program provides federal mortgage insurance to finance the construction and rehabilitations of rental property. HUD insures mortgages made by approved, private lending institutions for this purpose. To qualify, a property must contain a minimum of five residential rental units, and it should have the ability to accommodate families at reasonable rates. Through September of 1988, over 324,000 units were insured with values in excess of $4 billion.

Multifamily Rental Housing for Moderate-Income Families

The Multifamily Rental Housing for Moderate-Income Families program is designed to provide mortgage insurance to finance rental or co-op multifamily housing. This housing is intended for moderate-income families and may be designated for the elderly.

Under this program, the money for a project will come from a private lending institution, but it will be insured by HUD. Money may be borrowed for construction or substantial improvements. There must be a minimum of five units in the project for it to qualify, and its intended residents must be moderate-income or displaced families.

The project may comprise detached or semidetached dwellings. The units may be accessible by stairs or elevators. For most investors, HUD will insure up to 90 percent of the loan amount. Through September 1988, there were over 795,000 units insured for more than $22 billion.

Some Other Programs

Although the programs just described are generally the ones of most interest to investors and landlords, there are still more HUD-backed programs to look at. For example, the Mortgage Insurance for Housing the Elderly program is in place to finance the construction or renovation of rental housing for the elderly or handicapped. It requires a property to have a minimum of five units, and it considers people 62 or older as elderly.

Another program, the Housing Development Grant program, makes money available for building or renovating rental property, co-ops, and mutuals. Its purpose is to increase the availability of rental housing in areas where there are severe shortages. All projects participating in this program must reserve at least 20 percent of their units for families with low incomes. These units must remain available to such tenants for twenty years; they may not be converted to another use during that time. Program grants cannot exceed 50 percent of the project's cost and will not normally include the cost of acquisition of the subject property.

The Property Improvement Loan Insurance program insures loans for improvements, alterations, and repairs. Single-family and multifamily housing and nonresidential properties are all potentially eligible for this plan.

Loans for single-family homes may be made in amounts up to $17,500 for a term of fifteen years and thirty-two days. Apartment buildings may receive up to $8,750 per unit, so long as the total loan does not exceed $43,750, for a term not to exceed fifteen years. If more than $2,500 is being lent, a mortgage or deed of trust will be placed on the property to be improved.

The Rehabilitation Mortgage Insurance program provides help in financing the improvement of single-family homes and small multifamily buildings with less than four units. It insures loans for the rehabilitation of existing properties. It also insures refinancing of an existing debt for landlords in the process of rehab work and aids landlords attempting to acquire a property to rehab.

The Flexible Subsidy program provides federal aid to multifamily projects with financial problems. It can assist in restoration work and maintenance matters; it can provide immediate cash to correct deferred maintenance and replacements; and it can assist with financial deficiencies and the replacement of reserve and operating capital. Improved management is another of its goals.

What Can You Do with These Programs?

Are you surprised at all the ways your government can help you with your rental property? Many landlords go through their entire career never knowing how to take advantage of these programs. However, a few learn of them and go on to perfect their use. They turn a government program into a money machine. Of course, some investors abuse the system and hurt the programs. If you learn to work with these programs, you can greatly increase your net worth. Low-interest loans and grants are strong tools in the right hands.

There are numerous possibilities for using these programs. You could convert your existing building into specialized housing for the elderly and in doing so see a considerable increase in your rental income. Or you might rehab your building to build net worth and see nice profits that way. Suppose you became a general contractor, what would that do for you?

The General Contractor Advantage

If you become a general contractor, you open the door to higher profits. Let me show you how you might structure a deal as a general contractor and investor using these plans.

For my example, assume you are both a real estate investor and general contractor. You don't work for the public, of course; all of your contracting work is done for your rental business. Ideally, these two businesses will be separate corporations.

As an investor, you see a need for additional housing in your area to serve the elderly and the handicapped. So you explore all the programs described above and settle in on the Mortgage Insurance for Housing the Elderly program, which will insure a loan for up to 90 percent of the cost of your venture. You decide to rehab a 12-unit building you own for the elderly and handicapped.

At this point, you take off your landlord's hat and put on your hard hat. You are going to be working as a general contractor for a while. You develop your plans and specifications for the rehabilitation. After receiving price quotes from material suppliers and subcontractors, you estimate the total renovation costs to be $180,000, an amount that will allow you to replace existing fixtures with handicap fixtures in selected units and install grab bars and improve access to the dwellings.

You have confirmed the viability of this venture with appraisals, demographic studies, cost projections, and market research. You know the project will work, and you have convinced a private lending institution to agree with you. The approved lender has agreed to lend you the $180,000 with the backing of HUD.

As the general contractor, you arrange and supervise the rehab work. Charging your rental business a fair market value for your services, you earn 20 percent of the cost of the improvements, amounting to $36,000. By being your own general contractor, you have saved $36,000 that you would have otherwise had to pay to someone else.

You could have borrowed $36,000 less on the loan and kept your payments lower. Instead, you borrowed the full amount and generated a $36,000 income for yourself. You are responsible for this money as part of the loan, but it should be recovered in the sale of the property.

Suppose you had built the facility from the ground up. What would this type of building be worth in your area? Deduct the value of the land from the full appraised value, and you have the cost to construct the property. Say it was $600,000. As a general contractor, your income for arranging the construction might reach $120,000, but since the general contractor's percentage goes down as the cost of construction goes up, a more realistic income on this type of job would be between $60,000 and $75,000.

Final Words

As you can see, the programs shown in this chapter can provide wealth. If you expand your operations to include contracting, maintenance, and other service-related businesses, you can begin to stack up the cash. But even if you have no interest in playing all the roles, you can still do very well doing what you do best, landlording. Look into these programs and see if you can find a use for any of them. Contact your local housing authority and confirm the terms, conditions, and availability of the ones you are interested in. Times change and so do government programs.

Chapter 15

Time Management Is Money Management

We have all heard the old saying "Time is money." There is much truth to be found in those three simple words. Your time is a valuable commodity that should not be wasted. If you run your properties in a way that loses time, you are losing money. Strong time management is an admirable trait for any businessman, but for a property manager, it is essential to higher profits.

Many people go through life never realizing how much money they lose by not managing their time efficiently. For landlords and property managers, the day-to-day struggles of the business create a blind spot. The rental business can get crazy; there are vacancies to fill, maintenance tasks to tend to, and countless other unexpected duties. These things that must be taken care of but are not planned for rob property managers and landlords of their valuable time.

Some rental managers don't consider their time wasted even when it is. They think that if the phone isn't ringing and the paperwork is done, they have nothing to do. This group will not get far above the crowd. The business owner who runs out of productive work is not working to her best ability. Planning, forecasting, marketing, and numerous other jobs can be accomplished in the so-called slow times.

When it comes to time management, there are three distinct categories to consider: time to fulfill the daily requirements of the business, time to plan for the future, and time to relax and relieve the stress of a demanding job. In assessing your time management, take all three into consideration.

Consider this. Do you want to run around in an unorganized way just to feel busy, or do you prefer to refine the time spent on your duties to allow for a long weekend with your friends or family? If you had an extra six hours to work with each week, how much more money could you make? Unlike the payroll employee, who gets the same paycheck regardless of what she accomplishes, your income is directly related to your performance. If you can increase production, you should see higher earnings.

As your own property manager, you own the profits from your rental business. The more you make, the more you have. By honing your time-management skills you can accomplish more in less time, which will translate into higher profits and more free time for recreation. In either case, the results are better than running around in circles without accomplishing much. Time management is simple once you know how to allocate time for all your needs. No, nothing always goes according to your plans, but a good time-management plan will work in the overall picture.

This chapter is going to give you advice and examples of how effective time management can give you more money and more free time. The rental business is filled with situations that drain time from your day, such as long-winded tenants, maintenance repairs, and broken appointments with prospective renters. As you go through this chapter, you will discover other time thieves you have been a victim of and never knew existed. If you pay attention to the suggestions and put a time-management plan into effect, I believe you will notice substantial changes in less than a month.

Setting a Goal

Goals help many people achieve success. Without them, some people become complacent. If you want to ensure successful time management, set goals for yourself. They can take any form so long as they motivate you to make better use of your time. For example, would having every Friday afternoon off from work make you happy? If you had four extra hours each week to search for new properties to buy, do you think you could find some good deals? What you do with the time you save is up to you, but it is important to make the most of it.

Making a Plan

Making a viable plan is the most critical element of early success in time management. If your plan is not realistic, you will quickly become discouraged and discard the idea of using time more effectively. Creating a plan for time management can seem overwhelming, but it doesn't have to be oppressive.

Start making your plan by compiling data on your present habits. Make a list of your routine duties and assign each one an estimate of the time needed to complete it. For example, how many hours do you spend paying bills each month? How long does it take for you to drive to and from your office? What percentage of your time is spent collecting past-due rents? Address each aspect of your rental business with questions like these. Make a comprehensive list of all your responsibilities. If your list is sketchy, your results will not be effective.

It may be difficult to set a time limit on some of your chores. For example, do you know how many hours you spend handling inquiries to rent vacant apartments? While it may be easy to say you spend three hours a month paying bills, identifying the time spent on phone calls can be more difficult. In the early stages of your plan, you may have to estimate the time spent on many duties. As you begin to put your plan to work, you can keep accurate track of the time spent and do some fine-tuning.

Time management requires frequent adjustments. When you take on new challenges, you must allow for them in your schedule, but as you refine your plan, many original time allotments will be reduced. Time-management plans are under constant change, so don't be discouraged when your first attempt at one doesn't work out. With good tracking of your time, you can produce an accurate plan. There will be more on laying out a working plan near the end of this chapter.

Read the following pages with an open mind. Put yourself in the examples and rate your performance. As you read, make notes of your strengths and weaknesses. While not all the examples and advice may hit home for you, they will certainly make you think. This chapter is a catalyst; it will enable you to get your thoughts together for your personal plan. Now, let's dive in and explore the often-overlooked facts revolving around poor time management.

Collecting Current Rents

We have already talked about the various ways to collect rent. In Chapter 9, we discussed the pros and cons of the various methods as they relate to cash flow. Here, we discuss them as they relate to time. The most time-efficient way to collect current rents is by mail. Having a resident manager collect the rents also saves time, but not as much as mail collection does. The cycle in which you collect rents—weekly or monthly—has an impact on your time needs. If you collect weekly, your time spent on collection and bookkeeping is much greater than if you collect monthly. There are fifty-two weeks in the year, but only twelve months. Think of that when you consider that every collection period requires time spent on bookkeeping and time spent making bank deposits, as well as the time spent actually collecting. All of this time adds up quickly, as the following example shows.

Assume you own three buildings, each of them having six apartments. Thus, you have a total of eighteen tenants from whom to collect and process rent. Your rent is collected weekly, by mail and you have established that it requires forty minutes to process each rental payment, including making bank deposits, updating your ledgers, and performing all other associated tasks. Forty minutes per check means that 12 hours are required to complete your weekly collection duties. On an annual basis, this is 624 hours.

Now, if you collect your rent monthly, it still requires 12 hours to process your collections in each cycle. However, on an annual basis, you spend 144 hours processing rental collections instead of 624. This means you save 480 hours each year, which is the equivalent of 12 weeks of vacation.

What is your time worth? If you are conservative and say it is only worth $12 per hour, the time you have saved is equivalent to $5,760. If you are a successful investor, your time is probably worth much more than that. While you have not saved the money, you have saved the time to allow you to *make* the money.

Let's add a few more dimensions to the examples already given. Say you own three buildings in three separate locations and you prefer to collect your rents in person. Assume it will take a total of an hour and a half to drive to and from your buildings. In addition, you will spend time with each of your eighteen tenants when picking up the rents. Even at only five minutes per tenant, this adds another hour and a half to your collection time. In all, you spend an extra three hours in each rental cycle.

By collecting weekly, you spend 156 hours in travel time and time spent with your tenants, but if you collect monthly, you reduce this time to 36 hours. There is another 120 hours you could save by collecting monthly instead of weekly. I imagine you can think of a lot of ways to spend the additional three weeks saved with the monthly collection cycle.

Gossiping Tenants

Tenants who enjoy talking can ruin your time-management plans. They can consume most of your day when you go to collect your rents. Instead of the five minutes per visit allotted in the above example, you might well spend half an hour with some tenants. This type of casual conversation destroys your production rate.

It is good to spend time talking with your tenants, but you must be in control. Thus, if a tenant goes off on a talking spree, be prepared to break off the conversation without being rude. Collecting your rents in person does have its benefits, but beware of gossiping tenants.

Collecting Past-Due Rents

Past-due rents are a problem most property managers will have to deal with at some time. How you deal with them will affect your bank account and your time management. Chapter 9 told you how to collect your past-due rents. Here I will tell you how to collect them in the most time-efficient way.

By following the advice in Chapter 9, you can develop a system for dealing with delinquent rent. When you have your system on-line, it can be as simple as filling in the blanks on form letters or as complicated as taking eviction actions. If the rents are very much overdue, you may decide to hire a collection agency.

To make the most of your time, organize a system for this part of your business. If you do, you will minimize the time lost in going after old money. When you don't have a system, you lose time, money, and leverage; when you do have one, you know what notices to send, when to send them, and what to do. Without a system, you waste time on fruitless phone calls, trying to decide how to handle the situation and whether or not to seek legal advice. Go through the motions once with your attorney and perfect the procedure. From there on out, the system will pay for itself in many ways.

Filling Vacancies

Keeping your apartments rented is what it is all about in landlording. The time spent here is worthwhile, but you cannot afford to waste any of it on activities that will not help you get and keep tenants. Here are some examples of how to make the most of this time.

How Advertising Affects Your Time

Whenever you advertise for tenants, you can expect to lose time—it is just part of the job. There will always be curiosity calls and unqualified tenants to weed through. You can reduce the time lost on this task with a few procedures.

First, write descriptive ad copy. Give readers enough information to eliminate the majority of curiosity calls. I believe all the key issues pertaining to your property should be in the ad. This includes the price, number of bedrooms, at least a general location, whether or not pets are allowed, and anything else you think a tenant will be interested in. An ad like this will be longer and more expensive than a tickler ad, but it will greatly reduce the number of phone inquiries.

Time spent talking to unqualified prospects is wasted time. Thus, if you don't put the price of your rental unit in an ad, people must call to see if they can afford it. By listing the price, you eliminate such calls. The same is true for the location of your property. For security reasons you may not want to disclose its exact location, but you can give a general description of the area. This information will reduce the number of phone calls that waste your time. The more you tell your prospects in the ad, the less you will have to tell them on the phone. Descriptive ads pull more, and better, responses than ticklers.

Telephone Screening

Showing vacant units to prospective tenants can account for a large portion of a rental manager's time. Good telephone tactics can keep this time under control. There is no reason to show your units to people who cannot rent them. If you screen your prospects on the phone, you can reduce the number of showings you must attend.

Even if your units are close by, you will spend approximately thirty to sixty minutes with each showing you schedule. And the amount of time could be much more, depending on how long you talk and how far you have to travel. How many times do you normally show a vacancy before finding a suitable tenant? Unless you are very fortunate, you probably see at least ten people before you find the right one. This means you are probably wasting a full day of production every time you have to rent a unit.

I know landlords who show apartments to an average of twenty-five people to get one tenant. There may be times when this is necessary, but it usually means the landlord is not doing enough in the preliminary stages. If you qualify your prospects early, you greatly reduce lost time.

When a prospect calls to inquire about your rental ad, how do you handle her? Do you answer all her questions without asking questions of your own? If you do, you must change your ways. Develop a list of questions to ask each caller, and get all of them answered before you schedule a meeting to show your vacancy. This procedure will allow you to sort through the prospects without spending time traveling and showing apartments.

What questions should you ask? Your rental policy is a good place to start when listing the questions you need answered. If you don't allow pets, ask if the tenant has pets. If he does, you can rule him out. If you don't allow waterbeds, ask if the prospect has a waterbed. By following this line of questioning, you can reduce your showings to include only qualified tenants. Then, if you learn some sales skills, you can make your time even more efficient. The most important thing is prequalifying the tenant before showing the rental unit.

Showing Apartments

Even after you have done your best to prequalify prospects, some will not keep their appointment with you for a showing. Location is often the reason. If you have to drive to your rental building to show a vacancy, it is inconvenient and a waste of time when your prospect doesn't show up. You can prevent this from happening in two ways.

If the street address of your building is in the ad, you reduce the likelihood of broken appointments, but they still happen. To reduce them even more, have the prospect do a ride-by inspection to see if the location is acceptable. Then have her call you after her inspection to schedule a showing. This tactic works.

If a prospective tenant goes to the building for an outside inspection and calls for a showing, she is serious. Before leaving the comfort of your chair, you know she approves of the location and the exterior of the property. You also know she can find the property and will not get lost on the showing day. You may lose a few prospects by requiring the ride-by inspection, but the tenants you show the building to will be serious.

Scheduling Multiple Showings. Another way to reduce the effect of broken appointments is to schedule all of your appointments on the same day. Many property managers show vacancies without an organized plan—when a prospect calls, they run right out for a showing. If you are desperate for a tenant, you may have to do this, but there is a more productive way to fill your vacancies.

Group all of your showings on the same day, about fifteen minutes apart. Let's say you have four showings scheduled for Thursday evening and the first appointment is set for 4:30. If one of your prospects is a no-show, you will only have to wait fifteen minutes for the next one. And if the prospects overlap, you are creating competition. A tenant who might otherwise think about the unit overnight may make an on-the-spot decision to rent your unit if he feels someone else may beat him to it.

This type of showing strategy will reduce your travel time and the time lost with broken appointments. Moreover, the competition factor may increase your effectiveness in getting quick, affirmative action from the prospects. Whenever you can, schedule your appointments close together for best results.

Emergency Repairs

Emergency repairs are tough to plan around; you never know when a water heater will die or a heating system will quit working. When these things happen, you must interrupt your schedule to deal with them, but this is not to say they must ruin your day. Preliminary planning can reduce the effect of emergencies on your schedule.

Decide in advance how you will handle various emergencies. Know which tradesperson to call and have backups in each category. I always maintain a list of at least three companies in every trade I use. For example, I have a primary, a secondary, and a last-chance plumber, which gives me three known plumbers to call on. You cannot predict when your first choice will be too busy, too sick, or too hard to find to fix your problem. With a list of backups, you improve your odds of getting the emergency under control with minimal effort.

Make a list of every type of repair you may have a need for. Carpenters, electricians, and other tradespeople will all be needed from time to time. Also, establish accounts with your vendors. There is nothing worse than crawling out of your warm bed on a cold night to take a check to the heating technician before she will fix the furnace in your investment property. Not only is being on a C.O.D. basis inconvenient, it robs you of precious time.

The Question of Keys

Your contractors will need access to the building to do their work. If you have a trusted tenant who is usually home, you can leave a set of keys with her, or you can leave them with a resident manager. If these methods are not practical, you might consider giving each of your tradespeople a key to the building.

Some security risks arise when there are numerous keys floating around. And hide-out keys are rarely a good idea, since it is too easy for the wrong person to discover their location. If you cannot arrange to have someone on the premises with keys and you don't want to hand keys out to your contractors, you must be available to provide the needed access.

Scheduled Maintenance

Scheduled maintenance is easier to deal with than emergency calls. If you schedule, you can have your contractors pick up and return keys at your office. If you insist on being the only person handling your keys, arrange to have all of your routine maintenance done on the same day. This will allow you to make one trip to the building to open it up instead of several trips on various days.

Meetings

Meetings with bankers, lawyers, accountants, and vendors can consume much of your time. They cannot be avoided, but lost travel time can. Arrange your meetings to take place in your office. You cannot always do this, but every meeting you don't have to commute to means time saved.

Think about the last five meetings you attended. How many started at the scheduled time? It is not uncommon to sit in a waiting room while the person you are to meet with finishes up other things. When meetings are scheduled in your office, you can remain productive even if the person you are meeting with is late. You may not always be able to arrange for meetings on your turf, but it never hurts to ask.

There is a side benefit to having meetings in your office. Mentally, you will have an advantage because the people you meet with will feel you are in control. This can work against you in some cases, though; if the person you are meeting is too intimidated, you may not achieve the desired results. If you have good people skills, you will be able to sense when your meeting partner is uneasy. If this happens, make gestures to reassure her, perhaps by coming out from behind your desk. Having a desk between the two of you can act as a barrier. When you move out of your command position and onto common ground, the tension should ease.

Typically, holding meetings in your office will save you time. In particular, if you have a secretary, you can prearrange for him or her to interrupt a meeting that is running long. This ploy can get you off the hook politely if the person you are with is rambling.

If you are out of your office, a pager can help end nonproductive meetings. Set a time for your answering service or secretary to page you. When the pager goes off, you have a built-in excuse to cut the meeting short, but you also have the option of continuing. If you want to impress the person you are meeting with, let him hear you tell your secretary or service that the meeting is important and you don't wish to be disturbed again. This can be a real ego-builder for some people. If you make meeting with them seem important, they may be more inclined to see things your way.

Annoying Phone Calls and Drop-In Vistors

Every businessperson gets annoying phone calls. The callers range from sales-people to real estate brokers. When someone calls to sell you something you don't want or need, don't linger on the phone. This type of call ties up your phone line and consumes time you could put to better use.

Be prepared to end unwanted phone calls quickly. With the proper tech-nique, you can do this without being rude. Have you ever gotten a call from a person who talked nonstop, never giving you a chance to speak? How about those people selling advertising who want to read you the copy they have written for your business? To terminate these calls quickly, you must be assertive. Inter-rupt such callers and explain that you are not interested in what they have to offer.

When they make their second run at you, stand firm. Give them one more chance to get off the phone with dignity. If they persist, treat them with the same respect they are giving you—none. I don't recommend hanging up on people, but there are times when it is the only thing harassing callers understand. If you are polite and listen to every sales pitch that comes over your phone line, you lose a lot of time. What is worse, the phone is unavailable to callers you could be making money with. Reduce nonessential calls and you will have more time and more opportunity to make more money.

Drop-in visitors can also rob you of precious time. I am put in a compromis-ing situation when people I deal with on a regular basis drop by to shoot the breeze. I must take a few moments to talk with them, but doing so can disrupt an otherwise perfectly scheduled day. If this is something that happens to you, what can you do about it?

The best way to avoid unwanted visits is to hide behind a receptionist. If you are fortunate enough to have one, you can limit the number of such interruptions. If you don't enjoy this luxury, you must be more creative. You must also be cautious not to offend your friends and associates. While it is perfectly acceptable to chat for a few minutes, don't let the talk drag on for too long.

I have found it best not to lie to your friendly callers. If you tell them you are just leaving for a meeting and don't, you can be caught in your lie. Don't be too quick to shove your visitor out the door. Impromptu meetings can result in unexpected results. What starts as an inconvenient meeting can result in valuable information. I have made many good deals this way.

You must walk a thin line in these situations. One way to end idle chitchat is to explain that you are working to meet a deadline on a project. This could be getting an ad placed in the next edition of the paper. It could be compiling information for a meeting you have scheduled in the next hour. With some thought, you can come up with a number of ways to control the time lost with walk-in meetings. However you do it, don't let people with nothing to do keep you from getting your job done.

Tools That Can Help You Save Time

Computers can do much to help you manage your time better. If you are not intimidated by them, they can streamline your many chores. Whether your rental business is small or large, computers can improve your time management. It will take a little time to learn to use the mechanical wizards, but the time invested will be recovered many times over.

Bookkeeping can be a breeze with a computer and the right software. So can keeping good records and staying organized. The possible uses for a computer in the rental business are mindboggling. You can design advertisements, create mailing lists, and maintain databases to stay on top of current market conditions. These are just a few of the jobs a computer can help you do better.

Another time-saver, mobile phones, were once a symbol of wealth. Today, anyone can have a phone in her car, since the costs have dropped dramatically over the last few years. When I bought my first mobile phone, it cost over $1,800. Now you can buy a good one for under $300.

Can a mobile phone improve your productivity? You bet it can. With a car phone you can tend to business out of the office without missing important calls. You can also call ahead to confirm meetings before driving across town, and you can make many of your required phone calls while traveling to and from appointments. Used properly, mobile phones can provide a noticeable increase in your productivity.

Some people object to car phones because of their high cost. True, the per-minute usage rate can accumulate into a formidable bill, but if you use your phone judiciously, the cost is recovered in the results of your calls.

How Do You Rate?

Now that you have read some examples of how time management works, how do you rate your present performance? Did any of the items discussed hit a nerve? Almost anyone can improve his efficiency. While it is not practical to squeeze every minute of every day to make a profit, it is logical to make the most of your time.

Make a list of all your habits and see if you have time-management problems. For example, do you start reading the morning paper with breakfast and become engrossed in the sports pages? Reading the paper is fine. It gives you current events to discuss during the day and keeps you informed. However, it can be stealing valuable time. If you cannot get out of the house until you have read the entire paper, you may have to get out of bed earlier.

Self-discipline is the most difficult trait for entrepreneurs to master. When you are your own boss, it is easy to let yourself fall into the trap of wasted time. I am not suggesting that you take a cordless phone to the bathroom with you, but you must define the criteria for your working hours. You are entitled to certain freedoms when you run your own business, but these freedoms can be abused.

Thinking versus Daydreaming

How often do you find yourself lost in deep thought during the day? Are you thinking of how you can lower your operating expenses or how to catch that big trout you saw last weekend? Daydreaming is a healthy way to avert stress and regain perspective, but if it becomes excessive, it will derail your profits. If you find yourself fantasizing too often, you need to refocus your attentions on business.

Many entrepreneurs fall victim to the think tank—they start thinking about business, but wind up daydreaming. Some do this to avoid dealing with their business problems. Others transform their thoughts without realizing they are doing it. As a businessperson who makes key decisions, you need time to think, but keep your thinking on track.

Build a thorough list of all your habits, actions, and procedures. Inspect them carefully for flaws, trim out the excess, and streamline your efforts to maximize your time. When you have a rough idea of where to concentrate your efforts, look for ways to make the best use of your time. Maybe you will only have a few soft spots to work on. The point is, find out where you can save time and do it.

The Plan

The plan for how to spend your time can be simple or complex. Individual plans will have different styles. If you carry time management to its furthest extent, you will have a plan accounting for every minute of your day, but such a plan, although effective, can also be too restrictive, raising rather than lowering your stress level. When designing your plan it is important to set guidelines you will be able to adhere to. It will do no good to make a plan and abandon it.

Allow some time in your day for yourself—not every second has to be spent making money. How frequently have you found yourself faced with a problem you couldn't solve? Whether your computer program isn't doing what you want it to do or your ads aren't filling vacancies, there are times when being too involved with the problem does more harm than good. When this happens, step back, away from the problem at hand, and concentrate on something else. This is a good time to daydream about that big trout just waiting to be caught. By getting away from the problem for a while, when you go back to it you will be more apt to find a solution.

Controlling your time is much like controlling your weight; it requires discipline and patience. It is likely your first few plans will fail—this is to be expected. With perseverance, however, you will learn to get the most from your time.

Why Bother?

Some people will think creating a time-management plan is too much work and will take too much of their time. These are the very people who need a working plan the most. You may invest several hours in developing a plan, but think of all the time it will save you in the future. If it is easier for you to think in terms of dollars, refer back to the examples on rent-collection cycles in chapter 9.

The fact that you are actively engaged in managing your own rental properties shows that you have drive. It demonstrates your ability to be a self-starter. Moreover, the fact that you have purchased investment property shows you are willing to gamble. With all this to consider, it is evident that you are motivated to improve your income and living conditions. Effective time management will allow you the opportunity to meet both goals.

Chapter 16

Eviction: The Ugliest Word in Landlording

Eviction is the ugliest word in landlording. Going through the eviction process is one of the most miserable experiences you are likely to have. The costs involved can be staggering; the process can easily take months; and during the eviction proceedings you will probably not be able to collect rent from the hostile tenant. Add to this attorneys and the fees associated with eviction, which are expensive, and it all adds up to a financial disaster for you, the landlord.

It doesn't get much worse than eviction in your day-to-day responsibilities as a property manager. Can it be avoided? Not always—when you manage rental property you must be prepared to evict tenants.

This chapter will help you to understand the eviction process and the practices commonly employed in eviction proceedings. More important, you will be given suggestions to help you avoid eviction actions.

What Is Eviction?

What is eviction? It is the act of removing a tenant by legal procedures. This is a simple definition, but it carries mammoth consequences. Inexperienced landlords do not know what they are risking when they threaten to evict a tenant. Many think it is no big deal until they attempt to do it. Once you find yourself in the middle of eviction proceedings you begin to understand the formidable task you have undertaken.

Unfortunately, by the time most landlords realize their mistake, it is too late to reverse the procedure. It is not until their course of action is all but carved in stone that they appreciate how much time and money is being lost by their actions.

Once you have experienced the pain of evicting a tenant, you will probably do everything within your power to avoid doing it again. If you have never evicted anyone, you are lucky. If you have firsthand knowledge of the eviction process, you understand why I call eviction the ugliest word in landlording.

What Does It Take to Evict a Tenant?

What does it take to evict a tenant? Eviction requires money, time, and an organized approach. Do you need a lawyer to evict a tenant? There is no rule that says you must engage an attorney to evict someone, but it is a wise investment. Evictions can get down and dirty. Having legal representation is advantageous for all landlords, and it is especially beneficial if you are inexperienced. Unless you handle evictions on a regular basis, you should retain an attorney to assist you in your actions.

How long does it take to remove a bad tenant? It is not unreasonable to assume you will be dealing with some aspect of the eviction process for four months or more. Why does it take so long to remove a problem tenant? The process is time-consuming because of the steps required to remove the tenant legally. There are notices to be delivered, hearings to be held, and legal action to be taken. All of these factors add up to make the process long and arduous.

Let's take a look at some of the specific requirements involved in the eviction process. Before we begin, however, remember that the information you are about to read is not legal advice, and that the procedures for conducting a legal eviction in different jurisdictions may vary. Before you commence any eviction action, become well informed of the laws in your area. I advise you to consult an attorney before putting yourself into jeopardy with any actions that may compromise your position.

The Last Step before Starting Eviction Proceedings

The last step before starting eviction proceedings is usually the issuance of a final notice. Evictions are normally used to remove tenants who are not paying their rent, but they can also be used against tenants who have not adhered to the terms of their lease. In either case, you should issue a final warning to a tenant before beginning the eviction ritual.

These warnings normally give the tenant a prescribed period of time to comply with the terms of her lease. If she does not comply within the given time, more formal steps will have to be taken. These steps are the beginning of your eviction process.

The Eviction Process

The first step in an eviction is the filing of eviction papers, usually with the county court. When you file, you will be given a court date. The date could be a few weeks into the future, but it could be much more distant. Depending on your court system, the first court date could be more than a month away. Remember, in most evictions, the tenant will not be paying rent while you are in the process of removing him from your building.

Going to Court

When your date arrives, you must sit around the court and wait for your case to be heard. Expect to lose a full day from your business. If you are lucky, the tenant will not appear in court, and if that happens, the judge will generally order an eviction. Such a scenario is not unusual; tenants frequently fail to appear at their eviction hearing.

If the tenant does appear, you could be in for more delays and problems. Depending upon the grounds for your eviction, the court could rule in favor of the tenant, but if you have all of your paperwork in order and have obeyed the laws in your actions, you should win. Winning is not always what you might think it is, however. The judge could throw you a curve.

Court-Ordered Continuances

Often, if the tenant can impress the court with his reasons for being evicted, he may be granted a continuance. This allows him time to resolve his conflict with you. If he is behind in his rent, the continuance gives him time to pay what he owes. Court-ordered continuations are normally given when a tenant claims a hardship case. Not having any place to relocate to can be considered a hardship, especially if children are involved. The judge may also go easy on the tenant if he can prove he is behind in his rent because of illness or unemployment.

If the court issues a stay, it may be for a couple of weeks or a month. So far, you are just getting started and the tenant has bled you for two months of free housing. You have invested money in the legal action and have lost time from work. See how this can get frustrating and expensive?

If the tenant does not comply with the terms of the court-ordered continuation within the continued time—and most of them won't—you will be going back to court for a second time. When you do, proving that the tenant ignored the court's requirements, the judge should order the eviction. If you are suing the tenant for money, the court may also enter a judgment against her. However, while this is what you hope happens, you cannot count on it. The tenant may be awarded another continuance by once again claiming hardship. Some tenants know as much about eviction laws as lawyers do. Don't be surprised if you leave your second day in court with a bad taste in your mouth.

Being Awarded a Judgment

If you are fortunate enough to be awarded a judgment against the tenant, don't count your money until it is in your hand. The judgment proves that the tenant owes you a determined amount of money, and the judge will set terms for the amount to be paid to you, but if the tenant does not have the money you must continue with legal actions to collect. You may never recover your cash if the tenant doesn't have much cash or valuable assets. What is worse, your expenses in pursuing the money may exceed the judgment's value.

Having the Eviction Order Served

Once you have an eviction order from the court, you must deliver it to the county sheriff's office. The sheriff will then schedule a date for the eviction, which could be two weeks or more into the future. Remember, you are paying legal expenses during this time, but you are probably not collecting rent from the tenant.

Once the sheriff has the eviction order, all you can do is hurry up and wait. By now your stress level is peaking and your blood pressure may be off the scale. When this whole mess started you had no idea of how long it would take and how much time and money it would cost you. You are in the right, and the tenant is in the wrong, and by legal standards you are winning the battle. Still, the tenant is living rent-free in your apartment. How is this fair?

When the sheriff serves the eviction notice, the tenant may leave voluntarily, but he may not. If he refuses to leave, you will have to spend more money. It has been my experience that by this stage of the game, the tenant usually moves out in the middle of the night. Professional deadbeats know how long they can squat on your property, without paying rent, before they have to leave. But what happens if the tenant doesn't move out under his own power?

Getting the Tenant Out and Regaining Your Property

When your problem tenant refuses to move, the sheriff will make arrangements for a moving company to remove her belongings, but you will have to pay for it. This can get expensive fast. When the moving company arrives, the sheriff will supervise the removal of the tenant's possessions and, if necessary will remove the tenant by physical force. Evictions rarely get to this stage, but when they do, it adds considerable expense to an already expensive proposition.

Once the sheriff has removed the problem tenant, you will regain access to your property. This was the purpose for the eviction. However, your rental unit will probably be in a shambles. The tenant may have destroyed it just to get revenge on you, and if so, you will lose substantial money in preparing it for a new tenant. You might initiate new legal action against the tenant for the damages, but don't count on recovering your losses.

What Does Eviction Cost?

The cost of an eviction will vary greatly depending upon the circumstances. If the tenant knows how to work the system, she might stay in your unit, rent-free, for four months or more, and you lose four months rent. You also lose a few days of pay because of your court appearances, and you lose more time from work in meeting with your attorney. Even more time is lost filing and delivering documents. Then there are the court fees, filing fees, and attorney fees. When you add it all up, a difficult eviction could cost you in excess of $5,000.

With so much money at stake, it is well worth your efforts to avoid evictions. The money is only part of it; the stress involved in a tough eviction can engulf you. Now that you know approximately how an eviction goes, we should examine ways for you to avoid gaining personal eviction experience.

The Causes for Eviction and How You Can Avoid It

The primary cause for eviction is the nonpayment of rent by a tenant. For such a situation, eviction is the only sure cure. Another cause for eviction is the violation of the terms of your lease agreement. Thus, if the tenant has brought two large dogs into your building when your lease does not allow pets, you may have to evict him. Any breach of your lease agreement could be cause for eviction.

How can you avoid evicting a tenant? Well, sometimes you can't, but many times you can. If I had to choose a single method to reduce my eviction rate, it would be communication. Clear, open communication is an excellent way to solve most landlord–tenant disputes. There are many other ways to reduce the number of evictions you are forced to endure. Let's take a look at some of the best.

Communication

Communication is one of the best defenses you have against evictions. It will resolve most problems unless you are dealing with a hard-core, professional squatter. Communication will not generate cash from a pauper, but it can lead to acceptable terms that are better than the results of an eviction.

Many tenants quit paying their rent because of a disagreement with their landlord. As the landlord, if you fail to respond to a reasonable request from your tenant, you must expect the tenant to react, and if you take fast legal action against a tenant for doing so, you are in the middle of an eviction that might have been avoided. Talking with her may solve the problem and get your rent checks flowing again. Never underestimate the power of open communication.

Making Concessions

While it may go against your grain to make concessions, sometimes giving in is less expensive than fighting an eviction war. I am not suggesting that you roll over and play dead, but rather that you handle each situation with care. Your other tenants will be observing the outcome of the conflict, and if you cave in for one tenant, others will try the same tactics.

By making concessions you can eliminate the troublesome tenant quickly. Eviction can take a long time, but cutting the right deal can have him out of your building in a flash. Face the facts; you are going to lose substantial money in obtaining an eviction order. You could pay the tenant to leave your building and come out money ahead.

The Approaches Not to Take

Certain approaches you must never take. Do not verbally abuse a tenant; you could be arrested and sued for this type of abuse. Also, never enter a tenant's rental unit without the proper notification and permission; even though you own the property, the tenant is entitled to her privacy. Don't get cute and change the locks on the tenant's doors; this is childish and improper. And don't even think of impounding any of the tenant's property to hold hostage for your rent. Finally, don't get lazy with your paperwork. When you get to court, your paperwork is what will win the case for you.

Examples of Avoiding Evictions

Since they will be easier to understand than words of wisdom, I am about to give you some examples of how you might avoid evictions, and work with the tenant if you have to. Most of these examples are true case histories of my past experiences.

Example 1

Imagine owning a single-family rental. The house is old but in good shape. Its only drawback is that the location, on the fringe of a bad area, limits the quality of tenant. You bought the house cheap and are hoping that neighborhood revitalization will increase its value. In the meantime, you are using your long-range investment as a rental property.

Being relatively new to the rental business, you rent the house to two young men—carpenters without much credit history. You are wise enough to know this is a questionable decision on your part, but you hope for the best.

Time passes and the carpenters find themselves out of work and unable to pay their rent. As a reasonable landlord, you arrange a meeting to discuss the situation. After talking with the carpenters, you decide to allow them to trade their labor in renovating the house for rent until they can find stable employment. This seems like a good plan, and you leave happy.

When you go over about a month later to inspect the progress of the renovations, you are shocked. Your rental home's kitchen was never gorgeous, but now it doesn't exist. The men completely gutted it. Further inspection reveals more damage. The carpenters began the renovations, as discussed, but the house is in a shambles. What is worse, while you are standing in the living room, you begin to itch. When you look down, you see that your legs are covered in fleas. Discarded personal possessions are scattered around the house, but there is no sign of human life. The carpenters have obviously moved on to better accommodations, and you are left with no rent and a destroyed, flea-infested house.

This story is based on true facts surrounding one of my first rental properties. I obviously made many mistakes in my early judgments. I should have never rented the property to the unqualified tenants in the first place, and after I did rent the property and they couldn't pay the rent, I should have forced them to move. Instead, I made a deal that cost me thousands of dollars to reconcile. I don't favor evictions, but there are times when it is the only acceptable course of action.

Example 2

You are the landlord of a nearly new, single-family home. Your tenant has been average with a decent payment history, but all of a sudden, her rent checks begin to be returned for insufficient funds. At first, you just redeposit them without making a big issue of the problem, but as time goes on, the checks start arriving late, past the grace period. Not wanting to let a bad situation escalate, you try calling the tenant.

When you tire of talking to the tenant's answering machine, you contact your lawyer. By this time the rent checks have stopped coming altogether, so the attorney writes a letter to the tenant advising her to pay up or get out. When there is no response, your attorney proceeds with the appropriate legal steps.

When the court date arrives, the tenant doesn't show up. You are awarded an eviction order and a judgment. While you are waiting for the sheriff to serve the eviction order, you ride by the house. All the window treatments are gone and so is the tenant. You are left without your rent and a judgment against a person you cannot find. What could you have done differently?

In this case, there is little room for criticism. You could have acted more quickly in starting legal action, but you did not procrastinate for an unreasonable time. You tried to reach the tenant by phone and by mail, but received no return communication. You engaged an attorney to ensure that the matter was handled through the proper legal channels. In this case, there wasn't much else you could have done.

This misfortune happened to me with the second property I owned. It is a wonder I continued to stay with the rental business, but as I became more experienced, I became better qualified to avoid the downsides of property management.

Example 3

As the landlord, you are faced with a tenant who has stopped paying his rent. Up until the rent stopped coming, it had always been paid promptly. You attempt to call the tenant, but there is no answer. After a ride-by inspection of your rental unit, it appears to still be occupied, but there is no evidence of the tenant's car. What do you do? You could begin eviction procedures, but we already know how expensive evictions are. Here are some tips on how to resolve your problem.

Post a notice on the tenant's door advising him of his default on the terms of the lease. The notice should also instruct the tenant to call you, immediately, to avoid legal action. Then, check your file for the tenant's rental application. It should have names and phone numbers of people you should call in case of an emergency. If the tenant doesn't respond to your notice within twenty-four hours, call those people. For all you know, the tenant may have been involved in a serious accident.

If the contact people cannot provide information on the tenant's whereabouts, call his employer. Don't say anything about the tenant's late rent. Simply say you are concerned because you cannot locate the tenant. The employer should be willing to verify if the tenant is still employed and reporting for work.

After conducting your missing-person investigation, you should be armed with new information. If the tenant is going to work regularly, you know he is still in the area. If phone calls, posted notices, and certified mail do not lead to making contact, begin eviction proceedings.

If the tenant does respond to your request and calls you, arrange a face-to-face meeting to discuss his financial problems. Maybe he has a family member who has taken ill, which could be a legitimate reason for being late with the rent. If the tenant has a good track record with you, arranging different terms may be effective in collecting your money.

Have the tenant sign a promissory note for the money he owes you. Talk with him and arrange a payment schedule he can live with until he is back on his feet. Document all of your dealings with the tenant. Your written documentation may be needed later. Follow up on the tenant's story to prove its validity.

Set a time limit on your new terms. If you agree to extend the special payment arrangements for sixty days, put the agreement in writing and have the tenant sign it. Don't allow the tenant to fall behind in the new terms. If he can't maintain his commitment to your new deal, ask him to leave. If he refuses, go for an eviction order.

Example 4

You have a tenant who is unable to pay her rent because she has run out of money. Your best efforts to resolve the problem have failed and you have asked the tenant to leave. She says she can't because of her lack of funds. Will you file for an eviction order?

This problem requires some thought. The tenant is not angry with you, she just can't pay her rent. She is willing to move to an apartment with lower rent, but cannot afford to move. You understand the tenant's plight, but you need your rental income. On the surface, it appears you have no choice except to evict.

Talk to the tenant and see how much money she needs to get out of your unit. You may be surprised at how little it will take. For the sake of this example, assume that the tenant would be happy to move if she only had $1,500. Granted, $1,500 is a lot of money, but consider your options.

If you evict this tenant, the process may cost you $5,000, not to mention the hassle. If you lend her the $1,500, you get rid of her quickly. Sure, the chances are good she will never repay the loan, but you are still $3,500 ahead of the game. This type of concession makes sense.

A word of caution: don't be foolish enough to just give the tenant $1,500; have her sign a note for the loan. That way, if she never repays you, you have a bad debt to write off. Also, instead of simply giving the tenant the money, work with her to make her moving arrangements. Make sure that by parting with your money, you are getting rid of her. The last thing you want to do is give her money and still be stuck with her.

The Side Effects of Eviction

Up until this point, we have talked about eviction in terms of its direct effects. Now, we are going to study its side effects.

The Cost of Finding Replacement Tenants

When you evict a tenant, you must find a new one to take his place. And you can never be sure if the new tenant will be better than the person you just got rid of. There is significant cost involved in the eviction, but there can also be a high price to pay in finding a replacement.

You will most likely have to advertise for new tenants, and ads can be expensive. You will also have to prepare the rental unit for new occupancy, which is never without its cost. Then, there are the hours invested in handling phone inquiries and showings and all the necessary paperwork to prepare. Total expenses for finding a replacement tenant can scare you. It will be in your best interest to find a workable solution to your tenant problems without relying on eviction procedures.

Your Reputation

Because rumors often do not accurately present the facts, you may be tagged as a person who indiscriminately throws defenseless tenants out into the cold streets. If you acquire a reputation as an eviction expert, tenants will shy away from your building. Maintaining a good reputation as a fair landlord is important to the longevity of your rental business.

There are no winners in an eviction. You lose time and money; the tenant loses his home and his dignity. Unless you are dealing with the lowest life forms, you should be able to find a better solution to your problems.

Summary

As you can see, eviction is not an act to be taken lightly. The cost takes its toll both financially and mentally. Do everything you can to avoid eviction procedures. By approaching your problems with an open, and sometimes creative, mind, you can find a way to solve them.

Many landlords are plagued with evictions, but for the most part, they are the victims of their own poor management. If you follow the rules of the game, you will eliminate many of the causes of eviction. In all my years in the rental business, I have only had to resort to eviction procedures twice. Considering the large number of properties I have owned and managed, you might make it through your career without ever having to go through this ordeal.

Chapter 17

Insurance, Taxes, and Building Security

Insurance, taxes, and building security are all important to the successful operation of your rental property. If you have been doing property management for long, you know the impact these issues can have on your profitability. If you are new to the rental business, first-hand experience is an expensive way to learn about them.

This chapter is going to show you how to provide security and insurance for your building at attractive rates, explaining the various types of coverage you need in both areas. It will also give you the questions to ask to keep your taxes under control. The completion of this chapter will mean the end of this book. Don't stop now; read on to see how insurance, taxes, and building security will affect your profits and future.

Insurance Needs

What are your insurance needs? How much insurance is enough? How can you cut your best deal on the most advantageous insurance? These three questions bear heavily on your long-run success as a landlord.

Poor insurance coverage can force you into bankruptcy. Not having enough can be as bad as not being insured at all and having too much insurance or the wrong kind, on the other hand, can erode your net income. Learning to find the most affordable rates will take some research, but it will pay for itself.

You are about to receive a crash course in the insurance most landlords use. You won't need all of the various policies discussed, but each type will be explained, so you can decide what is right for you.

Fire Insurance

Do you need fire insurance? Yes—every property owner should carry it on her property. If your property is financed, your lender probably requires you to be covered in an amount sufficient to pay off the loan if the building is destroyed. The lender will also probably be named as the first insured on your policy.

The amount of coverage required by the lender is rarely enough to cover a landlord's financial interest in a property. A $200,000 building should not be insured for $300,000, but for its appraised value. If you carry only enough coverage to satisfy the lender, you may lose a minimum of 20 percent of the property's appraised value in the event of destruction. Your loss could be much more depending upon your equity position.

In deciding how much coverage to buy, consider the land value of your property, and deduct that from the total appraised value. By fire insurance standards, your land cannot be destroyed, so you would be wasting your money to insure it.

Some fire policies leave you holding the bag in the case of a partially destroyed building. Make sure that your policy will pay current, going rates to repair or replace your loss.

Extended Coverage

Look into the advantages of extended coverage when you set up your fire insurance. Most insurance companies offer a long list of coverages for any imaginable loss. By adding these as extended coverage, the cost of your premiums may be greatly reduced. Some companies refer to their extended coverage as package policies. Here are a few examples of what you might choose.

Windstorm coverage insures your building from damage from windstorms. Do you need it? To answer this question, consider how often windstorms wreak havoc on properties in your area. Most landlords can do without this coverage, but you may need it.

I do recommend lightning coverage, however. Lightning may never strike the same place twice, but if it hits your building once and you are not insured for it, you will learn an expensive lesson. On the other hand, unless your building is made of glass, hail insurance probably isn't necessary. It may come as a part of a package, and no insurance is bad to have, but it would not be high on my priority list.

What are the odds that your building will be victimized by rioting and looting? If your property is out in the country, they are probably very small, but if it is in the inner city of a major metropolitan area, you might be wise to invest in riot insurance.

Insuring your property against vandalism is a good idea, no matter where the building is located. You never know when some deranged mind is going to take pleasure in trashing it. Hostile extenants commonly seek revenge against landlords. Protect yourself from vandalism with the proper coverage. The cost should not break the bank.

Explosion coverage is another good idea. Many landlords prefer to gamble on their building not blowing up, but I am not one of them. If your building explodes, there is going to be hell to pay. Apart from the property damage, there may be personal injuries and untold damage to cars and other buildings. Gas leaks, defective relief valves on water heaters, gas cans for lawn mowers, and a number of other possibilities create explosion hazards. I don't see how you can avoid having this coverage.

Even in a new building, you can never be certain when the plumbing system may turn into a sprinkler system. Since water can cause severe damage, I recommend you invest in your peace of mind by buying broken pipe insurance.

As for falling tree coverage, if your building is in Oklahoma, I doubt you will need such protection. If your property is in Maine, however, falling trees could present a problem. Take a look at your property. If it is in danger of falling trees, consider the coverage, if not, forget about it.

Freeze-up coverage is a reasonable consideration for buildings subjected to cold weather. As with falling trees, your location will dictate the likelihood of freeze-ups.

For the most part, common sense will tell you if you need a particular type of coverage. Some coverages not yet mentioned that you may find available are smoke damage, falling objects, collapse, landslides, and flooding plumbing fixtures.

Other Types of Extended Insurance

Theft. Theft insurance is usually a good investment, since there never seems to be a shortage of crime. However, you may not need it if you don't have anything of much value at, or in, your rental property. Your tenants should have tenants' insurance to cover their possessions, but if all you have on the premises is appliances, I wouldn't worry about theft coverage. On the other hand, do buy it if you keep equipment, supplies, and other valuables on site.

Glass Breakage. Coverage for glass breakage can come in many forms. For example, it might be addressed in vandalism insurance. Talk with your insurance agent to determine your needs for this coverage, but do give it serious consideration. It may not be important for a small building in a good location, but big buildings in rough neighborhoods can lose a lot of glass.

Mechanical Systems. It is possible to obtain insurance to cover various aspects of your mechanical equipment. Some policies, for example, will cover you for the full replacement value of your heating system if it dies. Other types of mechanical coverage might offer a loss-of-rents benefit. Typically, inspections of your equipment will be made before these coverages are offered.

Remember, insurance companies play the odds. If they offer inexpensive insurance, they don't expect to pay claims. If their rates are high, they have been burned. Evaluate your risks, your worst-case out-of-pocket expenses, and decide for yourself if you want to pay to insure your mechanical systems.

Flood and Earthquake Insurance. Flood insurance is expensive, but if your property is located in a designated flood zone or flood plain, you may have to buy it to appease your lender. Standard insurance policies do not cover flood damage;

you must purchase a separate policy. Finding companies that offer flood insurance may be a little difficult, although they are out there.

A good mortgage survey will indicate if a property is in danger of flooding. Assess your situation and make your own call, but if you are in a high flood risk area, have your property covered for flood damage.

Earthquake insurance is much like flood insurance. Follow the advice given above, substituting "earthquake" for "flood."

Outside Improvements. If your property has outside improvements, such as swimming pools, fences, or parking lots, you may need additional insurance. However, the cost may prove to be prohibitive. Check with your insurance agent and determine if such insurance is worth its premiums.

Liability Insurance and Workers' Compensation. Liability insurance is something you cannot afford to be without. If you don't have it, you could lose all of your assets and future plans to a single lawsuit. Liability insurance can protect you and your assets from countless legal battles. It may not be cheap, but it is a bargain. Don't do business without extensive liability insurance.

Workers' compensation insurance also demands hefty premiums, but most states require an employer to carry it on all employees, with only a few exceptions. Even if you use only the services of a resident manager in exchange for a deduction in your normal rent, you may be deemed to be the manager's employer. Don't play around with this issue. Investigate the laws and abide by them. One injury claim could wipe you out.

Mortgage and Title Insurance. Mortgage insurance against the payment due on a mortgage used to be popular. Today, its cost prohibits most people from obtaining it. Basically, this insurance will pay off the mortgage on your property in the event of your death. Most people find a decreasing-term life insurance policy to be just as effective and not as expensive.

Title insurance is sometimes referred to as mortgage insurance, but that is not what it is. Title insurance insures the title you possess for your property. It is a one-time expense and not very costly. I would never buy real estate without it.

Title insurance provides some guarantee of your ownership of a property. It protects against unknown heirs or other people with a legal right to the property you think you own. If a lost heir turns up pressing his rightful claim, you may have to hand over your building to him. If you have title insurance, you will at least be reimbursed for your loss. If you don't have it, you must simply give up your property and move on.

Lenders in many states require title insurance. Even if you live in a state that does not require it, insist on it anyway. The possible repercussions of doing without it are scary.

Fidelity Insurance. Fidelity insurance is essentially a bond. It assures an employer that she will not be the victim of theft from her employees. If you don't have employees, you may not benefit from fidelity insurance, but if you have a maintenance person who enters tenants' apartments, especially when they aren't home, it could be a consideration. Talk to your insurance agent to see if you are a candidate for fidelity insurance.

Auto Insurance. In my opinion, anyone driving a car should carry auto insurance. Even if you are not concerned about the cost of repairing or replacing your car, you should be concerned about lawsuits that may steal your property. If you are sued for an accident and lose, the winner may be awarded a judgment against all of your assets. This, of course, includes your rental holdings. Don't risk it; get good auto insurance.

If you allow an employee to drive your car while doing work for you, you need nonowned auto insurance. This protects you if you are sued for damages caused by your car while your employee was driving it. Check out this coverage if you allow outsiders to drive your vehicle.

Loss-of-Rents Insurance. I feel every investor should consider purchasing loss-of rents insurance. If your building were to be rendered uninhabitable, how long could you make the mortgage payments? Consider that if a fire sweeps through your apartments, the tenants will not be likely to pay their rents for the period of time they are displaced. How will you meet your hard expenses like debt service? Loss-of-rents insurance can bail you out in these circumstances.

Such coverage is designed to assist you when, due to extenuating circumstances, you cannot collect rents for your units. Talk to your agent and see if you can justify the premiums for loss-of-rents insurance. If you can, go for it. It will provide comfort and peace of mind.

Waterbed Insurance. I am including waterbed insurance because I believe tenants with waterbeds should be required to pay for them. As a landlord, you can obtain insurance to protect you from waterbed damages. However, most savvy landlords stipulate in their leases that tenants must pay for this insurance themselves to protect the landlord's property. Use you own judgment, but give some thought to having your waterbed owners pay your premiums. After all, if the tenants didn't own waterbeds, you wouldn't need the insurance.

Identify Your Needs

When it comes to insurance, the first thing you must do is identify your needs. This will tell you which forms of insurance can be scratched from your list. For example, if you own an apartment building in the middle of a desert, you don't need flood insurance. You have been given enough fuel to fire your imagination. Look over the various types of insurances we have discussed and determine what your needs are.

Shop Around

I despise insurance payments as much as the next guy, maybe more so, but I keep paying them. You have to. As disgusting as they are, you need insurance, and premiums are the price you pay for peace of mind. This is not to say that having insurance will save you, but it can't hurt.

With that in mind, you must shop " 'til you drop" to find the best price for suitable insurance. Prices fluctuate greatly between different companies. A company that gives you a dynamite quote on liability may gouge you on fire. Also remember that premiums usually go up every year. Once you are established with a company, they seem to take you for granted. At each anniversary date, they see an opportunity to strip you of your money.

Take a hard look at package policies. Also known as extended coverage, they can be a great value as far as insurance deals go. By lumping your coverages into a package, you may be able to reduce your overall costs.

Deductible amounts can make a huge difference in the price you pay for insurance. Depending upon your cash reserves and financial standing, policies with high deductibles can be your best bet. Insurance is always a gamble. The companies are gambling that you will not make a claim. You are gambling that you will. By choosing a policy with a high deductible, you can be covered for situations you can't handle financially, without having to pay premiums that burden you.

One last thing. There is no point in buying more insurance than you need. If you insure a $200,000 building for $300,000 and it burns down, you are only going to get $200,000 at best. Overinsuring yourself is a waste of money.

Tax Matters

Taxes may be the second ugliest word in landlording, preceded only by eviction. I have never met anyone who enjoyed paying taxes. In fact, tax shelters are the reason many investors enter the rental business. Shelters were much easier to find before the change in the tax laws. Today, they can be quite limited for landlords, but they do still exist. Tax matters are similar to legal matters. You should consult experts within the field before making any decisions.

If you own real estate, you are well aware of property taxes. For most landlords, they are responsible for a big piece of the pie when it comes to expenses. There is no getting around property taxes—they are a cost of doing business. Don't forget them when you project your profits and possible losses.

Doing Your Own Income Taxes

Do you prepare your own income taxes? If you do and you have more than a couple of rental properties, you are probably losing money. Tax angles are complicated; that is why accountants are paid so well. Having done my own taxes and having hired experts to do them, I have learned that a good accountant doesn't cost you money; she saves you money. As a thriving landlord, you can't afford not to hire a professional to find the tax advantages you are entitled to.

Keeping Good Records

Regardless of who does your taxes, keeping good records is critical in beating the tax bite. Well-organized records are also comforting during an IRS audit—I know, I have been there. For the record, my files stood the test. Most investors envision a tax audit as their worst nightmare, and I felt this way too until I went through my first. If you have good records, and haven't monkeyed the numbers, an audit is nothing to lose sleep over.

In case you haven't heard, the tax laws have changed a great deal in the last few years. These changes have forced me to restructure my way of doing business. If you are reading outdated books, you could be getting bad information. The new tax laws do not allow the freedoms once associated with being a real estate investor. Talk with your CPA before you plot a course based on old tax information. Be sure you are playing by the current rules—if you aren't, you are in for some unpleasant surprises.

Building Security

Building security is more of an issue in some areas than in others. Most landlords think of criminal activity when they visualize security, but although crime is certainly one consideration, it is not the only one. Fire and tenant safety are also key aspects. Even if your property is located in an Iowa corn field, you should take the proper building security measures.

Fire Protection. Fire protection should be a predominant concern when it comes to building security. The safety of your tenants and the structure of your property is at stake. Most jurisdictions conduct routine fire inspections. If you are an insensitive or ignorant landlord, the officials inspecting your property will make you wise to the ways of fire protection fast, and unlike my advice, theirs will come as formal warnings, written violations, and cash fines. You can wait and learn their way, the hard way, or you can pay attention and learn from this book how to avoid the loss of money and, potentially, life.

If your building has more than one story holding rental units, you are more than likely required to provide a fire escape. Most fire codes require an acceptable route of escape for upper-level tenants in case of fire. Smoke detectors are probably required in the hallways of your building. They should also be installed in the halls and near sleeping areas in your apartments. Clearly display fire extinguishers in your hallways as well. Your rental units and your mechanical room should also have them.

Outside Lights. Outside lights provide many benefits. They light your building and discourage vandalism; they also illuminate the common areas surrounding your building, thus helping to prevent accidental injuries to tenants and visitors that might result in lawsuits. A well-lighted building is less enticing to a burglar than a dark one, and tenants appreciate the comfort of coming home to lighted walkways and parking areas. All in all, outside lights answer many building security needs.

Security Doors and Intercoms. The level of protection security doors and intercoms provide is not necessary in every rental building. However, in big cities and areas with high crime rates, these security measures do have their place. In such areas, they can pull higher rents and more tenants. If your building will benefit from these additions, add them; if not, don't. The same is true for alarm systems.

Locked Doors and Key Control. What do you think of when you hear the words "locked doors?" Most people think of locking the entry doors to their building or apartments. This is a reasonable assumption but not the only one. Lock the doors to your building's basement, mechanical room, and landlord storage areas. By doing so, you prevent mischief and possible injury to unauthorized people. There is no reason why your tenants should have access to your private areas. Lock the doors and remove the risks of damage and injury.

When tenants vacate a rental unit, change the unit's locks. Also be mindful of who you hand keys out to. The person who services your furnace in the afternoon may steal you blind in the night. Keep a tight lid on the distribution of your keys.

Rent Collection Security

Landlords who collect their rent in person run some risks of personal injury. If you go to your buildings on a regular schedule to collect rent money, you may be a target. Street thugs are not stupid. If they see you making routine trips to your building, they will put the pieces together.

The rent you collect for a six-unit building may not seem like a fortune to you; however, it could put a spark in the eye of a stressed-out junkie. People have taken a knife in the back for much less. If you collect your rents personally, mix up the days and times you do it. Never set a pattern; always keep changing your habits because they can get you into trouble fast when a bad guy is keeping track of your movements. Don't underestimate the value of your life to some street punk. There are people who will kill you for the change in your pocket, and to this group, the monthly rent from a six-unit building is like winning the lottery.

Epilogue

I hope this book will be a useful manual for all residential landlords and property managers. It is a compilation of many years of experience, pain, good fortune, and luck. I wish I had more time and space to share some more experiences with you.

My life has not been charmed, but I have done well considering my circumstances. With a little luck and a lot of hard work, you can enjoy the rewards I have received from the real estate business.

My career has taken many turns, but real estate has always been a guiding light along the road. I am sure you will do well if you take the time to consider your actions. When I got started in this business, I had no formal training or education. Yet at one time I controlled a stable of more than fifty properties for my own account. Today, I have downsized my operations, but I still play the game. Once you get the real estate bug, you can never get it out of your blood. Good luck with all your endeavors.

Sample Forms Used in Property Management

NOTICE

Intent to Access Your Rental Unit

Be advised, your landlord requires access to your rental unit on
_____, at _____ A.M./P.M. As
stipulated in your lease, this notice is your formal notification of
the landlord's intent to enter your dwelling. If you wish to be
present during this access, you are welcome. If you would like to
attempt to arrange a more convenient time for the entry, please
contact your landlord by calling _____. In the
event you are unable to be available for this access, your landlord
will be present during the time your rental unit is open. In addition
to this notice, an additional notice has been mailed to your address.
Thank you for your cooperation.

Date _____
Time _____ A.M./P.M.
Notice posted by _____

RENTAL ADDENDUM

This rental addendum shall become an integral part of the lease/
rental agreement dated _____, between the
landlord, _____, and the
tenant, _____, for the real estate
commonly known as _____.
The undersigned parties hereby agree to the following:

_____
_____
_____
_____
_____
_____
_____
_____
_____

_____   _____
Landlord   Date   Tenant   Date

NOTICE TO PERFORM COVENANT

To _____,
tenant in possession:

Please take notice that you have violated the following covenant in your lease/rental agreement: _____

_____
You are required to perform the aforesaid covenant or to deliver up possession of the premises now held and occupied by you, being those premises situated in the city of _____,
county of _____, state of _____,
commonly known as _____.
If you fail to do so, legal proceedings will be instituted against you to recover said premises and such damages as the law allows.

This notice is intended to be a _____ notice to perform the aforesaid covenant. It is not intended to terminate or forfeit the lease/rental agreement under which you occupy said premises. If after legal proceedings, said premises are recovered from you, the landlord will attempt to rent said premises for the highest possible rent, giving you credit for sums received and holding you liable for any deficiencies arising during the term of said lease/rental agreement.

Dated this _____ day of _____, 19____.

_____

Landlord

PROOF OF SERVICE

I, the undersigned, being of legal age, declare under penalty of perjury that I served the notice to perform covenant, of which this is a true copy, on the above-mentioned tenant in possession in the manner indicated below:

On _____, 19____, I served this notice in the following manner:

_____

Executed on _____, 19____, at _____.

By: _____
Title: _____

COMPARATIVE PROPERTY DATA SHEET

Address _____

Style _____ Rents _____

Amenities _____ Number of rooms _____

Number of bedrooms _____ Number of bathrooms _____

Siding _____ Heat type _____

Type of hot water _____ Water (public/private) _____

Sewer (public, private) _____ Basement (yes/no) _____

Utilities paid by landlord _____

Security _____ Storage _____

Laundry facilities _____

Deposit required _____ Pets allowed _____

Parking facilities _____

Proximity to shopping _____

School system _____

General condition of rental units _____

FLOOR PLAN

	1st	2nd	3rd	Basement
Living room				
Dining room				
Family room				
Bedrooms				
Bathrooms				
Kitchen				
Comments				

Other pertinent information:

_____
_____
_____
_____
_____
_____
_____
_____

SAMPLE OF SECURITY DEPOSIT RECEIPT

The landlord hereby acknowledges the receipt of a security/damage deposit from the tenant in the amount of $_____.
This deposit will remain in an escrow account during the term of the lease/rental agreement. The landlord has the right to apply this deposit to the costs incurred to offset any damages or financial responsibilities incurred, due to the tenant's lack of performance as agreed upon in the lease/rental agreement dated _____, between the landlord and tenant. If the tenant complies with the lease/rental agreement and does not cause damage to the landlord's property, this deposit will be returned to the tenant within 48 hours of the tenant's vacating the property. If the terms of the lease/rental agreement are breached by the tenant, or if the tenant causes damage to the landlord's property, the landlord may retain any portion of this deposit necessary to compensate the landlord for financial burdens caused by the tenant.

MONTHLY UTILITY EXPENSE LOG

Unit Number	Building Address	Date of Expense	Nature of Expense	Amount of Expense

FRIENDLY REMINDER

I wanted to take this opportunity to remind you that your rent for _____, 19____ is past due. I trust this is the result of an oversight. If you have already mailed your rent, please disregard this notice. If you have not mailed your rent, please do so immediately. If your rent has not been received by _____, 19____, you will be assessed a late charge, as allowed by your lease. I don't wish to charge you for being late, but the late-fee policy must be enforced on all tenants to be effective. Thank you for your prompt attention to this matter. If for some reason you are unable to pay your rent, please call me to discuss your circumstances. I can be reached from _____A.M to _____P.M. by calling _____.

Date _____

_____

Landlord

HELPFUL INFORMATION

This form is for your convenience. We know it can take awhile to get adjusted to a new home, and we will be happy to help you with questions you may have about the community. Thank you for renting with us.

Phone Numbers

Police (nonemergency)	_____
Police (emergency)	_____
Fire department	_____
Ambulance	_____
Emergency room	_____
Hospital	_____
Doctor	_____
Telephone company	_____
Utility company	_____
Water & sewer district	_____
Resident manager	_____
Landlord	_____

Notes

_____
_____
_____
_____
_____
_____
_____
_____
_____
_____
_____
_____

KEY LOG

Unit Number	Date Key Was Given	Person Given Key	Phone Number	Key Returned

RENTAL LEASE

This lease is between _____,
landlord, and _____, tenant, for a
dwelling located at _____, unit
number _____. The tenant agrees to lease this dwelling for a term
of _____, beginning _____, and
ending _____, for $_____, per _____,
payable in advance on the first day of every calendar _____.
Rent shall be paid to _____. Payments shall be mailed
to _____, at _____. The
first _____ rent for this dwelling is $_____. The
entire sum of this lease is $_____. The damage deposit on this
dwelling is $_____ and is refundable if tenant complies with
this lease and leaves the dwelling clean and undamaged. If the tenant
intends to move at the end of this lease, the tenant agrees to give the
landlord notice, in writing, at least thirty days before the lease expires. A
deposit of $_____ will be required for two keys. This deposit
will be refunded to the tenant when both keys are returned to the landlord.
The landlord will refund all deposits due within ten days after the tenant
has vacated the property and returned the keys. Only the following
persons are to live in the above mentioned dwelling:

_____

_____.

Without the landlord's prior written permission, no other persons may
live in the dwelling, and no pets shall be admitted to the dwelling, even
temporarily. The dwelling may not be sublet or used for business
purposes. Use of the following is included in the rent, at the tenant's own
risk: _____

_____.

The tenant agrees to the terms set forth in the attached rental policy. This
attached rental policy shall be considered a part of this lease and the
tenant's signature on this lease indicates his or her acceptance of all terms
and conditions of the rental policy.

Violation of any part of this agreement, or nonpayment of rent when due,
shall be cause for eviction under appropriate sections of the applicable
code and law. The landlord reserves the right to seek any legal means to
collect monies owed to him. The prevailing party shall recover reasonable
attorney's fees incurred to settle disputes. The tenant hereby acknowledges
that he or she has read this agreement, understands the entire agreement,
agrees to the entire agreement, and has been given a copy of the
agreement.

_____		_____	
Landlord	Date	Tenant	Date

MAINTENANCE EXPENSE LOG

Unit Number	Building Address	Date of Expense	Nature of Expense	Amount of Expense

MOVE-IN CHECKLIST

Please inspect all areas of your rental unit carefully. Note any existing deficiencies on the form below. The information on this form will be used in determining the return of your damage deposit. Please be thorough and complete all applicable items.

Tenant: _____

Rental unit: _____

Item	Location of Defect
Walls	_____
Floor coverings	_____
Ceilings	_____
Windows	_____
Screens	_____
Window treatments	_____
Doors	_____
Light fixtures	_____
Cabinets	_____
Countertops	_____
Plumbing	_____
Heating	_____
Air conditioning	_____
Electrical	_____
Trim work	_____
Smoke detectors	_____
Light bulbs	_____
Appliances	_____
Furniture	_____
Fireplace	_____
Hardware	_____
Closets	_____
Landscaping	_____
Parking area	_____
Storage area	_____
Other	_____

Comments

_____

_____

Inspection completed by: _____
                                Tenant   Date

MUTUAL TERMINATION AGREEMENT

For good and valuable consideration, _____, landlord, and _____, tenant, agree to terminate the lease/rental agreement presently in force and dated _____. Said lease/rental agreement for the property located at _____ _____, shall become null and void, once consideration has been given and terms and conditions are complied with, as described below, and this document is executed by all parties.

Terms of Consideration

_____
_____
_____.

In this mutual termination, both landlord and tenant agree to the disposition of deposits and financial responsibilities in the following manner:

_____
_____
_____

_____   _____
Landlord   Date   Tenant   Date

PET ADDENDUM

This pet addendum shall become an integral part of the lease/ rental agreement dated _____, 19____, between _____, tenant, and _____, landlord, for the dwelling located at _____. The tenant is allowed under the following terms and conditions to keep _____ pet/s described as _____, in the above-mentioned dwelling. The tenant shall maintain control of the pet at all times. The tenant agrees to treat the pet in a humane manner at all times. The tenant agrees to clean up after the pet, both in and out of the rental unit. The tenant may not create a condition where other animals are drawn to the property because of the pet. The tenant agrees to guarantee peace and quiet for other tenants, as it relates to the pet. If complaints are filed by other tenants, the tenant will make appropriate arrangements to cure the cause of the complaints of the pet. If pet delivers offspring, the tenant will remove the young animals within ten weeks of their birth. The tenant agrees to pay an additional damage deposit of $_____, for damage that may be caused by the pet. This deposit will be held in an escrow account and returned to the tenant within five days of vacating the property, if no damage has been caused by the pet. The tenant agrees to pay an additional monthly rent of $_____ for the privilege of housing the pet. The tenant agrees to remove the pet from the rental unit if any of these terms or conditions are broken.

_____   _____
Landlord   Date   Tenant   Date

PROMISSORY NOTE

City _____

State _____

Date _____

Face amount of note $_____

For value received and or services rendered, the undersigned promises to pay to _____, at the following address, _____ the principal sum of $_____ ($_____) with interest thereon at the rate of _____ percent per annum, said interest to be paid in monthly payments of $_____ ($_____) for _____ months. The balance is due in full and payable on _____. This note shall be secured by the personal guarantee and all assets of the undersigned and their heirs.

_____   _____
Debtor   Date   Debtor   Date

_____
Witness   Date

LEASE RENEWAL SCHEDULE

Unit Number	Date Leased	Lease Expires	Tenant Contacted	Will Renew	Will Not Renew

RENTAL AGREEMENT

This rental agreement, dated _____, is between _____, tenant, and _____, landlord, for the rental unit located at _____
_____.

Under this agreement, the tenant agrees to rent the above-mentioned dwelling on a month-to-month basis, with a monthly rental amount of $_____ _____. The monthly rent will be due and payable on the first day of each month, starting on the first day of _____, 19____. A damage deposit is required at the signing of this rental agreement. The deposit will be placed in an escrow account. The amount of this deposit shall be $_____ _____. If the rental unit is returned to the landlord in a clean and good condition, this deposit will be refunded to the tenant within _____ days of vacating the property. An additional deposit of $_____, will be required when keys are issued to the tenant. This deposit will also be placed in escrow and returned to the tenant within _____ days from the date the tenant returns said keys to the landlord. The tenant or the landlord may terminate this agreement with a 30-day written notice to the other party. The attached rental policy shall be made a part of this agreement and shall be binding on all parties.

The tenant acknowledges reading and understanding this agreement and the rental policy that is a part of this agreement. The tenant's signature below indicates acceptance of all terms and conditions of this rental agreement and the rental policy.

_____   _____
Landlord   Date   Tenant   Date

RENTAL INVOICE

J. P. Landlord
P.O. Box 001
Bucksville, ME 60322
(207) 696-5555

Date: October 14, 1992

To:
Jay Winkle
12 Wilkmont Rd.
Bucksville, ME 60322

Re:
Rent payment

Amount of rent due: $600.00
Date due: November 1, 1992
Period covered: The month of November, 1992

Thank you for your prompt payment of October's rent.

Sincerely,

J. P. Landlord

NOTICE TO TERMINATE TENANCY

To _____ ,
tenant in possession:

You are hereby required within thirty days from this date to remove from and deliver up possession of the premises now held and occupied by you, being those premises situated in the city of _____ , county of _____ , state of _____ , commonly known as _____ .

This notice is intended for the purpose of terminating the lease/rental agreement by which you now hold possession of the above-described premises, and should you fail to comply, legal proceedings will be instituted against you to recover possession, to declare said lease/rental agreement forfeited, and to recover rents and damages for the period of the unlawful detention.

Please be advised that your rent on said premises is due and payable up to and including the date of termination of your tenancy under this notice. This notice complies with the terms and conditions of the lease or rental agreement under which you presently hold said property.

Dated this _____ day of _____ , 19_____ .

_____

Landlord

PROOF OF SERVICE

I, the undersigned, being of legal age, declare under penalty of perjury that I served the notice to terminate tenancy, of which this is a true copy, on the above-mentioned tenant in possession, in the manner indicated below:

On _____ , 19_____ , I served the notice to the tenant in the following manner:

_____

_____ .

Executed on _____ , 19_____ , at _____ .

By: _____

Title: _____

NOTICE

Final Notice to Vacate

Be advised, this is your final notice to vacate these premises. All of my attempts to resolve your breach of our lease have gone unanswered. You have five days to vacate this property. If you have not delivered the property to me within five days, eviction proceedings will be started. Eviction is not an enjoyable experience for anyone. I am giving you this final notice to allow you the opportunity to leave these premises under your own power. If you fail to vacate, I will take all actions available to have you removed from the property.

Date: _____

Time: _____

_____

Landlord

WATERBED ADDENDUM

This addendum shall become an integral part of the lease/rental agreement dated _____, 19_____, between _____, _____ tenant, and _____, landlord, for the property located at _____. Under the terms and conditions of this agreement, the tenant may use a waterbed in his or her rental unit. The terms and conditions for the use of a waterbed in the above-mentioned dwelling are as follows: The tenant must allow the landlord to inspect and approve the quality and installation of the waterbed. The tenant shall provide the landlord with proof of insurance naming the landlord as first insured for damages caused in regards to the waterbed. The minimum amount of liability coverage acceptable to the landlord is $100,000.00. In addition to the insurance coverage, the tenant agrees to make an additional damage deposit in the amount of $_____. This deposit will be held in an escrow account and returned to the tenant within five days of vacating the property, if no damage has been caused in conjunction with the waterbed. The tenant agrees to remove his waterbed immediately if any of these terms or conditions are broken.

_____   _____
Landlord   Date   Tenant   Date

BALLOON PROMISSORY NOTE

City   ——————————————————————————

State ——————————————————————————

Date   ——————————————————————————

Face amount of note $———————————————————

For value received and or services rendered, the undersigned promises to pay to ————————————, at ————————————, the principal sum of $———————— ($————————), with interest thereon at the rate of ———————— percent per annum, said principal and interest to be paid in full on ————————. This note shall be secured by the personal guarantee and all assets of the undersigned and their heirs.

————————————————   ————————————————

Debtor   Date   Debtor   Date

————————————————

Witness   Date

TENANCY CHANGE ORDER

This tenancy change order addendum shall become an integral part of the lease/rental agreement dated _____, 19____, between _____, tenant, and _____, landlord, for the dwelling located at _____. This tenancy change order addendum shall serve to change the original terms of tenancy as dictated by the above-mentioned lease/rental agreement. The tenant and the landlord agree to the following changes and amendments to the existing lease/rental agreement for the property located at _____.

Changes in Tenancy

_____

_____

_____

_____

_____

_____

_____

_____

_____

The above-detailed changes are the only changes agreed to and in force. Other than for the above changes, the original lease/rental agreement is in full force. By signing below, both the landlord and the tenant agree to the detailed changes in the existing written agreement between them.

_____   _____
Landlord   Date   Tenant   Date

COSIGNER ADDENDUM

Addendum to rental agreement/lease dated: ——————,
between ———————————————————————
and ——————————————————————. This addendum shall
become an integral part of the above-mentioned agreement for the
rental unit located at ————————————————————. The
undersigned has read and understands the above-mentioned
document and agrees to abide by the agreement in the capacity of
a cosigner. In affixing his or her signature below, the cosigner may
be held accountable for all terms and conditions of the rental
agreement/lease described above.

———————————————————————————————

Cosigner   Date

RECORD OF DEPOSITS

Unit Number	Tenant's Name	Amount of Deposit	Date of Deposit	Type of Deposit	Deposit Returned

NOTICE

Final Notice

Be advised, this is your last opportunity to resolve your breach of our lease. You have been mailed many notices. All previous notices have gone unanswered. Other means of communication have failed to produce a response from you. If you do not comply with the terms of your lease within the next 48 hours, legal proceedings will be started to resolve this matter. If in doubt, refer to your lease. You will see that you may be held responsible for the fees incurred in these legal proceedings. If you fail to comply with your lease, all legal actions allowable by law will be used to correct this situation. It is not my desire to proceed legally, but you are leaving me with no options. If I have not been contacted by you within the next 48 hours, the next notifications you receive will be from my attorney. Please contact me immediately to avoid legal action. I can be reached from _____A.M. to _____P.M. at _____. A copy of this notice has also been mailed to you at this address.

Date: _____

Time: _____

_____

Landlord

PAST-DUE RENT NOTICE

Please take notice, your rent, which was due on _____, 19____, is past due. Unfortunately, you will be assessed a late charge for allowing your rent to become delinquent. If you have already mailed your rent, please disregard this notice. If you have not mailed your rent, this is your formal, and final, notice of your past-due rent. If your rent is not received within the next 48 hours, collection and eviction actions will be taken. If you are having trouble paying your rent, I will be happy to talk with you to see if we can come to amicable terms. If you dispute this notice, I will gladly meet with you to discuss the circumstances. If you do not pay your rent or contact me within the next 48 hours, you will be notified by the appropriate legal channels of the upcoming proceedings. I can be reached between _____A.M. and _____ P.M. at _____.

Date: _____

Time: _____

_____

Landlord   Date

SAMPLE OF A LEASE RENEWAL CLAUSE

If the tenant is not in default of the existing lease/rental agreement, dated _____, between the landlord and tenant, the tenant may renew the lease, under the existing, current rental terms, conditions, and rates in effect at the time of renewal. The tenant's lease renewal is subject to new rules, regulations, terms, conditions, and rates that may apply at the time of renewal. The tenant's lease renewal is subject to the review and approval of the landlord.

LIEN WAIVER

The undersigned has full knowledge of his right to a lien on the property of _____, located at _____, for labor performed and or materials supplied. The undersigned hereby acknowledges receipt of $_____, as good and valuable consideration for the labor and or materials supplied. The undersigned knowingly and voluntarily waives any right of a lien and all claims he or she may now have to the above-mentioned property. The undersigned has signed this agreement on this date, _____, in the presence of a witness, _____.

_____

Witness

By _____

Title _____

ANNUAL MAINTENANCE REMINDER

Item	Date for Attention	Completed
Clean heating system		
Clean flue		
Clean chimney		
Service heating system		
Clean air conditioning unit		
Service air conditioning unit		
Inspect water heater		
Inspect toilet tanks		
Inspect faucets		
Inspect caulking at fixtures		
Inspect attic		
Inspect basement/crawl space		
Inspect safety equipment		
Inspect parking area		
Inspect lighting		
Inspect for fire hazards		
Inspect porches		
Inspect balconies		
Interview tenants		

MARKETING MEMOS

Ad Number	Ad Placed in	Calls Received	Number of Showings	Number of Leases Signed

MOVE-OUT CHECKLIST

Tenant: _____

Rental unit: _____

Item	**Location of Defect**
Walls	_____
Floor coverings	_____
Ceilings	_____
Windows	_____
Screens	_____
Window treatments	_____
Doors	_____
Light fixtures	_____
Cabinets	_____
Countertops	_____
Plumbing	_____
Heating	_____
Air conditioning	_____
Electrical	_____
Trim work	_____
Smoke detectors	_____
Light bulbs	_____
Appliances	_____
Furniture	_____
Fireplace	_____
Hardware	_____
Closets	_____
Landscaping	_____
Parking area	_____
Storage area	_____
Other	_____

Comments

_____

_____

_____

_____

Inspection completed by: _____

                                   Landlord   Date

NOTICE TO PAY RENT OR QUIT

To _____

tenant in possession:

You are hereby notified that the rent is now due and payable on the premises now held and occupied by you, being those premises situated in the city of _____, county of _____, state of _____, commonly known as _____.

Your account is delinquent in the amount of $ _____, being the rent for the period from _____ to _____.

You are required to pay said rent, in full, within _____ days. If rent is not paid, you must vacate and deliver the above-mentioned premises, or legal proceedings will be instituted against you to recover possession of said premises, to declare the forfeiture of the lease or rental agreement under which you occupy said premises, and to recover rents and damages, together with all fees allowed by the lease or rental agreement in effect.

Dated this _____ day of _____, 19____.

_____

Landlord

PROOF OF SERVICE

I, the undersigned, being of legal age, declare under penalty of perjury that I served the notice to pay rent or quit, of which this is a true copy, on the above-mentioned tenant in possession in the manner indicated below:

On _____, 19____, I served this notice in the following manner:

_____

_____

Executed on _____, 19____, at _____.

By: _____

Title: _____

PHONE CHECKLIST FOR PROSPECTIVE TENANTS

1. How many bedrooms do you need?   ——
2. Do you prefer a ground-level unit?   ——
3. How many people will occupy the property?   ——
4. Do you have pets?   ——
5. How much parking space do you require?   ——
6. Do you work in this area?   ——
7. Do you require laundry facilities?   ——
8. Are you new to the area?   ——
9. Do you have a waterbed?   ——
10. Do you work in this area?   ——
11. When would you like to see the property?   ——
12. Will your spouse be attending the showing?   ——
13. Have you seen the exterior of the property?   ——
14. May I have your name and phone number?   ——
15. Do you have any other questions?   ——

Comments

_____

_____

_____

_____

_____

RENTAL APPLICATION

Name _____

Social Security # _____ Home phone _____

Current address _____

How long at present address _____

Landlord's name _____

Landlord's phone _____

Reason for leaving _____

Previous Addresses

Address _____ from _____ to _____

Landlord's name _____ Phone _____

Reason for moving _____

Address _____ from _____ to _____

Landlord's name _____ Phone _____

Reason for moving _____

Address _____ from _____ to _____

Landlord's name _____ Phone _____

Reason for moving _____

Credit References

Name _____ Account # _____

Address _____ Account # _____

Name _____ Account # _____

Address _____ Account # _____

Name _____ Account # _____

Address _____ Account # _____

Name, address, and phone number of nearest relative not living with you:

_____

Name, address, and phone number of personal reference not related to you:

_____

_____

Names of all people planning to reside in your rental unit:

_____

_____

I hereby give my consent for the landlord or property manager for the property located at _____, to verify any information on this application. I understand a request for verification may be sent to any of the names and addresses listed above. I further understand and consent to a credit report on my credit history being released to the landlord or property manager.

_____

Prospective Tenant   Date

RENTAL POLICY

1. The tenant shall keep all areas of his or her rented portion of the property clean.
2. The tenant must not disturb other people's peace and quiet.
3. The tenant may not alter the dwelling, without the landlord's written permission.
4. Parking of vehicles must be confined to those areas designated for the tenant.
5. The tenant must keep the parking area assigned to him or her clean and unsoiled by oil drippings.
6. The tenant may not perform major repairs on motor vehicles while the vehicles are parked on the premises.
7. The landlord has the right to inspect the dwelling with 24 hours verbal notice given to the tenant.
8. The landlord has the right to access the rental unit to have work performed on the property.
9. The landlord, or his or her agent, may show the dwelling to prospective tenants for purchasers at reasonable times, with 24 hours verbal notice to the tenant.
10. The tenant must receive written permission from the landlord to use a waterbed or other water-filled furniture.
11. The tenant shall pay all costs of repairs and or damage, including, but not limited to, drain stoppages, he or she or his or her guests cause.
12. The tenant shall prevent the plumbing in the rental unit from freezing.
13. The tenant shall provide the landlord with a completed move-in checklist, to be furnished by the landlord, within five days of taking occupancy of the rental unit.
14. The tenant shall inform the landlord of any defects or safety hazards that may cause damage to the property or the occupants.
15. Pets are not allowed, without the written permission of the landlord.
16. Violation of any part of this rental policy or nonpayment of rent as agreed shall be cause for eviction and all legal actions allowed by law.

SUBCONTRACT AGREEMENT

This agreement, made this _____ day of _____, 19_____ shall set forth the whole agreement in its entirety between the contractor and the subcontractor.

Contractor: _____, referred to herein as the contractor.

Subcontractor: _____, referred to herein as the subcontractor.

Job name: _____
Job location: _____

The contractor and the subcontractor agree to the following:

Scope of Work

The subcontractor shall perform all work as described below and provide all material to complete the work described below:

_____
_____
_____
_____
_____

Commencement and Completion Schedule

The work described above shall be started within three days of verbal notice from the contractor. At present, the anticipated start date is _____, 19_____. The subcontractor shall complete the above work in a professional and expedient manner by no later than a reasonable time from the start date. The subcontractor shall work on the job each consecutive day, except for weekends and legal holidays. Time is of the essence of this subcontract. No extension of time will be valid without the contractor's written consent. If the subcontractor does not complete the work in the time allowed, and if the lack of completion is not caused by the contractor, the subcontractor will be charged one hundred dollars ($100.00) per day. This charge will be deducted from any payments due to the subcontractor for work performed.

Contract Sum

The contractor shall pay the subcontractor for the performance of completed work, subject to additions and deductions as authorized by this agreement or attached addendums. The contract sum is $_____.

PROGRESS PAYMENTS

The contractor shall pay the subcontractor once an acceptable insurance certificate has been filed by the subcontractor with the contractor and the contractor approves the finished work. The payment schedule will be as follows:

_____

_____

All payments are subject to a site inspection and approval of work by the contractor.

Before final payment, the subcontractor, if required, shall submit satisfactory evidence to the contractor, that all expenses related to this work have been paid and no lien risk exists on the subject property.

Working Conditions

Working hours will be 8:00 A.M. through 4:30 P.M., Monday through Friday. The subcontractor may work additional hours if desired.

The subcontractor is required to clean his or her work debris from the job site on a daily basis and leave the site in a clean and neat condition. The subcontractor shall be responsible for the removal and disposal of all related debris from his or her job description.

Contract Assignment

The subcontractor shall not assign this contract or further subcontract the whole of this subcontract without the written consent of the contractor.

Laws, Permits, Fees, and Notices

The subcontractor shall be responsible for all required laws, permits, fees, or notices required to perform the work stated herein.

Work of Others

The subcontractor shall be responsible for any damage caused to existing conditions or other trade's work. This damage will be repaired and the subcontractor charged for the expense and supervision of this work. The amount charged will be deducted from any payments due to the subcontractor, if any exist.

WARRANTY

The subcontractor warrants to the contractor all work and materials for one year from the day work is completed.

Indemnification

To the fullest extent allowed by law, the subcontractor shall indemnify and hold harmless the owner, the contractor, and all of their agents and employees from and against all claims, damages, losses, and expenses.

This Agreement, entered into on _____, shall constitute the whole agreement between the contractor and the subcontractor.

_____   _____
Contractor   Subcontractor

VACANCY RATE DATA

Unit Number	Unoccupied	Month

Form Letters to Use in Property Management

J. P. Landlord
P.O. Box 001
Bucksville, ME 60322
(207) 696-5555

October 31, 1992

Able Contractors
42 Riskmore Lane
Cattail, ME 04392

Dear Sir or Madam:

I am planning extensive remodeling in one of my
rental properties. The renovations will be centered
around the kitchens and bathrooms. If your firm is
interested in submitting a bid for this work, I would be
happy to hear from you. Plans and specifications are
available in my office.

Feel free to call me between 8:00 A.M. and 4:30 P.M.,
Monday through Friday. Thank you for your attention
to this matter.

Sincerely,
J. P. Landlord

J. P. Landlord
P.O. Box 001
Bucksville, ME 60322
(207) 696-5555

October 31, 1992

Rita Renter
38 Nowhere Place
Bucksville, ME 60322

Dear Miss Renter:

I wanted to take this opportunity to introduce myself. I have recently purchased the property in which you reside. My goal, as the new landlord, is to improve your living conditions. To do this, I would like to arrange a meeting with you. Evaluations will be made to determine what property improvements are needed. During these evaluations, I will be reviewing existing leases and rental amounts. Of course, with the change of ownership in the property, new leases must be entered into. We have much to talk about, and I will value your input on the smooth operation of this property. Please contact me at your earliest opportunity.

Feel free to call me between 8:00 A.M. and 4:30 P.M., Monday through Friday. Thank you for your attention to this matter.

Sincerely,
J. P. Landlord

J. P. Landlord
P.O. Box 001
Bucksville, ME 60322
(207) 696-5555

October 31, 1992

Ms. Dorothy Yesser
Vice President
Golden Bank
123 Harpstown Road
Bucksville, ME 60322

Dear Ms. Yesser:

I am shopping for financing to renovate one of my rental properties. The type of loan I am seeking will be amortized for twenty years with an interest rate competitive with the market. I have substantial equity in the building to be improved and according to a recent appraisal of the property, the improvements will add more net equity to it. The loan amount will be $35,000.

I have complete plans and specifications for the work to be done. In addition, I have quotes from several contractors on the cost of the intended improvements. I would like to meet with you to discuss this project. Ideally, I would like to meet you in my office, where I have my computer and all of my projections and financial matters readily available. If you are interested in this type of loan and would be willing to meet at my office, please contact me at your earliest opportunity.

I can be reached in my office between 8:00 A.M. and 4:30 P.M. by calling 696-5555. Thank you for your time and consideration in this matter.

Sincerely,
J. P. Landlord

J. P. Landlord
P.O. Box 001
Bucksville, ME 60322
(207) 696-5555

October 31, 1992

Rodney Renter
38 Nowhere Place
Bucksville, ME 60322

Dear Mr. Renter:

In reviewing the current market conditions, I have
found it necessary to increase the rents being charged
in your building. This rent increase will not affect your
present lease, but if you choose to renew your lease,
the new rental rates will be in effect. The rent increase
will be five percent of your present rent. In your unit,
this increase will amount to $30 per month.

This increase will bring the rents being charged in
your building up to the current market average. If you
have any questions pertaining to this increase, please
feel free to call me. Your lease will be up for renewal
on December 1, 1992. You may contact me in my
office between 8:00 A.M. and 4:30 P.M. by calling
696-5555.

Sincerely,
J. P. Landlord

J. P. Landlord
P.O. Box 001
Bucksville, ME 60322
(207) 696-5555

October 31, 1992

EasyCheck Credit Agency
P.O. Box 465
Bucksville, ME 60322

Dear Sir or Madam:

As an owner and manager of several rental properties, I am interested in the services your firm provides. I am considering becoming a member of a credit reporting bureau. Please forward all available information on your services and fees to my address, as listed above. If you have any questions, I can be reached in my office between 8:00 A.M. and 4:30 P.M. by calling 696-5555. Thank you for your time and consideration in this matter.

Sincerely,
J. P. Landlord

Glossary

Accrued Interest Interest that is earned but not paid until the maturity of the loan. For example, a balloon loan is structured so that the interest on the note accrues until maturity. During the loan's term, the borrower pays no interest. The loan amount builds up interest, at the rate described in the loan agreement, to be paid when the loan is paid off.

Acquisition Cost The cost of obtaining a property.

Addendum A document that becomes a part of another document, such as a lease. Addendums may be used to alter the terms and conditions of a lease. When properly prepared, addendums become an integral part of an existing agreement.

Amenities Benefits or objects provided with a property. Examples of amenities include swimming pools, tennis courts, fitness rooms, etc.

Amortization The method of designing a payment schedule over an agreed term to repay a debt.

Amortization Schedule A table of periodic payment amounts for principal and interest payments required to repay a debt.

Annual Debt Service The amount of principal and interest payments required on an annual basis to repay a loan.

Annual Percentage Rate (APR) The effective rate of interest charged over a period of one year for a loan amount. The APR is normally higher than the note rate of a loan. For example, if your monthly payments are calculated with an interest rate of 10 percent, the APR may be higher. If discount points are paid, they increase the note rate of a loan to balance a higher annual percentage rate.

Apartment A residential dwelling contained in a multifamily building.

Apartment Building A building that contains multiple residential dwellings, with a common entrance and hallway.

Appraisal An estimated value of a property.

Appraiser A person who estimates the value of a property.

Appurtenance An item outside of a property but considered a part of the real estate. Examples of appurtenances are garages and private storage areas.

Arm's Length Transaction A transaction between parties seeking to fulfill their personal best interest. A transaction between husband and wife, parent and child, or corporate divisions would not be considered an arm's length transaction. There must be no combined interest in benefits derived from the transaction to either party when creating an arm's length transaction.

As Is A term used to acknowledge a sale or rental that is made based on existing conditions, without a warranty of the sale. An as-is property is accepted in its present condition, with no warranty or guarantee.

Asking Price The price advertised or presented in the initial offering of the sale or rental of a property.

Assessed Value The value of a property usually used to determine property taxes. An assessor assigns a tax value to a property. Assessed values are normally lower than appraised values.

Assessment The amount of tax levied by a municipality, or local authority, for property tax.

Assessment Ratio A formula used to determine a property's assessed value, based on the property's market value. For example, if the assessment ratio is 85 percent, a property with a market value of $100,000 will have an assessed value of $85,000.

Assessor An individual with the responsibility of determining the assessed value of real property.

Assignee A person, or entity, to whom a contract is assigned. For example, if you sold your rental property and assigned the existing leases to the purchaser of the property, that purchaser would be the assignee.

Assignment The act of transferring rights or interests in a contract to another party.

Assignor A person, or entity, who assigns rights or a contractual interest to another party.

Attachment The result of a legal act of seizing property to secure or force payment of a debt.

Attorney-in-Fact A person, or entity, authorized to act for another. This arrangement is commonly referred to as a power of attorney. The authorization may be limited to certain aspects or dealings, or it may be general in its scope with all aspects and dealings included.

Balance Sheet A financial report that shows assets, equity, and liabilities. These reports are laid out in double columns. At the end of the report, the two columns should have identical balances.

Balloon Loan A loan with a balloon payment due at a specified time. The balloon payment is usually large and must be paid in one lump sum.

Balloon Payment A lump sum payment paid to satisfy a balloon loan.

Bankruptcy A court action exercised to protect debtors. In many cases, people filing bankruptcy will be insolvent and will forfeit any assets they have to the court for dispersement to creditors.

Bilateral Contract A contractual agreement requiring both parties of the contract to promise performance.

Blind Pool A term used to describe a group of investors placing funds in a program to buy unknown properties.

Broker A person properly licensed to act on the behalf of others for a fee. Real estate brokers and mortgage brokers are two examples.

Brokerage A business involving the use of brokers.

Building Codes Rules and regulations adopted by a local jurisdiction to maintain an established minimum level of consistency in building practices.

Building Permit A license issued by an authorized agency to allow a person to build or alter a building.

Cash Flow The money received during the life of an investment.

Certificate of Insurance Physical evidence from an insurer proving the type and amount of coverage held by the insured. All subcontractors should present a certificate of insurance to the person they will be working for before work is started.

Certificate of Occupancy A certificate issued by the codes enforcement office of a municipality allowing a property to be occupied by humans. Without a certificate of occupancy, a property is considered uninhabitable.

Certificate of Title An opinion of title, generally provided by an attorney, to address the status of a property's title, based on recorded public records.

Chain of Title A report that discloses the history of all acts affecting the title of a property.

Chattel Personal property, for example, a range and refrigerator. If you are buying or selling a rental property, all chattel that will convey with the transaction must be detailed in the purchase and sale agreement. When left silent in a contract, chattel does not convey with the sale of real property.

Chattel Mortgage A mortgage loan secured by personal property. For example, if you own a furnished apartment building, you might pledge the furniture as security for a loan under a chattel mortgage. The chattel mortgage does not encumber the real estate, but it can use all personal property as security.

Clear Title A title free of clouds or liens. To be marketable, a title should be clear.

Cloud of Title A dispute, encumbrance, or pending lawsuit that, if valid or perfected, will affect the value and marketability of the title.

Collateral The property or goods pledged to secure a loan.

Common Area The area of a property used by all people involved with the property, such as tenants. Typical common areas include halls, parking areas, laundry rooms, and the grounds of the property.

Consideration An object of value given when entering into a contract. Examples of consideration include an earnest money deposit, love and affection, or a promise for a promise.

Contractor A person or entity contracting to provide goods or services for an agreed upon fee to another person or entity.

Convey To transfer an object to another.

Conveyance The act of conveying rights or objects to another.

Covenants Promises or rules written into deeds and leases or placed on public record to require or prohibit certain items or acts. For example, a covenant in a lease might prevent tenants from housing pets in rental units.

Default A term used to define the breaching of agreed upon terms.

Defect of Title A recorded encumbrance prohibiting the transfer of a free and clear title.

Deferred Payment A payment made at a later date.

Deficiency Judgment A court action requiring a debtor to repay the difference between a defaulted debt and the value of the security pledged to the debt. For example, if a tenant causes $2,000 in damages to your property, but you only have a $600 damage deposit, you can sue the tenant for a deficiency judgment for the remaining $1,400 to repair the damages.

Demographic Study The research done to establish characteristics of the population of an area, such as sex, age, size of families, and occupations.

Discrimination The act of showing special treatment, good or bad, to an individual based on the person's race, religion, or sex.

Due-on-Sale Clause A clause found in modern loans forbidding the owner from financing the sale of the property until the existing loan is paid in full. These clauses can be triggered by some lease-purchase agreements. They give a lender the right to demand the existing mortgage be paid in full, upon demand.

Duplex A residential property with provisions to house two residential dwellings.

Dwelling A place of residency in a residential property.

Equitable Title The interest held by a purchaser of a property that has been placed under contract but not yet closed upon.

Equity The amount of value between the market value of a property and the outstanding liens against it.

Escrow The act of placing certain money or documents in the hands of a neutral third party for safekeeping until a transaction can be completed. Security and damage deposits are frequently placed in escrow accounts.

Escrow Agent A person or entity receiving escrows for deposit and disbursement.

Eviction The legal method for a property owner to regain possession of his real property from tenants in default of lease agreements.

Fair Market Rent The amount of money a rental property may command in the present economy.

Fair Market Value The amount of money a property may be sold for in the present economy.

Feasibility Study A study done to determine if a venture is viable.

First Mortgage A mortgage with priority over all other mortgages.

Hypothecate To pledge an item as security for a loan without relinquishing possession of the item.

Income Property Real estate used to produce rental income.

Insurable Title A title to property that is capable of being insured by a title insurance company.

Landlord A person who leases property to another.

Leasehold The interest a tenant holds in rental property he or she is paying rent to occupy.

Lessee A person renting property from a landlord.

Lessor A person renting property to a tenant.

Letter of Credit A document from a lender acknowledging that lender's promise to provide credit for a customer.

Leverage The use of equity and borrowed money to increase buying power.

Lien A notice filed against property to secure a debt or other financial obligation.

Life Estate An interest in real property that terminates upon the death of the holder or other designated individual.

Life Tenant An individual allowed to use a property until the death of a designated individual.

Line of Credit An agreement from a lender to lend a specified sum of money, upon demand, to a borrower without further loan application or approval.

MAI An appraisal designation meaning, Member, Appraisal Institute. Appraisers with this designation are well-regarded professionals.

Marketable Title A title to real property that is free from defects and enforceable by a court decision.

Mortgage Banker An individual who originates, sells, and services mortgage loans.

Mortgage Broker An individual who arranges financing for others for a fee.

Mortgagee A person, or entity, holding a mortgage against real property. For example, if a bank lends a landlord money to buy a building, the bank is the mortgagee and the landlord is the mortgagor.

Mortgagor A person, or entity, pledging property as security for a loan.

Net Income The amount of money remaining from income after all expenses are paid.

Net Worth The amount of equity remaining when all liabilities are subtracted from all assets.

Net Yield The return on an investment after all fees and expenses are subtracted.

Novation An agreement in which one individual is released from an obligation through the substitution of another individual.

Passive Investor An investor who provides money, but does not provide personal services in a business endeavor.

Pro Forma Statement A report projecting the outcome of an investment.

Secondary Mortgage Market A market in which mortgages are bought and sold by investors. A majority of the loans originated in banks are sold in the secondary mortgage market.

Zoning The legal regulation by approved authorities for the use of private land.

Index